English Unlimited

A1   **Starter**
Teacher's Pack

Adrian Doff & Johanna Stirling

With Rachel Thake, Cathy Brabben & Mark Lloyd

Acknowledgements

Adrian Doff would like to thank Karen Momber and Keith Sands at Cambridge University Press for overseeing the project and for their invaluable help and support throughout the development of this course. He would also like to thank his editor, Andrew Reid, for his commitment and hard work and help in bringing the book into its final form.

He would like to thank Dr Astrid Krake and Donna Liersch at the Volkshochschule München for giving him an opportunity to teach there and try out new ideas.

He would also like to thank Gabriella Zaharias for consistently supporting and encouraging him during the writing of this book.

Johanna Stirling would like to thank her colleagues and students for all their help and inspiration. She also acknowledges the contribution of those in her online social network who often rallied to the cry of help. Thanks to Andrew Reid for simplifying the over-complicated. Above all, she would like to thank Daryl for his unfailing support and for doing more than his fair share of the washing-up.

Rachel Thake and **Cathy Brabben** would like to thank their colleagues and students in the ESOL department at Thames Valley University, Reading Campus, for their help and support with Writing Essentials. Special thanks go to Mary Langshaw, Angela Buckingham, Sue Laker and Sue Allan.

Mark Lloyd would like to thank the teachers and staff of IH Bath/WELS Bath for their suggestions and ever-constructive criticism, as well as all those students who have, knowingly or otherwise, acted as enthusiastic guinea pigs. Above all, however, he would like to thank Rosa – for her patience and for doing far more than her fair share of the parental duties – and Gabriela, for her smiles and giggles!

The authors and publishers are grateful to:

Text design and page make-up: Stephanie White at Kamae Design
Video content: all the team at Phaebus Media Group
Video scripts: Nick Robinson

Illustrations by:

Mark Duffin, Clare Elsom, Paul Moran and Kathy Baxendale.

The authors and publishers acknowledge the following sources of copyright material and are grateful for the permissions granted. While every effort has been made, it has not always been possible to identify the sources of all the material used, or to trace all copyright holders. If any omissions are brought to our notice, we will be happy to include the appropriate acknowledgements on reprinting.

For the tables on the DVD-ROM and the text on pages 4 and 20 of the Teacher's book © *Common European Framework of Reference for Languages: Learning, teaching, assessment* (2001) Council of Europe Modern Languages Division, Strasbourg, Cambridge University Press

Contents

Introduction

Teaching notes

The thinking behind *English Unlimited*

The aim of *English Unlimited*

The aim of *English Unlimited* is to enable adult learners to communicate effectively in English in real situations. To achieve this, *English Unlimited* is:

1 a **practical** course
2 an **authentic** course
3 an **international** course
4 a **flexible** course

1 A practical course

Each unit of *English Unlimited* is designed to help learners achieve specific **communicative goals**. These goals are listed at relevant points throughout the coursebook. For example, in Unit 3, learners focus on how to arrange to meet people: this is the **unit goal**. Arranging to meet people involves saying where places are in a town, talking about days and times and saying when you are free: these are the specific **goals** of each of the main lessons.

So for example, at the top of the first lesson in Unit 3 you and your learners will see these goals:

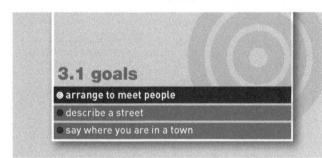

3.1 goals
- arrange to meet people
- describe a street
- say where you are in a town

All the goals describe what learners will learn to **do**, rather than listing, for example, vocabulary sets or grammar points. Of course, learners will learn both vocabulary and grammar in each unit – but the goals come first. We've chosen goals which we think will be useful for Starter-level learners to work on and then selected vocabulary and grammar to help them do this.

Where exactly do the goals come from?

The goals for the course have been taken from the **Common European Framework of Reference for Languages (CEF)**, and adapted and supplemented according to our research into the needs of Starter-level learners.

The goals in this coursebook are based on CEF goals but have been reworded to make them less 'technical' and more motivating and accessible for you and your learners.

What is the CEF?

The CEF uses 'can-do' statements to describe the abilities of learners of English (or any other language) at different levels. The focus is on **how to do things in the language**, rather than on abstract knowledge of the language itself. For example, here are some CEF goals which describe learners' speaking abilities at the end of Starter:

- Can describe him/herself, what he/she does and where he/she lives.

- Can understand questions and instructions addressed carefully and slowly to him/her and follow short, simple directions.
- Can discuss what to do, where to go and make arrangements to meet.

The CEF originated in Europe but is used increasingly widely around the world as a guide for curriculum design and assessment. It can be used with learners of any nationality or first language.

What's the level of the course?

The CEF is divided into six main **levels**, sometimes with 'plus' levels in between. This table shows the CEF levels and how they relate to the Cambridge ESOL exams:

CEF levels		Cambridge exams
C2	'Mastery'	CPE
C1	'Operational proficiency'	CAE
B2+		
B2	'Vantage'	FCE
B1+		
B1	'Threshold'	PET
A2+		
A2	'Waystage'	KET
A1	'Breakthrough'	

English Unlimited Starter **completes A1**, and moves into A2.

2 An authentic course

Because it is based on practical goals, *English Unlimited* teaches authentic language – that is, the kind of language which is really used by native speakers and proficient non-native speakers of English in everyday situations. An important tool for identifying useful language to include in the course has been the **Cambridge International Corpus (CIC)**.

What is the CIC?

The CIC is an electronic collection of more than a billion words of real text, both spoken and written, which can be searched by computer to discover the most common words, expressions and structures of the language, and the kinds of situations in which they are used.

How has it been used in the course?

The CIC has been used throughout *English Unlimited* to ensure that, as far as possible given the level of the course, learners are taught the most frequent and useful **words and expressions** for meeting their communicative goals.

The CIC has also been used in the preparation of **grammar** sections to identify realistic contexts for presenting particular structures. For example, corpus research suggests that a common use of the past simple is 'talking about a place you visited' (Unit 8), while the present progressive is often used for the function of 'saying you're busy' (Unit 9).

A further use of the CIC is in the **Keyword sections** which appear in every unit. Each Keyword section focuses on one or more of the most frequently used words in English, and teaches its most common meanings, as well as useful expressions based around it.

How else is English Unlimited *an authentic course?*

In addition to being informed by the CIC, *English Unlimited* as a whole contains a large amount of unscripted audio material, recorded using non-actors, both native and non-native speakers. Even at Starter level, there are one or more **authentic recordings** in most units – 'real' people speaking about themselves (saying where they live, talking about their family, saying what they like and don't like, etc.), using natural, spontaneous speech.

At Starter level, many other recordings are of simple conversations. Although these are scripted, they have been checked against the CIC to ensure that the language used is as natural and authentic as possible.

What are the benefits for learners of using 'authentic' listening material?

Listening to spontaneous, unscripted speech is the best way to prepare learners for the experience of understanding and communicating in English in the real world. Our observations have shown not only that Starter-level learners are capable of following spontaneous speech, but that authentic recordings are more motivating and engaging for learners in general.

3 An international course

In what ways is English Unlimited *'international'?*

Firstly, the course aims to be **inclusive**, to cater to learners of different backgrounds from all around the world. Care has been taken to select topics, texts and tasks which will appeal to a broad range of learners rather than learners from one particular country or region. We don't assume that learners have knowledge of British or American culture, but instead focus on universal topics and themes that are accessible to all learners. The course is therefore suited to both mixed and single-nationality groups.

English is most often used nowadays between non-native speakers from different places. How does the course take this into account?

A second strand to the 'internationalism' of the course is that it includes features which will help learners become more effective communicators in international contexts.

Every unit features a section called **Across cultures,** which focuses on a particular topic of cultural or international interest. The aim of these sections is to encourage interest in other cultures, and also to heighten learners' awareness of how the values and background of the people who they talk to in English might differ from their own. These sections also provide an opportunity to read more extended texts and include language which goes slightly beyond what has been introduced in the unit.

Listening sections use recordings of speakers using **different varieties of English**. These include both native speakers (British, US, Canadian) and also speakers whose own language is not English. The aim of this is to familiarise learners with the experience of hearing both native and non-native speakers from a wide variety of places, reflecting the fact that English is increasingly used as an international language.

Care has been taken to ensure that recordings are of appropriate speed and clarity for learners at this level, and that all the speakers are competent users of English who can provide a good, accurate model of the spoken language.

Although the language taught in the book is standard British English, the **language forms** which are taught reflect the way English is used internationally. So, for example, in Unit 3 both the word *flat* (which is common in British English) and the US English word *apartment* (which is more common internationally) are taught. To talk about possessions and family, we teach the forms *I have* and *Do you have ...?* which are widely used internationally, rather than *I've got* and *Have you got ...?*, which are mainly used by people in Britain.

4 A flexible course

The next five pages show how a typical unit of *English Unlimited* is organised.

As you'll see, the first six pages are connected to each other and make up the 'core' of the unit. After that, there is the **Explore** section, activities which have a topical or linguistic link to the unit, but which can be used separately. On the last page of each unit is the **Look again** section, comprising review and extension activities, which can either be done by learners in the classroom or for homework.

This means that *English Unlimited* can be adapted not only for lessons of different lengths, but also for shorter and longer courses. For example, just using the 'core' of each unit would be suitable for a course of about 40 hours, while using all the material, including the **Explore** and **Look again** sections, would give a course length of 50–60 hours.

The flexibility of *English Unlimited* is further enhanced by an extensive range of supplementary materials. These include **extra conversation practice** at the back of the coursebook, the **Teacher's DVD-ROM** containing four printable worksheets for each unit of the Coursebook, **Achievement and Progress tests**, and the **Self-study Pack**, which offers more than 40 hours of additional language and skills practice material in the Workbook and on the Self-Study DVD-ROM.

In the rest of this introduction you'll find:
- a plan showing how a typical unit is organised *pages 6 to 10*
- more detailed notes on the different sections of the units *pages 11 to 14*
- information about the other components of the course *pages 15 to 18*
- more detailed information about the CEF *page 19*

I hope that you and your learners will enjoy using *English Unlimited*!

Adrian Doff

How a unit is organised

The course consists of 10 units.
Each unit has 8 pages.

The first two pages are a single lesson with goals based on the CEF. You can of course spread the material over more than one lesson if you want.
① *about 90 minutes*

Lessons include **vocabulary** and / or **grammar**, as well as practice in **reading**, **listening**, **speaking** and **writing**. Lessons always finish with a communicative speaking (or occasionally writing) task. *See pp11–12 for details of language and skills sections.*

At the end of the first two pages, there is a **Classroom language** section. This focuses on important words and expressions which you and your learners will use in class. *See p13 for details.*

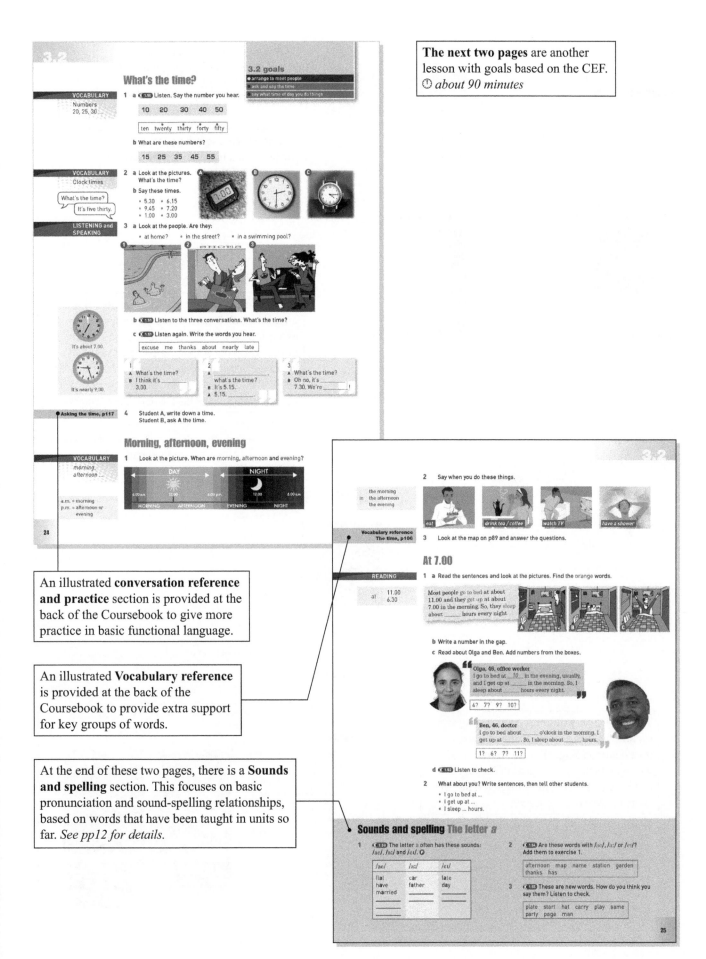

The **next two pages** are another lesson with goals based on the CEF.
⏱ *about 90 minutes*

An illustrated **conversation reference and practice** section is provided at the back of the Coursebook to give more practice in basic functional language.

An illustrated **Vocabulary reference** is provided at the back of the Coursebook to provide extra support for key groups of words.

At the end of these two pages, there is a **Sounds and spelling** section. This focuses on basic pronunciation and sound-spelling relationships, based on words that have been taught in units so far. *See pp12 for details.*

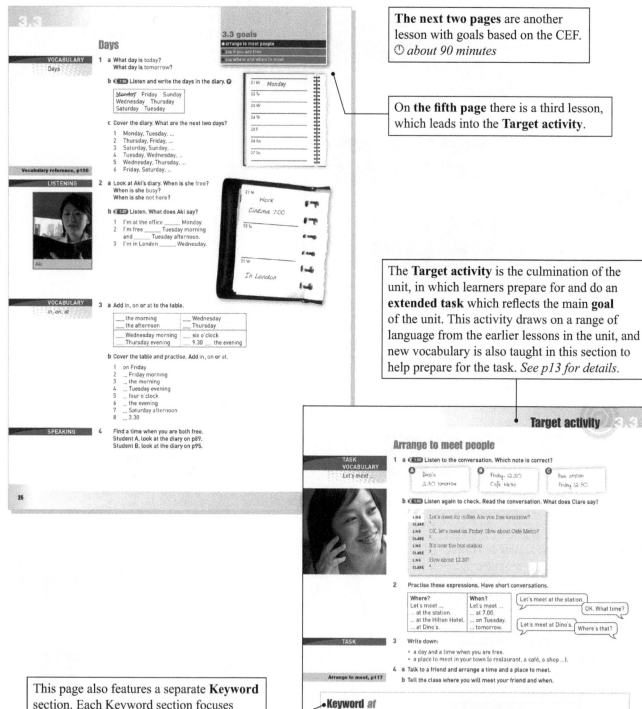

The next two pages are another lesson with goals based on the CEF. ⏱ *about 90 minutes*

On **the fifth page** there is a third lesson, which leads into the **Target activity**.

The **Target activity** is the culmination of the unit, in which learners prepare for and do an **extended task** which reflects the main **goal** of the unit. This activity draws on a range of language from the earlier lessons in the unit, and new vocabulary is also taught in this section to help prepare for the task. *See p13 for details.*

This page also features a separate **Keyword** section. Each Keyword section focuses on a common English word (or group of words) which has appeared in the unit, and practises using the word in a range of contexts. *See p13 for details.*

The seventh page of the unit has two sections: **Explore speaking** or **Explore writing** and **Across cultures**.

⏱ The **last two pages** of the unit will take about 45 minutes each.

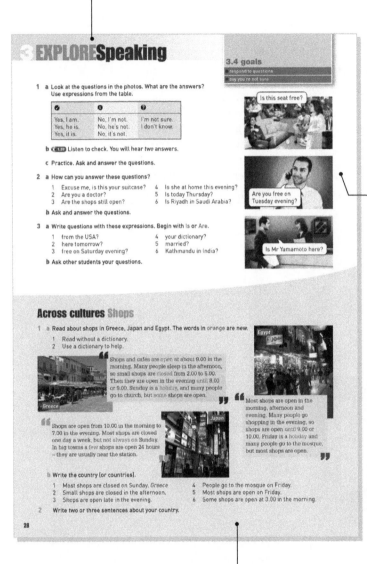

Odd-numbered units have an **Explore speaking** section which focuses on simple speaking skills and strategies. *See p14 for details.*

Even-numbered units have an **Explore writing** section which focuses on elementary writing skills. *See p14 for details.*

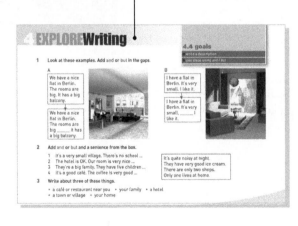

In every unit there is an **Across cultures** section which gives learners a chance to read and discuss aspects of different cultures and countries around the world. *See p13 for details.*

The last page of each unit, **Look again**, is a series of short activities for reviewing and the language from the unit. *See p14 for details.*

Review activities include **vocabulary** and **grammar** from the unit.

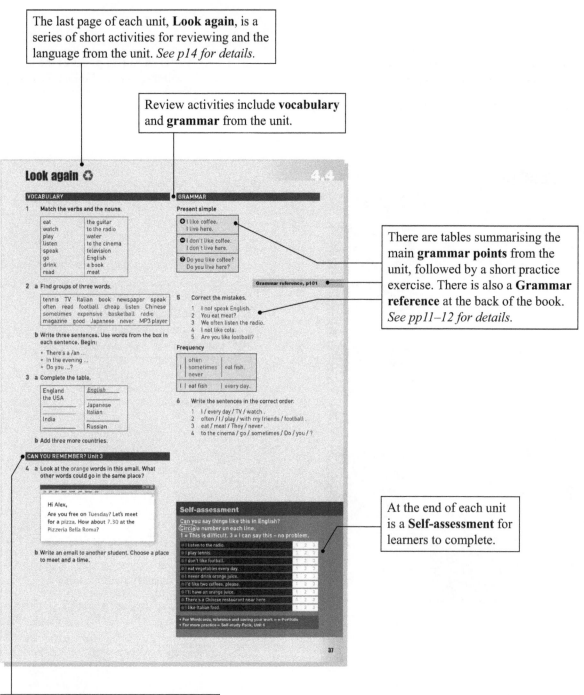

There are tables summarising the main **grammar points** from the unit, followed by a short practice exercise. There is also a **Grammar reference** at the back of the book. *See pp11–12 for details.*

At the end of each unit is a **Self-assessment** for learners to complete.

Can you remember? activities review a language point from the previous unit.

A detailed look at the features of *English Unlimited*

A real beginner's course

The Starter level of *English Unlimited* takes into account the needs of real beginner learners, and is based on the author's own experience of teaching absolute beginners from a range of different countries. So the units:

- assume **no previous knowledge** of English.
- introduce language in **easily managed stages**, so that learners can develop confidence and absorb what they have learned.
- focus on **frequently used words and expressions**, so that learners can express themselves and communicate straight away.
- **avoid** complex and unnecessary grammar rules and distinctions.

Vocabulary

As well as a full grammar syllabus, *English Unlimited* provides learners with **a wide variety of vocabulary** chosen to meet each unit's communicative goals. In most units, there are three or four vocabulary sections in the first two lessons and Target activity, and vocabulary is also presented and practised in Keyword sections, on Explore writing pages, and on Explore speaking pages.

Vocabulary includes:

- **words** like *pen, doctor, vegetables.*
- **collocations** like *an interesting book*, *watch football*, *leave school.*
- **phrases** like *by car, on Tuesday*, *at the station.*
- **fixed expressions** like *I don't know, I think.*

The focus on longer items as well as single words will enable learners to express themselves more fluently, naturally and effectively.

The course provides a balance of:

- **very frequent vocabulary**, selected and checked using the Cambridge International Corpus (CIC).
- **topical and functional items** which learners need in order to achieve particular goals. For example, food and drink words are not especially frequent statistically, but are obviously necessary for the fulfilment of goals like 'say what you eat and drink' and 'ask for a drink in a café'.

Vocabulary is always **taught in clear contexts** which help learners see what it means and how it is used. It is either presented through short reading texts or recordings, or through visual material.

Vocabulary reference

At the back of the Coursebook is an illustrated **Vocabulary reference** which lists key words and expressions from the units. There are clear references to this section in the lessons.

Grammar

Each unit of the course includes at least one major grammar point.

The points of the grammar syllabus have been selected and placed in particular units to help learners meet their **communicative goals**. For example, *I / we* forms of both the verb *be* and the Present simple are focused on in Unit 1 because they are useful in talking to someone for the first time (*I'm from China ..., I live ...*); *this / these* appears in Unit 5 because it is useful for choosing and buying things (*I like this bag*).

Grammar points have been checked in the Cambridge International Corpus to find **the most frequent and natural-sounding forms**. For example, the Starter level introduces the negative forms *He's not ..., They're not ...* rather than *He isn't* and *They aren't ...*, as they are not only simpler, but also more frequently used.

In grammar presentations, learners see or hear the grammar **in context** through short reading texts or conversations. Then learners are helped to **notice** the new form by means of a focusing exercise.

Thorough **controlled practice** is provided to check learners' understanding of the language and provide initial practice, while maintaining and developing the topic of the lesson:

Lessons end with a speaking task (or a writing task) which gives learners the chance to use the language of the lesson, including the grammar, in **freer practice**.

The key grammar points are **summarised** on the Look Again page at the end of each unit. On this page, there is also a reference to the **Grammar reference** section at the back of the book.

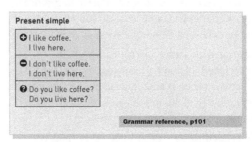

Each Grammar reference section sets out the **meaning, form and pronunciation** of the point in question:

Pronunciation

Pronunciation is focused on in two ways at Starter level:

1 **practising pronunciation** of new words, expressions and grammatical forms as they are presented. The symbol ❷ in Vocabulary and Grammar sections indicates that the items are recorded, and it may be useful to drill them to practise pronunciation. These recordings focus not only on individual words but also on rhythm and stress patterns of sentences and questions.

2 in the **Sounds and spelling** sections. These focus on words with similar sounds and spelling patterns, and aim:

- to help learners notice the different **sounds** of English, and differences between them.
- to help learners to see the relationship between sounds and common **spelling** patterns.
- to help learners **pronounce** words more accurately and with more confidence.

Note that, although native-speaker voices are used to model features of pronunciation, the primary goal of these sections is **intelligibility** and **awareness** and not (necessarily) achieving 'perfect' pronunciation.

Learners can also practise pronunciation in Sounds and spelling exercises on the Self-study DVD-ROM.

Listening

There are opportunities to listen to natural spoken English throughout the book. Short pieces of listening are often integrated into the presentation of vocabulary and grammar, and (especially in later units) there are also longer pieces of listening for more extended comprehension.

The book features **a wide range of recordings**, both **authentic** and **scripted**, including monologues, topical conversations between friends and colleagues, conversations in everyday situations (e.g. buying things, ordering drinks, making enquiries), phone calls and interviews.

The **authentic recordings** are unscripted recordings of both native and non-native speakers from a variety of backgrounds. These provide exposure to a range of accents and to features of real spoken English.

The **scripted recordings** are mostly of everyday conversations, and are based on real-world recordings and corpus data to guarantee the inclusion of natural expressions and features of English. They are often used to contextualise functional language, such as asking the time or making arrangements on the phone.

Texts are exploited using **a range of tasks** designed to develop specific listening skills, build confidence and focus on the language the speakers use. For example, this sequence includes:

- a pre-listening prediction task (2a).
- listening for main points (sequencing task) (2b).
- language focus (3a).

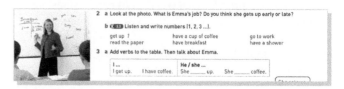

Reading

In the first few units, texts are kept short and within the range of language that has already been introduced. In later units, a **wider range of texts** is used, both **printed and electronic**: excerpts from magazines, newspaper and online articles, web postings, advertisements, brochures, notes, text messages and emails. Reading texts:

- are from authentic sources but simplified, ensuring that learners are exposed to natural language and preparing them for reading outside the classroom.
- recycle known language in order to build learners' confidence in reading.
- are slightly above learners' productive language level, so that learners have opportunities to notice new language.
- provide a context for taught vocabulary and grammar.

Texts are exploited using **a range of tasks** appropriate for the level and text type. These focus both on the meaning and on vocabulary contained in the text. For example, this sequence includes:

- a language focus task which helps to establish the general meaning (1a)
- a task where learners read for specific information (1b).

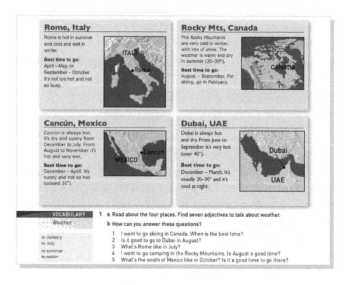

The **Across cultures** section in each unit provides a further opportunity for reading. Even in the early units, these reading texts go slightly beyond what learners know already, and so encourage them to guess unknown words from the start and to use a dictionary where necessary.

Target activity

The Target activity is an **extended speaking task**, which recycles some or all of the **goals, vocabulary** and **grammar** of the previous two lessons. It is the conclusion of the first five, topically-linked pages of the unit.

The Target activity has either **two** or **three sections**. These usually include:

Task listening. This provides a model for the task which learners will do themselves. It also provides further development in listening skills:

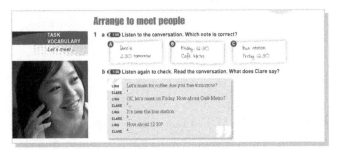

Preparation. Before doing the task, learners are given the chance to think about the ideas and the language they want to use before they begin, so that they will be able to focus on accuracy as well as fluency when doing the task itself:

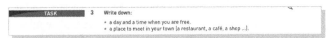

The task itself. Learners do an activity, usually in pairs or groups, and then report back to the whole class.

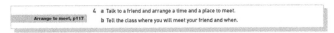

Classroom language

An extremely important source of **English-language input** for Starter learners is the language the teacher uses in giving instructions, using the book and asking questions. To help learners notice and understand this language, there is a **Classroom language** section at the end of the first lesson in each unit. These sections focus not on the classroom language the learners will need to use themselves (which at this level is very limited) but on the language they will need to **understand** as part of the lesson. This includes:

- vocabulary involved in using the coursebook (*picture, box, conversation; cross, underline*)
- simple classroom instructions (*open, close, look, listen; again, together, everyone*)
- words for talking about language (*noun, verb, adjective; sentence, question, answer*)
- expressions used to introduce stages of the lesson (*Let's ..., now*)
- language used to talk about pictures (*Where is she? What's she doing?*)
- questions about meaning (*What does ... mean? What's ... in English?*)

Each Classroom language section introduces a set of words or expressions to focus on, often using recordings of classroom interactions.

Keyword

English has a number of very common words (such as *have, go, this, at*) which are used again and again with a range of different meanings. Each unit of *English Unlimited Starter* has a separate **Keyword** section which focuses on one common word that has been taught in the unit, and shows how it can be used in different contexts.

For example, Unit 2 introduces expressions with *have*, such as *have two children, have a flat*. The Keyword section shows other common words that can be used after *have*. This is followed by a practice stage.

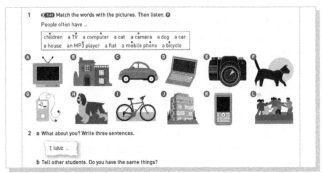

Across cultures

Increasingly, learners use English to communicate with people from other countries and cultures. This means that **intercultural awareness** is becoming an important aspect of learning the language. With this in mind, all levels of *English Unlimited* feature regular **Across cultures** sections as part of the units. These sections are intended to help learners to:

- communicate better with people from a range of cultural backgrounds.
- be more aware of the kinds of differences and similarities that can exist both between and within cultures.
- reflect on aspects of their own and other cultures in an objective, non-judgemental way.
- contribute to an exchange of ideas about cultures by drawing on their own observations and experiences.

At Starter level, there is an Across cultures section in each unit. These sections focus on a particular topic from an intercultural perspective, usually picking up on a main theme from the unit.

Unit	
1 Students	6 Journeys
2 Families and children	7 Housework
3 Shops	8 Hostels
4 Tea	9 Family weekend
5 Office clothes	10 Birthdays

Across cultures sections usually include a brief lead-in, a reading text for further skills development, and some vocabulary input to support learners in a final speaking stage where they talk about their own and other cultures.

Explore speaking

Explore speaking sections occur in **odd-numbered units** (alternating with Explore writing).

Explore speaking is a free-standing section which aims to equip learners with **skills and strategies for improving their spoken interaction** in a range of situations. It covers the essential language that Starter learners will need when interacting with other people:

- saying hello and goodbye.
- responding to questions.
- expressing uncertainty.
- apologising and interrupting.
- making requests and replying to them.

As elsewhere in the course, the language included in these sections is based on the CEF.

Each Explore speaking page includes:

- **a listening section, focusing on key expressions**. Often the focus is on what language to use in particular situations.
- activities in which learners **notice the target language**, often by noting down the words or expressions they hear.
- **controlled practice exercises** which build familiarity with and confidence in the target language.
- (in later units) **a freer practice activity**, such as a role play, which gives learners the chance to use the target language in a real-life situation.

Explore writing

Explore writing sections occur in **even-numbered units** (alternating with Explore speaking).

These sections aim to develop basic writing skills which are essential at this level:

- dictating and writing names and numbers using the English alphabet.
- writing a simple description (using *and, but, or*).
- joining ideas and giving reasons (using *so, because*).
- describing a sequence of events (using *and, then*).
- describing when things happened (using *when, after*).

Explore writing sections usually follow these stages:

- learners see **examples of sentences or short texts**, focusing on ways of joining ideas and linking sentences together.
- they do exercises which help them to **notice** specific language features.
- they **practise** using the new language in writing.
- they **write** simple sentences and short paragraphs, usually about themselves or people they know.
- they **read out** their sentences and compare them with other students.

Look again

The Look again page is divided into sections: **Vocabulary**, **Spelling**, **Can you remember?** and **Grammar**. Although some sections can be set as homework, the page is intended as a series of simple review activities for learners to do in class. The Look again page also includes a final **Self-assessment** for the unit.

Vocabulary

These exercises provide further practice of words, expressions and functional phrases from the unit.

Spelling

This section consists of one exercise, focusing on the spelling of words from the unit and from previous units.

Can you remember?

This is a review of key language from the preceding unit to help learners reactivate and better retain what they have learned.

Grammar

This section contains:

- summary tables of the key grammar points taught in the unit.
- simple exercises giving controlled grammar practice.

Self-assessment

Each unit concludes with a Self-assessment box for learners to complete either in class or at home. Many learners find it useful and motivating to reflect on their progress at regular intervals during a course of study.

For teachers, the Self-assessment will be a valuable means of gauging learners' perceptions of how much progress they've made, and of areas they need to work on further. Self-assessments can also be useful preparation for one-to-one tutorials in which the learners' and teacher's perceptions of progress are compared and discussed.

The Self-study Pack

About the Self-study Pack

English Unlimited Starter Self-study Pack has been designed to offer flexibility and depth to your English teaching, whatever the specific needs of your learners. The Workbook and Self-study DVD-ROM provide a wide range of language and skills practice activities to accompany each unit of the Coursebook, so you can:

- set homework tasks based on the Coursebook lessons
- supplement your lessons with further language and skills practice
- use video activities in class, or get learners to watch at home.

Your learners can:

- consolidate their knowledge of language and skills taught in class
- practise and check their pronunciation
- learn and practise essential speaking skills
- create tests on specific language areas quickly and easily
- check their progress and get feedback on their level of English and any specific areas of difficulty
- record and listen to themselves speaking in everyday dialogues.

In the Workbook

The *English Unlimited Starter Workbook* contains:

activities which practise and extend the vocabulary and grammar taught in the Coursebook units; further reading, writing and listening skills practice; and numerous opportunities in each unit for learners to personalise what they are learning to their own interests and situations.

The first two pages of each unit consist of further **vocabulary and grammar practice** activities which can either be used in class or set for homework. **Over to you** activities suggest ways for learners to personalise the language and skills they have learnt.

Time out, in odd-numbered units, offers a fun way for learners to practise and remember vocabulary sets.

Explore writing, in odd-numbered units, gives learners key pointers on spelling and joining ideas in sentences.

Explore reading, in even-numbered units, offers practice in reading and understanding a range of everyday texts, such as forms, adverts, and web pages.

The last page of each unit, **DVD-ROM Extra**, links up with the video on the **Self-study DVD-ROM**. Each video recycles the language taught in that unit and shows everyday situations involving characters who learners can follow through the course. These can be used in class or by learners on their own at home or in the school multi-media room.

A **Writing reference and practice** section is at the back of the Workbook. This gives more support and practice in key areas of basic literacy, such as punctuation, capital letters and joining ideas in sentences.

On the Self-study DVD-ROM

The *English Unlimited Starter Self-study DVD-ROM* offers your learners over 200 **interactive activities** which they can use to practise and consolidate what they've learned in class, while providing a number of **easy ways to check their progress** at every step of the course.

Just click on the icon for each unit and the learners will find fun and easy-to-use activities, from picture matching and drag-and-drop category exercises to **opportunities for learners to record themselves** and play back the result to check against an audio recording.

Each unit's activities practise and extend the **vocabulary**, **grammar**, **Classroom language, Sounds and spelling** and **Keyword** areas focused on in the Coursebook. Learners can also generate tests quickly and easily, using the **Quick Check** question bank. They can choose which units they want to test and how many questions you want the test to consist of, and Quick Check will randomly select from the 300 questions in the bank.

Learners can also **keep track of their progress** as they work through the course. The Progress page shows them which scored exercises they have attempted and how they've done. Learners can see which language areas they need to do more work on and can go back and try again.

In addition to language practice, each unit of the Self-study DVD-ROM also contains **Explore speaking** or **Explore writing** activities, which offer practice and extension of the speaking and writing skills taught in the Coursebook.

In most language courses, it is rare for learners to get the chance to **listen to themselves in conversation**, but if there is a microphone available, this can be done easily using the record and playback activities on the DVD-ROM. Learners listen to the clips, take a closer look at the language used, and then have the opportunity to record themselves in the conversations and play it back to hear how they sound.

On the Self-study DVD-ROM, you will also find the **DVD-ROM Extra** video, described above, which can be used in or outside class, using the last page of each unit of the Workbook, or just watching them to get extra exposure to real language.

The Teacher's Pack

We understand that no two teachers or classes are alike, and that the role of a Teacher's Pack accompanying a language course is to cater for as diverse a range of pedagogical needs as possible. The materials in this Teacher's Pack serve to enhance the flexibility of *English Unlimited* to meet the needs of teachers who:

- are teaching courses of different lengths
- want to supplement the Coursebook materials
- have different class sizes and types
- are teaching in different parts of the world
- are addressing different assessment needs
- want to use DVD materials in the classroom.

English Unlimited Starter Teacher's Pack offers a **step-by-step guide to teaching** from the Coursebook, **38 photocopiable activity worksheets** to extend and enrich your lessons and a **complete testing suite**. The Teacher's Pack consists of the **Teacher's book** and the **Teacher's DVD-ROM**.

In the Teacher's book

Teacher's notes

In the Teacher's book, there are more than 70 pages of teacher's notes (pp20–92) to accompany the Coursebook material. These notes are a comprehensive and easy-to-follow guide to using the *English Unlimited Starter Coursebook*, and have been written with a broad range of class-types and teaching styles in mind.

Each unit's notes take you smoothly through the different stages of the Coursebook lessons. Answers are clearly highlighted, and the Individual, Pair and Group work symbols show at a glance what interaction is suggested for each stage.

On every page, there are instructions for alternative activities, clearly boxed, to offer greater variety and interest. There are also suggestions throughout for adapting activities to stronger and weaker classes, multi-lingual and mono-lingual classes, and to large and small class sizes.

On the Teacher's DVD-ROM

Photocopiable activities

There are 20 photocopiable activity worksheets on the Teacher's DVD-ROM (two for each unit) ready to print out and use straight away. These offer extra vocabulary and grammar practice, extra reading and writing work, role plays and games which further activate the language that learners have been introduced to in the Coursebook, and build their fluency, confidence and communication skills.

Each activity is accompanied by a page of clear, step-by-step instructions, with answer keys and extra teaching ideas. At the end of each unit of the Teacher's notes, there is a page to help you find the activities you need.

Writing Essentials

The Writing Essentials activities (described in more detail on pp93–96) consist of 18 sets of photocopiable activity worksheets specially designed for non-Roman alphabet learners of English. Each activity teaches a vital writing or reading skill, such as letter formation or recognition of common words, and supports learners in the process of reading and writing in a new script. These activities can be used alongside the Coursebook and other material, or as part of a separate course for non-Roman alphabet learners.

Progress and Achievement Tests

The *English Unlimited* testing suite consists of 10 unit-by-unit Progress Tests and 3 skills-based Achievement Tests to motivate your learners and give you and them a clear idea of the progress that they are making. These and other methods of assessment are discussed in detail on pp17–18.

DVDs

Two DVDs per level from the Self-study Pack are also included on the Teacher's DVD-ROM, as they are easily adaptable for use in class.

Assessing your learners with *English Unlimited*

There are many ways of assessing learner progress through a language course. For this reason *English Unlimited* offers a range of testing and assessment options, including progress tests, skill-based achievement tests, assessment using the e-Portfolio, self-assessment and continuous assessment.

Tests on the Teacher's DVD-ROM

There are two types of test available as PDFs on the Teacher's DVD-ROM: progress and achievement tests.

Progress tests

There is one progress test for each of the 10 units of the course. These assess the learners' acquisition of language items taught in the main Coursebook material. Each test carries 40 marks and includes questions assessing grammar and vocabulary items taught in the unit. These are not intended to be 'high stakes' tests but rather quick checks that will help the teacher and learner judge which language points have been successfully acquired and understood, and which areas individual learners or the whole class may need to study again.

We suggest that each test should take no more than 30 minutes in the classroom. Tests can be copied and distributed to each learner and taken in class time. The tests are designed for quick marking with the provided Answer key. Teachers may choose to mark tests, or, alternatively, learners can mark each other's work. A mark can be given out of 40. If particular problem areas are identified, learners can be directed to do extra work from the Self-study Pack.

Achievement tests

There are three Achievement tests, designed to form the basis of formal learner assessment.
- **Achievement test 1** can be taken after unit 4.
- **Achievement test 2** can be taken after unit 7.
- The **End of Course Achievement test** can be taken after unit 10.

These tests are based on the four skills: Reading, Listening, Writing and Speaking.

Reading tests

Each test is based on a short text and we advise allowing no more than 15 minutes for each test. As with the Coursebook texts and Listening tests, there may be a few unfamiliar items in the text but the tasks are graded so unknown items should not hinder the learners' ability to answer the five questions. The teacher may mark the tests or it may be acceptable for learners to mark each other's work.

Listening tests

The audio tracks for these are found at the end of the two Class Audio CDs. Achievement Test 1 is track 92 on CD1; Achievement Test 2 is track 68 on CD2; the End of Course Achievement Test 3 is track 69 on CD2.

We suggest carrying out tests under controlled conditions with the recording played twice. Each test should take no longer than ten minutes. As with the Coursebook audio, there may be a few unfamiliar language items in the listening text but tasks are graded to the level of the learner, so unknown items should not hinder the learners' ability to answer the questions. The tests are simple and quick to mark. They can be marked by the teacher or it may be acceptable for learners to mark each other's work.

Writing tests

Learners are set a writing task based on themes from the Coursebook, and the teacher assesses work using the analytical marking scales provided. Tasks are designed to simulate purposeful, real-life, communicative pieces of writing. The teacher should endeavour to identify the band the work falls in for each category. This marking scheme can give learners a profile of the strong and weak points of their written work, helping them improve their writing skills over the length of the course.

If the tests are to be used under timed conditions in class, 30 minutes should be allowed for the learners to produce their texts – planning and redrafting may be encouraged by the teacher at the outset.

Another way is to set the tasks as assessed writing assignments to be done as homework. In these cases, the teacher should interpret the band scales according to the time available and the availability of dictionaries and other reference materials.

The option chosen will depend on your learning environment. A timed test may help you assess learners under equal conditions, but can be a rather artificial, pressured environment. Written homework assignments are less controlled, but could be a better way of encouraging learners to work at their writing and feel satisfied with a polished piece of written work. The *Explore Writing* tasks in the Coursebook and Self-study Pack may also be used as assessed assignments and marked using the analytical scales.

Speaking tests

These are designed to be carried out by an assessor, who may be the learners' regular teacher, or another teacher in the institution. Learners do the tests in pairs. The ideal environment is for the test to take place in a separate room from the rest of the class, who can be engaged in self-study work while the testing is taking place. It is best if seating is set up as a 'round table' if possible, rather than the teacher facing both learners across a desk, so as not to suggest an interrogation! Each test takes eight minutes.

The assessor should be familiar with the Analytical Scales for the speaking tests before the test and have a copy of the Mark Sheet for each learner with their names already filled in. Screen the mark sheets from the learners.

The assessor will need the Teacher's Notes, which provide a script of prompts for the test. Each test is in two parts. In the first Task (four minutes), the assessor puts the learners at ease with warm-up questions, before asking the learners in turn a selection of questions from the Notes, based on themes from the Coursebook. The assessor may depart from the script to elicit further responses, maintaining a friendly, encouraging manner. The assessor may begin to note down some marks based on the scales for each learner.

In Task 2 (four minutes) learners are provided with prompts for a communicative task, which they carry out between themselves. Learners may need some encouragement, or to have the instructions explained more than once.

During this section the teacher should withdraw eye contact, making it clear that the learners should talk to each other, listen closely and revise the marks from Task 1, gradually completing the grid.

The assessor should not correct learners at any point during the test.

Filling in the Mark Sheets

Once all four papers of the Achievement Tests have been carried out, the teacher can provide marks for each learner. This includes analytical marks for the Speaking and Writing tests, and an average mark out of five for each one; and marks out of five for the Reading and Listening tests. This gives the learners a snapshot of their performance in the four skills. The learners should be encouraged to reflect on what they found easy or difficult, and given strategies to improve performance in different skills. The marks can be used as the basis for course reports or formal assessment.

Self-assessment

Assessment is not just about tests. Self-assessment encourages more reflective and focused learning. *English Unlimited* offers a number of tools for learner self-assessment:

- each unit of the Coursebook ends with a self-assessment grid in which learners are encouraged to measure their own progress against the unit goals, which in turn are based on the can-do statements of the *Common European Framework of Reference for Language Learning*.
- progress with the activities on the Self-study DVD-ROM can be analysed in detail on the Progress screen.
- the Self-study DVD-ROM also contains Quick Check tests, using a bank of 300 multiple choice questions. Learners select which units they want to be tested on and how long they want the test to be – new tests will be randomly generated each time.

Using the e-Portfolio

Portfolio-based assessment is a useful tool both for self-assessment and formal assessment, particularly for teachers seeking an alternative to traditional timed writing tests. The e-Portfolio allows learners to do the following.

- Assess their progress against can-do statements and revise their assessments later in the course depending on progress made.

- Build up a personal e-Portfolio of written work associated with the course. The learner may then select their best work, as an alternative to tests, or at the end of the course to be provided as a Portfolio. This may include word-processed documents, project work and even audio files. Some of the *Explore writing* tasks may lend themselves well to portfolio work, and in some classrooms, learners may be asked to record personal audio files based around speaking tasks in the book. The satisfaction of producing a polished *spoken* text is a rare one in a language course, but if the learner or the centre has access to a microphone, it is relatively easy to do.

Written texts and audio in a learner's e-Portfolio may be assessed using the same analytical scales as the Writing and Speaking Achievement tests.

Continuous assessment

Finally, some teachers and institutions may prefer to dispense with tests and adopt a form of continuous assessment. This can be demanding of a teacher's time but perhaps no more so than the marking load created by frequent formal tests. The important thing is to explain the system to learners early in the course, and regularly show them their marksheets to indicate how they are getting on. How actual assessment is carried out may differ between institutions, but here are some guidelines and ideas.

- It is possible to assess learners using the Speaking analytical scales regularly though the course. The *Target activity* sections, where learners are involved in more extended discourse, offer an opportunity for this.
- Tell learners when their speaking is being assessed, and the teacher can monitor particular groups.
- Learners should be assessed several times during the course or they may rightly feel they were let down by a single bad performance, even if the assessment was not 'high stakes'.
- An atmosphere of gentle encouragement and striving for improvement should always accompany this kind of assessment. Some learners can get competitive about this, which can have a negative effect on class atmosphere and demotivate less confident learners.
- The *Explore writing* tasks can be used for continuous written assessment, using the Analytical scales for writing.

A final word

Testing and assessment can be a vital tool for teachers and learners in assessing strengths and weaknesses, building awareness and encouraging improvement. But it can be frustrating for a learner to feel that they are being assessed too often, at the expense of actually learning; and whilst there are certainly learners who like being tested, there are many others who certainly don't!

English Unlimited aims to help learners communicate in real-life situations, and the testing and assessment tools provided should be used with that purpose in mind. Testing and assessment should never take precedence over learning, but serve as useful checks on the way to increasing confidence, competence and fluency.

The Common European Framework of Reference for Languages (CEF)

A goals-based course

English Unlimited is a practical, goals-based course for adult learners of English. The course goals are taken and adapted from the language-learning goals stated in the Common European Framework of Reference for Languages (CEF).

The goals of the CEF are divided into a number of **scales** which describe abilities in different kinds of communication. We've chosen the scales which we felt to be the most useful for adult general English learners at Starter level. These are:

Speaking
Describing experience
Conversation
Goal-oriented co-operation
Transactions to obtain goods and services
Information exchange

Writing
Creative writing
Correspondence
Notes, messages and forms

Listening
Overall listening comprehension
Listening to announcements and instructions

Reading
Overall reading comprehension
Reading correspondence
Reading for orientation
Reading for information and argument

Where the goals are met

As you can see in the example unit on pp6–10, goals are given for the three main lessons of each unit (culminating in each unit's Target activity) and on the Explore speaking and Explore writing pages. These are closely linked to the Self-assessment, which learners do at the end of the Look again page.

Listening and reading goals are not usually given on the page as they are addressed repeatedly throughout the course. The CEF tables on the Teacher's Pack DVD-ROM show which parts of the course deal with the listening and reading goals.

Find out more about the CEF

You can read about the CEF in detail in *Common European Framework of Reference for Languages: Learning, teaching, assessment* (2001), Council of Europe Modern Languages Division, Strasbourg, Cambridge University Press, ISBN 9780521005319.

Hello

Unit goal: talk to someone for the first time

1.1

Goals: talk to someone for the first time
introduce yourself
say where you are from
ask people where they are from

Core language:

VOCABULARY	Hello, I'm …; I'm from …; my, your
	My name is …; What's your name?
	Countries: England, Russia, China; the USA
GRAMMAR	be present – questions: Are you …?; Are you
	from …?; Where are you from?

I'm …

VOCABULARY Hello, I'm …, My …

Optional lead-in with books closed

Introduce yourself to the class. Say *I'm (John).* a few times.
Point to yourself to show the meaning of *I.* Say to one
learner: *Hello. I'm (John).* Get the learner to give his / her
name in the same way. Go round the class, getting learners
to give their names, using *I'm … .*
Write on the board: *I'm John. = I am John.*
Say both sentences to show how *I'm* is a short form of *I am.*
Introduce yourself again. This time say *My name is (John).*
Say a few common names to show what *name* means.
Go round the class, getting learners to give their names,
using *My name is … .*

1 a *Presentation of 'I'm …, My name is …; Hello. Hi.'*
Look at the photo and play recording **1.1**. Ask learners
what words go in the gaps.

> Hi. I'm Carlos Puente.
> Hello. My name is Peter Newman.

b If they haven't already done so, get learners to give
their own names, using the same expressions.

LISTENING

2 a *Numbers 1–3.* See if learners know the numbers. If
not, say them and learners repeat. Play recording **1.2**.
Pause after each conversation and ask learners to say
which photo it is.

> A 2 B 3 C 1

Optional extra

Use the photos to teach *school, café* and *airport.* Ask *Where
is it?* to elicit the words. Write them on the board.

b *Presentation of 'My, your; What's your name?'.* To
teach *your* and the question *What's your name?*, point
to yourself and say *My name is (John)*, then point to
a learner and say *Your name is (Ali).* Then ask a few
learners *What's your name?*.

 / Learners read conversations A, B and C and fill
in the gaps. If necessary, play the recording again to
check.

> A your; My
> B I'm; I'm
> C your; your; My

Check that learners know *new* and *teacher.*
To demonstrate the meaning of *Nice to meet you,* say
hello to a learner. Shake his / her hand and say:
Nice to meet you. You could give an equivalent in
learners' own language, or ask them for one.

c *Short forms.* Look at the table and say both forms to
make the difference clear. Then play recording **1.3**
(or say the sentences yourself) and get learners to
repeat. Focus on the stress pattern of:
– *What's your name?*

Language note

It isn't essential to use short forms, but they are very
common in spoken English, especially *I'm.*

SPEAKING

3 a Learners read the sentences and choose the best
order. Go through the answers together by listening to
recording **1.4**.

> 1 Hello, I'm Luis.   2 What's your name?   3 I'm Ali.
> 4 Hi, Ali.   5 Nice to meet you.

b *Mingling activity.* To demonstrate, choose one learner
and have a conversation. Then have a conversation
with a second learner, getting him / her to ask you
What's your name?.

Learners move freely round the class, introducing
themselves and asking other learners' names.

Alternative

If it is difficult for learners to move freely around the class,
you could ask them to stay in their seats and talk to the
people around them.

I'm from …

VOCABULARY Countries

1 *Presentation.* Play recording **1.5** or say the names of
the countries. Ask learners to identify them.

> A China   B the USA   C England   D Russia

Learners repeat the countries. Focus on the
pronunciation of /juː‿es‿ˈeɪ/, and the /ə/ sounds in
/ˈɪŋglənd/, /ˈrʌʃə/, /ˈtʃaɪnə/. You could also practise
/ˈlʌndən/ and /ˈmɒskəʊ/.

GRAMMAR Questions

2 a *Presentation of 'I'm from …'.* Look at the picture and
play recording **1.6**. Establish what the people say:

> 1 I'm from the USA. I'm from New York.
> 2 I'm from England. I'm from London.

Get learners to repeat the sentences. Focus on the pronunciation of /frəm/.

> **Optional extra**
>
> Ask learners where the people in the picture are. Use this to teach *plane* (or *on a plane*) and *passenger*.

b *Presentation of 'Are you (from) ...? Where are you from?'*. Play recording **1.6** again. Learners say questions in the correct order. Write the questions on the board.

> **Alternative**
>
> Ask learners what the questions are. Then play recording **1.6** again to check.

To show how the word order changes in questions, write on the board:

   1   2   2   1

– <u>*You*</u> <u>*are*</u> *from England* → <u>*Are*</u> <u>*you*</u> *from England?*

Point out that *you* and *are* change round.

Look at the table. Read through the examples.
You could give other sentences and learners make questions:

– *I'm a teacher.* → *Am I a teacher?*
– *You are here.* → *Are you here? Where are you?*

c *Practice of questions and answers.* Look at the speech bubbles and learners say the questions and answers.

> 1 – *Where are you from?*
> – *(I'm from) China.*
> 2 – *Are you from the USA?*
> – *Yes, I'm from Miami.*
> 3 – *Are you from China?*
> – *No, I'm from the USA.*
> 4 – *Where are you from?*
> – *(I'm from) London.*

Go through the answers together by listening to recording **1.7**.

👥 Learners ask and answer the questions.

SPEAKING

3 a *Writing.* Ask learners: *Where are you from?* Check that they can say their country correctly. Write the country name(s) on the board for learners to copy.

b Ask each question to two or three different learners round the class. Expected answers:

> 1 *No. I'm from (Japan).*
> 2 *I'm from (Japan).*
> 3 *I'm from (Tokyo).*

c Get learners to ask you the questions. Give true answers.

👥 Learners ask and answer the questions in pairs. Instead of *I'm from London*, they should give their own home town.

> **Alternative: Mingling activity**
>
> Learners move freely round the class, asking and answering questions.

Classroom language: Letter, word, sentence ...

Goal: to understand simple words needed to use the Coursebook

Core language:
letter, word, sentence, number, question

1 *Vocabulary.* Use the examples to establish the meaning of the words.

> 2 *a question* 3 *a word* 4 *a letter* 5 *a number*

Focus on the pronunciation of the words, especially the reduced vowels in /ˈsentənts/ and /ˈkwestʃən/.

> **Optional practice**
>
> If necessary, write other examples on the board to make the meanings clear. Show that:
> – a sentence starts with a capital (big) letter and ends in a full stop (.)
> – a question starts with a capital (big) letter and ends in a question mark (?)
> Learners could find examples of sentences and questions in the Coursebook.

2 👥 *Practice.* Learners do the exercise.

> 1 *word*   2 *number*   3 *sentence*   4 *letter*   5 *question*
> 6 *letter*   7 *number*

> **Language note**
>
> You could point out that *P* is a capital letter (or big letter) and *m* is a small letter. Write *capital letter* and *small letter* on the board.

1.2

Goals: talk to someone for the first time
ask and say where places are
say where you live

Core language:

VOCABULARY	*flat, apartment, house, room, car*
	big, small, nice
	in, near (London)
GRAMMAR	*a / an: a* (flat), *an* (apartment)
	be present: It's ..., Where is ...?
	Present simple – positive: *I / We* + verb

Where is it?

GRAMMAR *It's ..., Where is ...?*

1 *Presentation of 'It's .. (It is ...); I think ...'* Look on p86 of the Coursebook. Look at photo A and ask:
– *Where is it?* (England, or London).

Show the full and short forms of *It is* on the board:
– *It is ...* → *It's ...*

Then add *I think*:
– *I think it's ...*

Show the meaning of *I think* with gestures. Get learners to practise saying the sentence. You could help them with the stress pattern by 'back-chaining':
– *Éngland* → *It's Éngland.* → *I thínk it's Éngland.*

👥 Learners look at photos B–H and guess the countries, making sentences with *I think it's ... .*

> A England   B the USA   C Russia   D the USA
> E the USA   F China   G Russia   H China

2 a *Presentation of 'Where's ...? (Where is ..?) I don't know'.* Books closed. Ask: *Where's Manchester?* (It's in England.) Write the full and short forms on the board: *Where is ...?* → *Where's ...?*

Practise asking the question, using different places:
– *London* → *Where's London?*
– *Beijing* → *Where's Beijing?*, etc.

Open books. Look at the city names in the box. Give possible answers for one item, e.g.
– *Where's Shanghai?*
– *I don't know. / It's in China. / I think it's in China.*

Show the meaning of *I don't know* with gestures.

> Shanghai: It's in China.
> Miami: It's in the USA.
> Novosibirsk: It's in Russia.
> Beijing: It's in China.
> Oxford: It's in England.
> Los Angeles: It's in the USA.
> Moscow: It's in Russia.
> Manchester: It's in England.

b Read the full and short forms in the table or play recording **1.8**. Show on the board how we use an apostrophe (') to show that a letter is missing. Practise saying the short forms.

Language note

We usually use short forms (*It's*, *Where's*, etc.) in conversation, but not always. It is important for learners to understand them, but don't insist on them using short forms themselves at this stage.
After some nouns, it isn't possible to use a short form, e.g. *Paris is ...*, *Los Angeles is ...* .

Big, small ...

VOCABULARY *big, small*

1 *Presentation of '(It's) big, small; (It's a) house'.* Look at the picture and ask *What is it?* (a house). Then ask: *Is it big or small?* (big). Use gestures to show the meaning of *big* and *small*.

2 a *Presentation of 'It's a big house.'* On the board, write: *It's a house.* Then show how we can add *big*:
– *It's a big house.*

Read the sentences or play recording **1.9**. Ask learners to repeat. Make sure that they say *It's a house* and *It's a big house* (not just *It's big house*). Make sure they say *a* as /ə/.

Language note

For many learners, the use of *a* will be the same as in their own language.
If learners have no article system in their own language, tell them that *a* = 'one'.

---

b Look at the pictures on page 86. Use the pictures to present *car* and *room* (point to a picture and ask: *What's this?*).

👥 Learners take it in turns to choose a picture and say a sentence.

I live ...

READING

1 *Presentation of 'flat, apartment; a/an'.* Look at each photo. Ask: *What is it?*. Use this to present *flat* and *apartment*. Ask if they are big or small.

> A It's a flat (an apartment). It's small.
> B It's a flat (an apartment). It's big.
> C It's a house. It's big.

Language note

Flat is British English; *apartment* is US (and also international) English. They mean the same.

Point out that we say *an apartment*. This is because *apartment* begins with the sound 'a' (a vowel). If necessary, show that it is difficult to say *a apartment*, so we add /n/.

Note

Don't give a detailed presentation of *a / an* at this point. It is presented in Unit **4.2**.

---

b Learners read the sentences and match them with the photos. Then they fill in the gaps.

> 1 B – an apartment
> 2 C – a house
> 3 A – a flat

If necessary, quickly present *live* and *have* (it should be clear from the context), but wait till **2** to focus on these verbs.

c Play recording **1.10**.

d Learners cover the sentences in **1b** and listen again (either play recording **1.10**, or read them aloud). Then ask the questions round the class.

> Photo A – It's a flat. It's very small. It's in Paris.
> Photo B – It's an apartment. It's big. It's in Dubai.
> Photo C – It's a house. It's near Naples. It's a town in Florida, in the USA.

👥 *Sentences covered.* Learners ask and answer the questions.

GRAMMAR *I / We* + verb

2 a *Presentation of 'I have, We have, I live, We live'.* Give examples about yourself to present the meaning of *live* and *have*, e.g.
I live in (Rome). I have a house.
I live in a house in (Rome) / I have a house in (Rome).

To show the meaning of *we*, say *I live in (Rome)*, then stand with a learner and say *We live in (Rome)*.

Read the sentences in the table. Ask learners to repeat *I live, we live, I have, we have*, to check pronunciation. Alternatively, ask learners to read the sentences aloud. Check learners say /lɪv/ not /liːv/ and /hæv/ not /hæf/.

b 👤/👥 Learners write *live* or *have* in the gaps.

> 1 have   2 live   3 have   4 live   5 live   6 have

LISTENING

3 Read the sentences and look at plans A and B. Then play recording **1.11** and go through the answers.

> *1 Yes.*   *2 No (in Berlin).*   *3 No (it's very small).*   *4 Yes.*
> *It's Flat A (one room and a kitchen).*

If necessary, play recording **1.11** again.

WRITING

4 a To show what to do, write or say a few sentences about your own house / flat.

Learners write sentences about their house or flat. While they are writing, go round and check.

> **Note**
>
> If learners all live in the same town, ask them to write what part of town they live in.
> If they live alone or have their own house / flat, they should write *I have*. If they live with their parents or family, they should write *we have*.

   b 👥 *Speaking.* Learners tell their partner about their house or flat.

> **Optional practice**
>
> *1 Mingling activity*
> After writing, learners move freely round the class. They tell two or three other learners about their house / flat.
>
> *2 Writing for homework*
> Learners do this as a speaking activity and write the sentences for homework.
>
> *3 Add a photo*
> Ask learners to find (or take) a photo of their house or flat and add it to their sentences.

Sounds and spelling: The letter *i*

Goal: to recognise and pronounce the letter *i* with the sounds /ɪ/ and /aɪ/

Core language:

Words from Unit 1 with the letter *i*

1 /ɪ/ *and* /aɪ/. Say the words or play recording **1.12**. Focus on the two sounds:
  – /ɪ/ is said with lips neutral, not spread (it has a lower quality than in many languages).
  – show how /aɪ/ is formed from /a/ + /ɪ/. Get learners to say the sounds separately. Then run them together.
2 🧍/👥 Learners put the words in the correct group. Go through the answers together by listening to recording **1.13**.

/ɪ/	/aɪ/
it	five
in	China
big	I'm

> **Language note**
>
> Words with the spelling pattern *i...e* (*five, nice*) usually have the sound /aɪ/. *Live* (as a verb) is an exception because it is pronounced /lɪv/. Point this out to the class, if necessary.

3 a Play recording **1.14**. Learners listen and underline the words they hear. Check the answers and play recording **1.14** again if necessary.

> Hi
> it's
> I'm
> in
> Paris

   b A strong pair of learners have the conversation in front of the class. Check pronunciation.

👥 Learners have a similar conversation, but use their own name and choose a different place.

1.3

Goals: talk to someone for the first time
       ask and say if you are married
       say if you have children

Core language:

VOCABULARY	Numbers: 0–10
	boy, boys; *girl, girls*; *child, children*
	Family: *no (children)* = 'not any', *married*
GRAMMAR	*be* present – negative: *I'm, I'm not*;
	we're, we're not

Numbers

VOCABULARY Numbers 0–10

1 *Presentation of numbers 0–10.* Learners say the numbers. If necessary, say them (or play recording **1.15**) and get learners to repeat.

> **Option: Stronger classes**
>
> Learners may already know the numbers. Check this with books closed: write the numbers on the board, and learners say them. Then write the words. Focus on any that learners aren't sure of.

Focus on the sounds /wʌn/ and /θriː/.

> **Language note**
>
> To help students say /θ/, get them to say /t/, and notice where their tongue touches their top teeth. Then get them to make less contact, so air can pass their tongue and their teeth. This should produce a /θ/ sound.

Look at the words in the box. Learners read them aloud. Then learners write the numbers with the words beside them, in order.

To practise, say a number and learners say the next one. They could also do this in pairs.

2 👥 Learners cover **1** and practise saying the numbers in A–F. Then go through the answers together.

> **Language note**
>
> All these numbers would normally be said as separate digits in English. *0* can be said as *zero* or *oh*.

Families

VOCABULARY boy, girl ...

1 a *Presentation of vocabulary.* Look at the picture and see if learners know the words (*boys*, *a girl*, etc.). If not, read them out or play recording **1.16** and ask learners to repeat. You could also ask questions, e.g.
– *Look at C – a boy or boys?*

Use this to present plurals. Write *boy* and *girl* on the board, and say the words. Then add *-s* and say *boys* and *girls*. Get learners to repeat the singular and plural forms (check that they pronounce the *-s* as /z/). Point out that:
– to make a plural, we usually add *-s*.
– *children* is irregular.

Listening. Play recording **1.16**. Learners listen and say the expression they hear.

> A two boys   B a girl   C three girls   D a boy
> E seven children

b 👥 Learners take it in turns to point to a picture. The other learner says what it is.

GRAMMAR I'm not, we're not

2 *Presentation of 'married, no (children)'.* Read the sentences to the class or play recording **1.17**. Ask the class to find the picture.

> 1 C   2 E   3 A   4 D   5 B

As you go through, present *married* by showing or gesturing to a wedding ring and show on the board that *no children* = '0 children'.

3 a *Presentation of 'I'm not, we're not'.* Write on the board: *I'm married. We're married.* Then add *not*, to show how to make the sentences negative.

Say the sentences in the box or play recording **1.18** as a model. Ask learners to repeat.

Tell the class *I'm married* (or *I'm not married*). A few learners round the class say if they are married or not married.

b 👤/👥 Learners add words to the gaps. Go through the answers together by listening to recording **1.19**.

> 1 girl   2 married; children   3 child   4 have; girls

4 *Speaking.* Look on page 87. To show how the game works, say a few different sentences and learners say the picture, e.g.
– *I'm married. We have two boys.* (2)
– *I have one girl.* (1)

👥 Learners take it in turns to say a sentence. The other learner guesses the picture.

5 *Writing.* Show what to do by writing two sentences about yourself on the board.

Learners write true sentences. As they do this, go round and check. A few learners could read out their sentences.

Target activity: Talk to someone for the first time

Goal: Talk to someone for the first time

Core language:

1.1 VOCABULARY	Hello, I'm, my ...	
1.3 VOCABULARY	boy, girl	
1.1 GRAMMAR	Questions	
1.2 GRAMMAR	I / We + verb	

TASK LISTENING

1 a *Preparation for exercise 1b.* Read the expressions and ask learners to suggest what the people say.

> I'm / My name is Mark.
> I'm from the USA.
> I live in / near London.
> I have / live in a small apartment.
> I'm not married.
>
> I'm / My name is Claudia.
> I'm from / I live in Brazil.
> I have / live in a flat in São Paulo.
> I'm married.
> I have two sons.

To focus on the word *son*, tell the class: *I have one child – a boy. So he is my son.*

If you like, teach *daughter* in the same way.

b *Listening.* Play recording **1.20**. Pause from time to time to check what the speakers actually say. Don't focus on the questions at this stage.

c *Writing.* Establish what the questions should be. Either do this together, or let learners work alone or in pairs, then go through them together:

> 1 What's your name?
> 2 Are you married?
> 3 Where are you from?
> 4 What about you?

If necessary, play recording **1.20** again to check. Alternatively, play it and let learners follow the script on p120.

TASK

2 a *Role play.* To show what to do, take the role of either Mark or Claudia. Choose a strong learner and have a conversation (the learner should be him/herself). Then choose another learner. This time, the learner should be either Mark or Claudia and you are yourself.

    Learners have conversations in pairs. One learner takes the role of either Mark or Claudia (depending on whether they are male or female) and the other learner is him / herself.

b Learners change roles and have a second conversation. Learners could change partners to do this.

 You could use photocopiable activity 1A on the Teacher's DVD-ROM at this point.

Keyword *this*

Goal: identify things in a picture or a room

Core language:

This is ...
What's this? It's ...
mother, father, bed, desk, door, window, picture, room, chair

1 *Presentation of 'This is ...'.* Look at the pictures and check that learners understand *mother* and *father*.

    Play recording **1.21** and ask what Sophie says. Write *This is ...* on the board. To make it clear how we use *This is ...*, give examples using gestures, e.g.
– point to a learner and say *This is (Maria).*
– show your Coursebook and say *This is my book.*

2 a *Vocabulary.* Go through the words in the box and point to the things in the picture or in the classroom. Say *This is a door*, etc. If necessary, play recording **1.22**. Ask learners to repeat the words and focus on the pronunciation of /dɔː/, /tʃɛə/ and /ˈpɪktʃə/.

b *Practice of 'This is'.* Learners practise saying sentences with *This is*. Prompt them by saying *a door, a window,* etc.

3 *Practice of 'What's this?'.* Point to things in the picture and ask *What's this?* Learners should answer *It's a (door).*

    Learners cover the words and ask and answer questions.

Learners could point to the same things in the room.

1.4 Explore speaking

Goal: say hello and goodbye

Core language:

Hi, Hello
How are you?, Are you OK?
I'm fine, Fine, thanks
Goodbye, Bye, See you, Nice to meet you

1 a *'Hello' words and responses.* Play recording **1.23** and ask learners to repeat. Focus on the stress pattern of the question:

    Hi, how are you?

Practise the conversation with a few learners round the class.

b Read through the words in the box and learners repeat them. Point out that:
– *Hello* and *Hi* mean the same. *Hi* is more casual (so friends would say this).
– *thanks* means the same as *thank you*. It is slightly more casual.

Play recording **1.24**. Learners listen and underline the expressions they hear.

> Hi!
> Hello
> How are you?
> Are you OK?
> I'm fine.
> I'm OK.

2 *Speaking.* Have conversations with a few learners, using the expressions in **1b**. Sometimes start the conversation yourself, and sometimes get a learner to start.

Learners move freely round the class, 'meeting' other learners and using the expressions in **1b**.

3 a *'Goodbye' words*. Read the expressions and learners match them with the photos.

  b Play recording **1.25** to check. Point out that:
    – *Goodbye*, *Bye* and *See you* mean the same. *Bye* and *See you* are more casual.
    – we can say *Nice to meet you* when we say hello or when we say goodbye.

4 *Practice of 'goodbye' words*. Say goodbye to a few learners, using different expressions each time.

    Learners practise saying goodbye two or three times, using different expressions each time.

 You could use photocopiable activity 1B on the Teacher's DVD-ROM at this point.

Across cultures: Students

Goals: to give practice in reading short texts
to sensitise learners to ways of life in different countries and cultures

Core language:
student, *study*
Countries: *Vietnam*, *Germany*, *Ghana*

1 *Reading*. Use the photos to show the meaning of *student* and *study*. Point out that *study* is a verb, like *live* and *have*, so we say *I study* ... .

Learners read the quotes, either alone or in pairs. The first time, they should try to guess the meaning of new words.

Learners read again using dictionaries to check any new words (or go through the quotes together and present the new words).

2 *Speaking*. Ask learners what is normal in their country. In a single nationality class, ask: *Do you agree?*.

You could ask learners to write a sentence about students in their own country. To help, you could write on the board: *In my country* ... .

Look again

VOCABULARY

1 a 👥 *Similar words*. Learners find pairs of words and write them down.

> big – small; hello – goodbye; flat – apartment; door – window; five – three; the USA – China; boy – girl; yes – no; café – restaurant

  b Learners write sentences. Possible answers:

> 1 We're from the USA.
> 2 I'm a student (teacher / boy / girl).
> 3 We live in a (small / big) flat / apartment.

2 *Plural forms*. Learners write the plural forms.

> 2 rooms 3 windows 4 we 5 boys 6 children

3 *Numbers 0 – 10*. Learners write the numbers as words. Go through the answers by writing them on the board.

> 2 two 3 four 4 one

SPELLING

4 Learners correct the words.

> 2 have 3 teacher 4 goodbye 5 Russia 6 house
> 7 apartment

GRAMMAR

'be' present: am, is are. Read through the table.

Other verbs. Read through the table.

5 Learners correct the mistakes.

> 1 We are from the USA. (We're from the USA.)
> 2 Are you from England?
> 3 I have two children.
> 4 We have a small house.

6 Learners add a missing word to each sentence.

> 1 My name is Ahmed. (My name's Ahmed.)
> 2 I have a flat in Beijing.
> 3 Manchester is in England. (Manchester's in England.)
> 4 We live in a big house.

Self-assessment

To help focus learners on the self-assessment, you could read it through, giving a few more examples of the language they have learned in each section (or asking learners to tell you). Then they circle a number on each line.

Unit 1 Extra activities on the Teacher's DVD-ROM

Printable worksheets, activity instructions and answer keys are on your Teacher's DVD-ROM.

1A Who am I?

Activity type: Speaking – Information gap – Groups of six

Aim:
To practise talking about yourself and asking questions

Language: Talk to someone for the first time – Coursebook p11

Preparation: Make one copy of the two worksheets for every six learners. Cut each worksheet along the dotted line to make sets of six cards.

Time: 20 minutes

1B Conversation dominoes

Activity type: Reading – Dominoes – Pairs

Aim: To review conversation language

Language: Talk to someone for the first time – Coursebook p11; say hello and goodbye – Coursebook p12

Preparation: Make one copy of the worksheet for each pair of learners. Cut it along the dotted lines into a set of 16 dominoes. Shuffle each set.

Time: 15–20 minutes

Unit 1 Self-study Pack

In the Workbook

Unit 1 of the *English Unlimited Starter Workbook* offers additional ways to practise the vocabulary and grammar taught in the Coursebook. There are also activities which build reading and writing skills and a whole page of tasks to use with the DVD-ROM video, giving your learners the opportunity to hear and react to spoken English.

- **Vocabulary:** *Hello, I'm, My* ...; Flats and houses; Numbers 0–10; *boy, girl* ...
- **Grammar:** Questions; Questions and answers
- **Time out:** Crossword
- **Explore writing:** Capital letters
- **DVD-ROM Extra:** *Nice to meet you.*

On the DVD-ROM

Unit 1 of the *English Unlimited Starter Self-study Pack DVD-ROM* contains interactive games and activities for your learners to practise and improve their vocabulary, grammar and pronunciation, and also their speaking and listening. It also contains video material (with the possibility for learners to record themselves) to use with the *Workbook*.

- **Vocabulary and Grammar:** Extra practice of Coursebook language and Keyword
- **Classroom language:** Letter, word, sentence ...
- **Sounds and spelling:** The letter *i*
- **Explore speaking:** Say hello and goodbye
- **Video:** *Nice to meet you.*

2 People

2.1

Goals: talk about people you know
ask and say how old people are
talk about families

Core language:

VOCABULARY   Numbers: 11–20
Family: *mother, father, brother, sister, son, daughter, wife, husband*
GRAMMAR   be present: *He's ..., She's ..., They're ...*
Possessive adjectives: *my, his, her*

Numbers 11–20

VOCABULARY Numbers 11–20

1   *Review of numbers 1–10.* Books closed. Write numbers 1–10 on the board. Point to different numbers and ask learners to say them.

Presentation of numbers 11–20. Write numbers 11–20 on the board and see if learners know any of them. Play recording **1.26** or say the numbers and get learners to repeat. Focus on the sounds /əlevən/, /twelv/, /θɜːtiːn/, /fɪftiːn/.

Open books. Learners match the numbers to the words in the box. Read out the words to check.

> **Language note**
>
> *Thirteen, fourteen, fifteen*, etc. have roughly equal stress on each syllable. Encourage learners to make a long /iː/ sound in *-teen* (otherwise it sounds more like *thirty, forty*, etc.)

2   To demonstrate the game, think of a number between 1 and 20. Say: *I have a number. What is it?* Learners guess it.

When they make a guess, tell them *More* or *Less*. Write these words on the board and show what they mean by gestures. Demonstrate once or twice until learners get the idea of the game.

🗣 Learners take it in turns to think of a number and guess.

> **Alternative: Whole class activity**
>
> Learners come to the front of the class one at a time. The rest of the class guess the number.

3   *Listening.* Play recording **1.27**. Pause after each sentence and ask if the sentence is the same as the picture or not. If not, learners give the number in the picture.

> *1 No (19)   2 Yes   3 No (14)   4 No (11)   5 Yes   6 No (20)*

Birthday cards

GRAMMAR *He's ..., She's ...*

1   **a**   *Presentation.* Look at each birthday card and read what it says. Ask: *What is it?* Use this to present *birthday* and *birthday card* (the meaning should be obvious from the pictures). Practise saying /ˈbɜːθdeɪ/.

Learners complete the sentences.

> *A This card is for a girl. She's eight.*
> *B This card is for a boy. He's 16.*

To focus on *He's* and *She's*, write on the board:
– *Sonya is 8. Max is 16.*

Then cross out *Sonya* and *Max* and write:
– *She is 8. He is 16.*
Then cross out *She is* and *He is* and write:
– *She's 8. He's 16.*

b   Read the short forms in the table, or play recording **1.28**. Learners repeat. Focus on the sounds /hiːz/ and /ʃiːz/.

Quickly practise the forms by giving prompts, e.g.
– *Max is 16.* → *He's 16.*
– *a boy* → *He's a boy.*
– *from England* → *He's from England.*

SPEAKING

2   *'How old is he / she?'.* Look at the birthday cards in **1** again and ask: *How old is she? How old is he?* Learners repeat the questions. Write them on the board, focusing on the stress: *How old is she? How old is he?*

Play recording **1.29**. Learners read the conversations. They choose a card from the pictures.

> *Birthday card B*

> **Language note**
>
> Show the meaning of *for* with gestures (you could give a learner a book and say *This is for you*).
> Point out that *this one* = 'this card'.

3   *Role play.* Look on p88. Read through the conversation and learners complete it.

Demonstrate a conversation with two strong learners having the conversation in front of the class.

🗣 Learners have three conversations and choose a suitable card each time.

Round-up. Ask learners which card they chose.

Family

VOCABULARY Family

1 a *Vocabulary presentation.* Look at the photos and play recording **1.30**. Learners write numbers beside the words.

> 2 father   3 sister   4 son   5 husband   6 daughter

To check the meaning, you could use the words in a few simple questions, e.g.
– *I have a daughter. Is that a boy or a girl?* (A girl.) *How about you? Who has a daughter? What's her name?*

Focus on the other two words: *wife*, *brother*. Give an example to show the meaning (e.g. *I have a husband, John. He's my husband. I'm his wife.*)

Option: Stronger classes

Look at the photos and ask learners who the people are (Say: *This is Omar. So who is this woman?*). Use this to introduce the words before learners listen.

---

b *Pronunciation.* Learners write the words in the table. Then play recording **1.31**, and practise saying the words. Focus on the pronunciation of /ˈdɔːtə/; the /ʌ/ sound in /ˈmʌðə/, /ˈbrʌðə/ and /sʌn/; and also on the /ð/ sound in /ˈmʌðə/, /ˈbrʌðə/ and /ˈfaːðə/.

2 a *'His, her'.* Read the two sentences and ask learners to choose *his* or *her*.

> A his   B her

If necessary, give a few more examples, using things in the classroom.
– *I have a book. It's my book.*
– *Andrej has a book.* (Hold it up) *Is it my book or his book?*

b *Practice of 'his, her'.* To introduce the pair work, ask about the people in photos A and B:
– *Look, this is Omar. Who's this?* (His mother.) Do this with two or three items.

👥 Learners ask and answer questions about the photos.

3 a *'They're'.* To introduce *they're*, point to a learner and say *He's* (or *She's*) *a student.* Then point to two learners and say *They're students.* Write on the board: *They are students.* Then cross out *They are* and write: *They're students.*

Optional presentation

Books closed. Show a wedding photo or a photo of a well-known married couple from a newspaper or magazine. Ask questions to elicit *husband and wife* (*What are they? Are they brother and sister? Are they friends?*).
Write on the board:
_____ *husband and wife.*
Ask learners what goes in the gap. Use this to present *They're*.

Read sentences 1–4 and match them with the photos.

> 1 B   2 A   3 D   4 C

b *Pronunciation.* Play recording **1.32** and practise the pronunciation of *they're*: /ðeə/.

SPEAKING

4 Look on page 87 and look together at photo 1. Write on the board *I think they're ...* and learners give a sentence.

👥 Learners look at the other photos and say who they think the people are. They could write sentences. Possible answers:

> 1 brother and sister
> 2 husband and wife
> 3 mother and son
> 4 a family (father and mother / husband and wife / ...)
> 5 father and son
> 6 friends / sisters

Classroom language: *Look, read, write ...*

Goal: to understand simple classroom instructions

Core language:
Verbs for classroom activities: *look (at)*, *listen (to)*, *talk (to)*, *read*, *write*, *say*

1 *Vocabulary.* Go through the words and use mime and gestures to make the meaning clear. Alternatively, use the words in simple examples to show the meaning, e.g.
– *Look at the photo.*
– *Read this sentence.*
– *Say 'Hello'.*
– *Listen to me.*
– *Write 'Hello'.*
– *Talk to Maria.*

Learners write the words in their own language. If you don't know their language, encourage them to use a bilingual dictionary to check. Point out that:
– we say *Look at me. Look at the picture.* (not *Look the picture.*)
– we say *Listen to me. Listen to the CD.* (not *Listen the CD.*)

2 *Listening.* Play recording **1.33**. Learners write down the verb they hear.

> 1 look
> 2 write
> 3 read
> 4 listen
> 5 say
> 6 talk
> 7 listen

After each item, ask what the person said.

2.2

Goals: talk about people you know
ask and say where you work
say where other people work

Core language:

VOCABULARY	*I'm a ... I work in, I work for*
	Places of work: *shop, office, hotel, school, hospital, café, restaurant, supermarket, company*
	Jobs and occupations: *waiter, teacher, doctor, manager, student*
GRAMMAR	Present simple – positive: *I work, He / She works*

Work

VOCABULARY *work in, work for*

1 a *'I'm a ..., I work ...; work in, work for'.* Look at the picture and ask where the people are (At a party). Play recording **1.34** or read the sentences yourself. Learners match the sentences with pictures A–C.

> I'm a student. I'm at university in Hong Kong – B
> I work for Dell. It's a computer company. – C
> I work in a restaurant. I'm a waiter. – A

Check that learners know *company* (give examples of well-known companies).

b Read the sentences in the table. Check that learners:
– can say *work*: /wɜːk/
– understand that *work* is a verb, like *I have*, *I live*.

Give a few other examples to show the meaning of *work for* (you could mention local companies).

Alternative: Presentation with books closed

To introduce the verb *work*, tell the class about yourself: say *I'm a teacher* and then say a sentence with *I work* (e.g. *I work in a school, I work for International House*). Write the two sentences on the board.
If possible, use your own job to introduce both the expressions *work in* and *work for*.

---

c *Writing.* Look at **1**. Point out that before jobs we use *a* – so we say *I'm a student, I'm a teacher* (not *I'm teacher*).

👤 / 👥 Learners write sentences. Go round and check.

> 2 I work in a restaurant.
> 3 I work for Dell.
> 4 I'm a waiter.
> 5 I'm at university in Hong Kong.
> 6 It's a computer company.

LISTENING

2 a *'What's your job? What do you do?'.* Play recording **1.35** and ask what the questions are.

> 1 What's your job?
> 2 What do you do?

Write the questions on the board.

Language note

Teach *What do you do?* as a fixed expression at this point. Tell the class that it means *What's your job?*.

---

b *Practice of 'What's your job? What do you do?'.* Ask a pair of strong learners to have each conversation in front of the class.

👥 Learners practise the conversations together in pairs.

Places

VOCABULARY Places of work

1 a *Vocabulary.* Look at the photos and ask *What is it?*. Use this to present the words in the box. Practise pronunciation, focusing especially on the stress in *office, hotel, hospital*. Teach the word *place* (Tell the class: *These are all places in a town.*).

> A school   B hospital   C café   D office   E hotel   F shop

b *Listening.* Play recording **1.36**. Learners write the places.

> 1 shop   2 office   3 hotel   4 hospital   5 school   6 café

Ask learners for other details about 1–6.

> 1 It's a bookshop.
> 2 The office is in Paris.
> 3 It's a small hotel – 20 rooms. It's in Manchester.
> 4 It's a big hospital.
> 5 The school is in London.
> 6 She's a student.

If necessary, play recording **1.36** again to check.

2 👥 / 👥 Learners make sentences round the class or in pairs.

> 1 I'm a teacher. 2 I work in a hospital.
> 3 I work for Hitachi. 4 I work in a big hotel.
> 5 I work for Microsoft. 6 I'm a student. 7 I'm a doctor.
> 8 I work for a big company in New York.

SPEAKING

3 To show how to play the game, choose a job or a place from page 16. Learners guess by making sentences with *You ...*, as in the examples.

👥 / 👥 Learners take it in turns to choose a job or a place and to guess. Alternatively, do this with the whole class together.

Conversation practice

You could do the conversation practice exercises on p116 at this point.

He works, she works ...

GRAMMAR *He / She works ...*

1 a Look at the two photos. Learners complete the sentences.

> 1 She's a doctor.   2 He's a manager.
> 3 She works in a hospital.   4 He works for IKEA.

b Look at the table, and ask how A and B are different. Use this to focus on the -*s* ending: *He works, She works*. Write these forms on the board and underline the -*s*. Practise saying them.

c *Practice of 'He / She works'.* Look at photo A and ask learners to make a sentence using a word from the box. Possible answers:

> A She works in a supermarket. She works for Tesco.

👥 Learners look at photos B–F and make sentences. Sometimes only one sentence will be possible, sometimes two:

> B He's a teacher. He works in a school.
> C He's a waiter. He works in a café.
> D (She's a manager.) She works in an office.
> E (He's a doctor.) He works in a hospital.
> F He works in a hotel.

2 a To show what to do, think of two people you know (friends or people) in your family. Tell learners about their jobs (keeping to the language presented in this unit). Write sentences about them on the board.

Learners write sentences. Emphasise that they should find a *simple* way to write about the jobs (for example: *My father works in an office in Paris*, or *He works for Vivendi. – not He's the assistant sales manager!*). As learners write, go round and check.

b 👥 *Speaking.* Learners sit in groups of three or four. In turn, one learner tells the others in his / her group about the two people. Learners should try to do this without reading their sentences.

Round-up. A few learners tell you one thing that they heard.

Sounds and spelling: The letters *th*

Goal: to recognise and pronounce the letters *th* with the sounds /ð/ and /θ/

Core language:
Words from Units 1 and 2 with the letters *th*

1 *Presentation of /ð/ and /θ/.* Say the words or play recording **1.37**. Learners repeat the words. Focus on the sounds /ð/ and /θ/:
   – to pronounce /ð/, get learners to say /d/ and to feel how their tongue touches the back of their teeth. Then get them to loosen the contact and let air pass through. This should produce /ð/.
   – show how to produce /θ/ in the same way, but starting from the sound /t/.

2 *Practice in recognising /ð/ and /θ/.* Learners put the words in the correct group. Go through the answers together by listening to recording **1.38**.

/ð/	/θ/
the	three
father	thanks
with	birthday

3 *Listening.* Play the two conversations in recording **1.39**. Learners underline the words they hear.

> this; brother; thirteen; birthday; thanks

2.3

Goals: talk about people you know
            say where people live and work
Core language:
GRAMMAR   Present simple – positive: *lives, works, has*

Donna's family

READING and LISTENING

1 *Reading and listening.* Play recording **1.40**. Learners read the sentences. Pause after each part and ask: *Which photo?*. Check that students know *parents* (= mother and father) and *Australia*.

> A her parents   B her sister   C her brother and his family

2 Learners add verbs to the box. Write them on the board.

> lives; works; has

Practise saying the verbs. Focus on the /z/ sound in *lives* and *has* and the /s/ sound in *works*.

GRAMMAR *lives, works, has*

3 👤 / 👥 *Practice of 'lives, works, has'.* Learners choose the correct verb.

> 1 have   2 lives   3 has   4 live   5 have   6 works

4 Learners cover the top half of the page. They give a sentence each round the class.

> 1 I live in London.
> 2 I work in (for) a company in London.
> 3 My parents live in Halifax.
> 4 They have a house there.
> 5 My brother lives in Australia.
> 6 He has an Australian wife and three children.
> 7 My sister lives in Tokyo.
> 8 She works for Sony Corporation.

👥 In turn, learners cover the page and test each other.

Target activity: Talk about people you know

Goal: Talk about people you know

Core language:

2.1 VOCABULARY	Family
2.2 VOCABULARY	Work
2.2 GRAMMAR	*He / She works*
2.3 GRAMMAR	*lives, works, has*

PREPARATION

1 *Writing.* To show what to do, choose someone you know and write a sentence on the board.

Learners choose three people they know. They write sentences as in the examples. As they do this, go round and check. Give help where necessary.

TASK

2 Learners tell each other about their three people, if possible without reading their sentences.

Alternatives

1 *Whole class.* In turn, learners tell the class about the three people.
2 *Mingling activity.* Learners move freely round the class, telling three or four other learners about their three people.

Conservation practice

You could do the conversation practice exercises on p116 at this point.

Keyword *have* (1)

Goal: to use *have* and *has* to talk about possessions and family

Core language:

have, has
children, TV, computer, cat, camera, dog, car, house,
MP3 player, flat, mobile phone, bicycle

1 *Possessions.* Learners match the words in the box with pictures A–L. Go through this together and present any new words by listening to recording **1.41** or saying the words yourself. Focus on the pronunciation of *camera, mobile phone, bicycle.*

> *A a TV   B a house   C a car   D a computer*
> *E a camera   F a cat   G an MP3 player   H a dog*
> *I a bicycle   J a flat   K a mobile phone   L children*

Language note

We can say:
– *mobile phone* or just *mobile* (US English: *cell phone*).
– *bicycle* or *bike*.

Learners could test each other in pairs: one learner points to a picture and the other learner says what it is.

2 a Point out that we use *have* with these words: *I have a car, I have a cat*, etc. To introduce the activity, tell the class which things from the picture you have.

Writing. Learners choose three things from the picture and write sentences beginning *I have … .*

b *Speaking.* Learners tell their partner what they have. *Round-up.* Ask pairs if they have the same things.

3 a *Listening.* Play recording **1.42** to demonstrate the game. Ask what the people say.

> 1 *an old car*
> 2 *an old car and a computer*
> 3 *an old car, a computer and five children*

b *Speaking.* Put learners into groups of four or five. Check that everyone understands what to do: each learner adds a new word or expression.

Learners play the game round their group, going round twice.

Round-up. One person from each group remembers all the things their group said.

Alternative: Whole class activity

Play the game round the class.

 You could use photocopiable activity 2A on the Teacher's DVD-ROM at this point.

2.4 Explore writing

Goal: spell words aloud

Core language:
The alphabet

1 a *The alphabet.* Play recording **1.43** or say the letters yourself. Learners repeat. You could also write the alphabet on the board and point to the letters.

b To practise, point to the letters and ask learners to say them. First go through the alphabet, then jump around from letter to letter. Focus on letters that learners find difficult, e.g. *G, J, Q, R, V, W.*

Note

Don't expect learners to master the alphabet immediately. You can practise it frequently in later lessons by asking learners to spell words.

2 a *Listening.* Play recording **1.44**. Learners listen and write the words.

b To check the answers, learners spell the words. Write the words on the board.

> 1 *chair*   2 *table*   3 *eight*   4 *fifteen*   5 *India*   6 *camera*

3 This game is a version of the well-known spelling game 'Hangman'. Play it on the board with the class. Learners guess letters. After each guess, either add the letter to the word, or (if they guess wrong) write it in a separate box on the board.

> 1 *brother*   2 *mother*   3 *husband*   4 *wife*   5 *daughter*

Idea for later lessons

You could play this game as a 'filler' in later lessons. You can play it with any vocabulary you have recently taught (e.g. transport, colours, food).

Across cultures: Families and children

Goals: to give practice in reading short texts
to sensitise students to ways of life in different countries and cultures

Core language:
many, most, some

1 **a** *Reading for main idea.* Use the diagrams to show the meaning of *most* and *some*.

👤 / 👥 Learners read about the three countries. They should try to guess the meaning of new words.

   b Learners circle the correct number. Then discuss this together, referring back to the texts.

> *Japan: 1.5   USA: 2.0   Sudan: 4.5*

2 *Reading for detail.* Learners read again and answer the questions. They can use dictionaries to check any new words (or go through the text together and present the new words).

Go through the answers and ask learners to correct the sentences that aren't true.

> *1 No. She has no brothers or sisters.*
> *2 Yes.*
> *3 No. He has three children.*
> *4 Yes.*
> *5 No. He has two brothers, but no sisters.*
> *6 No. Most people have two children, or just one child.*

3 *Writing.* Learners write two sentences about their country. They read out their sentences.

Mixed nationality classes

Learners from the same country could work together as a group and decide what to write. Then one learner from each country reads out their sentences to the class.

Look again

VOCABULARY

1 **a** 👥 *Word pairs.* Learners find pairs.

> *boy – girl;   husband – wife;   ten – twenty*
> *shop – supermarket;   read – write;*
> *doctor – teacher;   his – her;   cat – dog*

   b Learners write sentences and read them out.

2 *Numbers 11 – 20.* Learners write the numbers as words. Write them on the board.

> *2 twenty   3 eighteen   4 twelve*

3 *Similar words.* Learners add words to the lists. Go through the answers by writing the words on the board. Possible answers:

> *1 teacher, manager, waiter*
> *2 restaurant, shop, station, hospital, school*
> *3 wife, brother, son, daughter, mother, father*
> *4 read, write, talk, say*
> *5 chair, table, bed, picture, window*

SPELLING

4 Learners correct the words. One learner at a time comes to the front of the class and writes an answer on the board. Check with the class: *Is this correct?*

> *1 fourteen   2 daughter   3 friend   4 hospital   5 school*
> *6 office*

CAN YOU REMEMBER? Unit 1

5 **a** Learners write sentences from the table. Go through the answers by writing them on the board.

> *1 I'm from China.   2 I live in a small apartment.*
> *3 I'm not married.   4 I'm a student.*
> *5 I have two children*

   b *Writing and speaking.* To demonstrate, say two sentences about yourself and ask learners if they think they are true or false.

Learners write one true and one false sentence. As they do this, go round and check.

👥 / 👥 Learners read out their sentences in pairs or small groups. The other learner guesses which is true and which is false.

GRAMMAR

'be' present: am, is, are. Read through the table.

Alternative: Presentation with books closed

Write the full forms on the board. Learners tell you the short forms (or come and write them on the board).

Present simple – positive. Read through the table.

Alternative: Presentation with books closed

Write on the board: *I live in London.* Then write:
– They ...
– He ...
Learners complete the sentences.
Do the same for *work* and *have.*

Pronouns and possessive adjectives. Read through the table.

Alternative: Presentation with books closed

Write the left-hand column (*I, you, he, she*) on the board.
Then write *my car* beside *I.* Learners say the other forms.

6 Learners choose the correct word.

> *1 live   2 has   3 They   4 her   5 He's*

7 Learners write short forms.

> *2 What's   3 I'm   4 Where's   5 Who's*

 You could use photocopiable activity 2B on the Teacher's DVD-ROM at this point.

Self-assessment

To help focus students on the self-assessment, you could read it through, giving a few more examples of the language they have learned in each section (or asking students to tell you). Then they circle a number on each line.

Unit 2 Extra activities on the Teacher's DVD-ROM

Printable worksheets, activity instructions and answer keys are on your Teacher's DVD-ROM.

2A Homestay families

Activity type: Speaking – Information gap – Pairs

Aim: To practise talking about people and their possessions

Language: Talk about people you know; Keyword *have* (1) – Coursebook p19

Preparation: Make one copy of the worksheet for each pair of learners. Cut each worksheet into A and B tables along the dotted line.

Time: 20–25 minutes

2B Three in a line

Activity type: Speaking – Noughts and crosses – Pairs

Aim: To review and personalise vocabulary and grammar from the Coursebook

Language: Review of vocabulary and grammar – Coursebook, Unit 2

Preparation: Make one copy of the worksheet for each pair of learners.

Time: 20 minutes

Unit 2 Self-study Pack

In the Workbook

Unit 2 of the *English Unlimited Starter Workbook* offers additional ways to practise the vocabulary and grammar taught in the Coursebook. There are also activities which build reading and writing skills, and a whole page of tasks to use with the DVD-ROM video, giving your learners the opportunity to hear and react to spoken English.

- **Vocabulary:** Family; Numbers 1–20; Work
- **Grammar:** *He's ..., She's ...; He / She works*
- **Explore reading:** Completing a hotel form
- **DVD-ROM Extra:** Family photos

On the DVD-ROM

Unit 2 of the *English Unlimited Starter Self-study Pack DVD-ROM* contains interactive games and activities for your learners to practise and improve their vocabulary, grammar and pronunciation, and also their speaking and listening. It also contains video material (with the possibility for learners to record themselves) to use with the *Workbook*.

- **Vocabulary and Grammar:** Extra practice of Coursebook language and Keyword
- **Classroom language:** Look, read, write ...
- **Sounds and spelling:** The letters *th*
- **Explore writing:** Spelling words
- **Video:** Family photos

3 Where and when?

Unit goal: arrange to meet people

3.1

Goals: arrange to meet people
describe a street
say where you are in a town

Core language:

VOCABULARY	Features of streets: *café, shop, church, mosque; house, flat/apartment; car, taxi, bicycle; tree; street*
	Places in towns: *station, bus station, airport, cinema, café, restaurant, hotel, shop, church, flat (or apartment), house*
	at + place: *at the station, at a café ...*
	Plurals: *shops, cafés, trees, cars,* etc.
	lots of
	Where are you? I'm ...
	Adjectives: *busy, quiet, noisy, nice, beautiful*
GRAMMAR	*there's / there are*

Streets

VOCABULARY Streets

1 a *Presentation of features of streets.* Look at photos A–D. Read the words in the box and check that learners can say them. Ask which photo(s) they are in, using the photos to present them.

> A cars, taxis, flats (or apartments), a mosque
> B people, houses, a tree, a café, bicycles
> C cars, a church, houses, people, shops
> D people, shops

b *Singular and plural forms.* Ask learners to give the singular and plural forms of all the words in **1a** (e.g. *a car → cars*).

> a car → cars
> a taxi → taxis
> a church → churches
> a house → houses
> a person → people
> a shop → shops
> a mosque → mosques
> a flat (an apartment) → flats (apartments)
> a tree → trees
> a café → cafés
> a bicycle → bicycles

Focus on the word *people* (= men, women, boys or girls). We say *one person, two people*.

c *Pronunciation.* Play recording **1.45** and practise saying the plural forms.

> **Language note**
>
> Point out the following features in passing, but don't go into too much detail at this point. Plural -*s* and -*es* endings are presented in Unit 5.
> – *shops, flats, mosques* have the sound /s/ at the end
> – *trees, cars, taxis, cafés* have the sound /z/ at the end
> – *houses* has the sound /ɪz/: /ˈhaʊzɪz/
> – *churches* adds -*es* and has the sound /ɪz/: /ˈtʃɜːtʃɪz/

> **Optional extra**
>
> Learners cover the words and ask and answer questions about the photos, e.g.
> – *What's this?* – *It's a shop.*
> Alternatively, you could bring in photos cut from magazines and use these to test the words.

GRAMMAR *there's / there are*

2 a *'There's / there are'.* Play recording **1.46**. Learners match the sentences with the photos.

> 1 C 2 A 3 B 4 D

Check that learners understand the meaning of *there's / there are*. If necessary, give other simple examples, e.g. *In this room there's a door, there are desks ... .*

Practise saying the sentences. Focus on the stress, and the reduced vowel sounds in /ðeəzə/ and /ðeərə/.

Point out that we use *There's* (= *There is*) with singular nouns and *There are* with plural nouns.

b *Practice of 'there's / there are'.* Learners make sentences with *There's / There are* from the prompts.

> 1 There's   2 There are   3 There are   4 There are
> 5 There's   6 There's   7 There are   8 There are
> 9 There's

Present *lots of* (cars) using gestures.

LISTENING

3 *Presentation of adjectives.* Play recording **1.47**. Ask which adjectives the speakers use and what they say.

> A It's noisy. It's a nice street.
> B It's a very quiet street. There are nice cafés.
> C It's a beautiful street.
> D It's a noisy street. It's always busy.

Check the meaning of the adjectives. To do this, give examples of parts of the town where you are, and ask *Is it quiet? Is it busy?*, etc. Check that learners can say /ˈbɪzi/, /ˈbjuːtɪfəl/, /ˈkwaɪət/.

SPEAKING and WRITING

4 a *Practice making sentences.* Build up a description together of the street where you are now. Prompt by asking questions, e.g.
– *Is it quiet / noisy / busy?* (It's busy.)
– *There are ... what?* (Cars.)
– *What else?* (Lots of shops.)

If there isn't a street outside the class, choose any well-known street in the town.

b *Writing.* Learners write sentences about their own street. As they do this, go round and check.

👥 *Speaking.* Learners tell their partner about their street.

Round-up. Ask a few learners to tell you about their street and their partner's street.

 You could use photocopiable activity 3A on the Teacher's DVD-ROM at this point.

Where are you?

VOCABULARY Places in towns

1 a *Listening.* Learners read the conversations and listen to recording **1.48**. After each conversation, ask which picture it is.

> 1 D   2 A

Check that learners understand *See you soon* (= maybe 5–10 minutes) and *See you there* (= at the café).

b *'at + place'.* Look at the other pictures and ask where the people are.

> B He's at a restaurant.
> C She's at the airport.
> E He's at the cinema.

Practise saying the expressions and focus on the stress pattern: /ət ðə steɪʃən/, /ət ði eəpɔːt/, etc.

> **Language note**
>
> We often use *at* to say where we are in a town.
> We usually say *at the airport, at the cinema, at the station* (because we know which one it is, or there is only one), but *at a restaurant, at a café* (because there are lots of them).

> **Optional extra**
>
> Choose a picture and write on the board: *Are you …?* Mime an action (e.g. drinking a cup of coffee, carrying a suitcase, looking at your watch). Learners guess which picture you chose by asking questions with *Are you (at a café)?*
> Then a learner chooses a picture and the others guess.

2 *Practice.* Look at the conversations in **1a** again and practise them with the class. Focus on the stress pattern in *Where are you?, See you soon, See you there.*

👥 Learners choose one of the places in the pictures and have a conversation.

It's near the station

READING

1 👤 / 👥 *'in, near, next to'.* Read the café reviews and find the three cafés on the map. At this point learners don't need to understand every word in the texts.

> Dino's – 1
> Mike's – 5
> Café Metro – 9

Look at the diagram and present *next to* and *near*. Give a few other examples to make the meaning clear, e.g. point to two people in the class (ask *Is he next to Juan?* Or *Is he near Juan?*), or well-known places in your town. Emphasise that we say *next to* (two words), but we say *near* (one word).

Practise saying the expressions, focusing on the stress pattern:
– *It's next to the cinema.*
– *It's near the station.*

Point out that we say *in* for streets:
– *in King Street.*
– *in Green Street.*

Learners read the texts again and underline any new words (*expensive, ice cream, drinks, sandwiches, garden, cheap, usually*). Write them on the board and show their meaning using examples or gestures.

SPEAKING

2 a Learners read the conversation and guess what the people say.

b Play recording **1.49** to check.

> LIAM Hi. Where are you?
> ALEX I'm at Café Metro.
> LIAM Where's that?
> ALEX It's in King Street, near the bus station.
> LIAM OK, see you there.

3 *Speaking.* Look on p88. To demonstrate the pair work, choose a place on the map and have a conversation like in **2a** with one learner. Make up a name for the café, but don't say the number, e.g.
– *Hi. Where are you?*
– *I'm at Café Miro.*
– *Where's that?*
– *It's in New Street, next to the hotel.*

Learners find the café on the map (3).

👥 Learners have similar conversations.

Round-up. A few pairs say the name of their café and where it is.

Classroom language: Your book

Goals: to understand simple instructions for using the Coursebook
to identify words for using the Coursebook

Core language:

Verbs: *open, close, cover*
Words for using the Coursebook: *sentence, picture, conversation, text, map, word, box, question, answer*

1 *Instructions.* Give the instructions and check that learners follow them (i.e. they should open their books, etc.). If necessary, show the meaning with gestures.

Learners write the words in their own language. In a single nationality class, check what learners are writing, or they can check with each other.

2 *Vocabulary for using the Coursebook.* Look at each word in turn and ask learners to find an example on pages 22 and 23. Present any words that learners don't know by showing an example on the page.

> **Optional extra**
>
> Learners could test each other in A/B pairs:
> A chooses a word, and says *Find a (question).*
> B finds an example from other pages in the Coursebook.

3.2

Goal: arrange to meet people
ask and say the time
say what time of day you do things

Core language:

VOCABULARY Numbers: 20, 25, 30 ...
Clock times: *five thirty, six fifteen,*
one o'clock ...;
about, nearly
What's the time? It's ...
in the morning, afternoon, evening;
It's 5.30 in the (morning)
at + time: at 11.00
Verbs: *work, study, eat, drink (coffee), watch*
TV, have a shower, sleep, get up, go to bed

What's the time?

VOCABULARY Numbers 20, 25, 30 ...

1 a *Numbers.* Play recording **1.50**. Pause after each
remark and ask learners to say the number they hear.

Practise saying the numbers, focusing on the stress:
thírty, fórty, etc.

b Look at the numbers *15, 25, 35 ...* . Ask learners to
say them. Write them (as words) on the board.

Practise saying the words. Point out the difference in
stress between *fiftéen* and *fífty.*

Alternative: Elicitation with books closed

Books closed. Write these numbers on the board and see if
learners know them: *5, 10, 15, 20, 25, 30, 35, 40, 45, 50, 55.*
Then open books and play recording **1.50**.

VOCABULARY Clock times

2 a *Presentation of clock times.* Look at the pictures. Use
it to present times:

> A *seven (seven o'clock)*
> B *two thirty*
> C *four fifteen.*

Focus on the pronunciation and spelling of *o'clock*:
/ə'klɒk/

Alternative: Presentation with books closed

Ask: *What's the time?* See if anyone understands and can
answer. Use this to present:
– the question *What's the time?*
– simple forms for telling the time.

---

b Do some quick practice round the class. Use the
exercise or write times on the board.

Option: Stronger classes

You could also present *half past, quarter past* and *quarter to,*
but only if learners ask about these forms. Increasingly (with
digital clock times) people say *eight fifteen, ten thirty,* etc.

LISTENING and SPEAKING

3 a *Preparation for the listening.* Look at the pictures.
Ask: *What can you see? Where are they?*

> 1 *two men; in a swimming pool*
> 2 *a man and a woman; in the street*
> 3 *a man and a woman; in a flat or at home.*

b *Listening.* Play recording **1.51**. Pause after each
conversation asking: *What's the time?*

> 1 *(about) 3 o'clock*
> 2 *5.15*
> 3 *(nearly) 7.30*

c Read the words in the box, then play recording **1.51**
again. After each conversation, establish which words
learners heard.

> 1 *about*   2 *Excuse me; thanks*   3 *nearly; late*

Show the meaning of *about* and *nearly*, using the
pictures in the margin or your own drawings on the
board. Practise saying *It's about 3 o'clock*, focusing
on the reduced vowels in /ə'baʊt/ and /ə'klɒk/.

Give examples to show the meaning of *late*
(e.g. *The class is at 6.00. It's 6.15 now = I'm late.*)

To show how we use *excuse me* to start a conversation,
go up to a learner and say *Excuse me ... .*

Optional extra

👥 Learners practise the three conversations.

---

4 *Practice in asking the time.* Learners write down a time.

To demonstrate, have a conversation with one learner.
Begin: *Excuse me, what's the time?*

Then have a second conversation. This time, write a
time on the board and choose a learner to ask you the
time. Reply using *about* or *nearly*.

👥 Learners ask each other the time and say the time
they wrote down.

Conversation practice

You could do the conversation practice exercises on p117 at
this point.

Morning, afternoon, evening

VOCABULARY *morning, afternoon ...*

1 *'Morning, afternoon, evening; day, night'.* Use the
diagram to focus on the meaning of the words. Point
out that:
– a.m. = before 12.00 (= the morning)
– p.m. = after 12.00 (= afternoon or evening)

Alternative: Presentation with books closed

To present the vocabulary, write on the board: *day, night.*
Ask: *Is it day now, or night?*
Then write on the board: *morning, afternoon, evening.*
Ask: *What is it now? Morning, afternoon, or evening?*

---

2 *Verbs; 'in the (morning)'.* Look at the pictures and
read the verbs and expressions. Learners repeat them.

To introduce the activity, tell the class when you
work. Then a few learners tell you when they work or
study. Use this to teach *in the morning / afternoon /*
evening.

👥 Learners say when they do the things in the pictures.

Round-up. Ask two or three learners when they do each activity.

3   *'It's 5.00 in the morning', etc.* Look at the map of time zones on p89. Establish what time it is where you are and write it on the board, e.g.
– *It's 10 o'clock in the morning.*

Show the stress pattern:
– *It's tén o'clóck in the mórning.*

Choose a place on the map. Ask:
– *Is it morning? Afternoon? Evening? Night?*
– *What time is it?*

👥 *Speaking.* Learners choose three other cities and answer the questions. Alternatively, choose three cities and write them on the board. Discuss the answers together.

At 7.00

READING

1 **a** *'at' + time; verbs.* Present the verbs *go to bed, sleep, get up* (use the pictures and gestures to show the meaning).

Check that learners understand the meaning of *most people* (= 70–90%).

Write on the board:

at	*11.00*
	7.00 in the morning

Alternative: Presentation with books closed

Tell the class: *At 11.00 in the evening I go to bed* (draw a bed and arrow on the board). *Then I sleep* (mime this). *Then at 7.00 in the morning I get up* (draw a bed and arrow). Write *go to bed, sleep* and *get up* on the board and practise saying them.
Ask the class: *What did I say?* Use this to present *at + time*. Write on the board: *I go to bed at 11.00 (in the evening).*

---

  b Read the sentences and ask the class what number goes in the gap (*eight*).

  c *Reading.* Learners read the two texts and guess the times. Ask learners to suggest answers.

  d Play recording **1.52** to check.

Olga – 7; 9
Ben – 1; 7; 6

2   *Writing.* Learners write three sentences about themselves. As they do this, go round and check. A few strong learners read out their sentences to the class.

Round-up. Find out who sleeps the most, who gets up earliest, etc. Do this by asking *Who goes to bed at 9.00? At 10.00? At 11.00?*, etc.

Sounds and spelling: The letter *a*

Goal: to recognise and pronounce the letter *a* with the sounds /æ/, /ɑː/ and /eɪ/

Core language:
Words from Units 1–3 with the letter *a*

1   *Common sounds with the letter 'a'.* Say the words or play recording **1.53**. Focus on the three sounds:
– /æ/ is a short sound, with the lips spread.
– /ɑː/ is a longer sound, with the mouth wider open.
– /eɪ/ is a combination of /e/ and /ɪ/.

2   *Practice.* Play recording **1.54**. Learners put the words in the correct group.

/æ/	/ɑː/	/eɪ/
map	afternoon	name
thanks	garden	station
has		

3   Learners guess how to say the words. Play recording **1.55** to check. You could also tell the class what the words mean (they are all taught later in this book).

3.3

Goals: arrange to meet people
say when you are free
say where and when to meet

Core language:
VOCABULARY Days: *Monday, Tuesday, Wednesday, Thursday, Friday, Saturday, Sunday, today, tomorrow*
in, on, at

Days

VOCABULARY Days

1 **a** Write *today* and *tomorrow* on the board. (If necessary, show the meaning by writing today's date and say *This is today*) Ask: *What day is it?* (Tuesday). Write: *Today is Tuesday.* Do the same for *tomorrow.*

  b Read out the days or play recording **1.56**. Learners repeat to practise pronunciation.

Learners write the days in the correct order in the diary. Check the answers and write them on the board.

Note

The diary begins with Monday, which is usual in modern diaries in Britain. Make sure that learners know which day is which.

---

c *Practice of days.* Say a day and ask learners to say the next one, e.g. *Wednesday → Thursday*.

👥 Then learners practise in pairs, following 1–6.

Stronger classes
Give more difficult sequences, e.g. *Monday, Wednesday ...*

LISTENING

2 a *'(She's) free, busy, not here'.* Look at Aki's diary and ask the questions.

> She's free – Tuesday
> She's busy – Monday
> She's not here – Wednesday

Use this to present *free* (= she's not at the office, she's not at the cinema, she has time) and *busy* (= She's not free, she has no time).

b *'on' + days.* Play recording **1.57**. Learners listen and fill the gaps.

> 1 on   2 on; on   3 on

Use this to present *on* with days. Write on the board:

on	Monday
	Monday morning

Point out that we say simply *on Monday morning*, not 'on Monday in the morning'.

Optional extra
Ask a few learners round the class when they are free or busy on different days. Ask: *What about tomorrow evening? What about on Saturday morning? Are you free or busy?*

VOCABULARY *in, on, at*

3 a *'in, on, at'.* Learners add words to the table. Use this to establish that:
– we use *in* before *the morning, the evening*, etc.
– we use *on* before days.
– we use *at* before times.

<u>in</u> the morning	<u>on</u> Wednesday
<u>in</u> the afternoon	<u>on</u> Thursday
<u>on</u> Wednesday morning	<u>at</u> six o'clock
<u>on</u> Thursday evening	<u>at</u> 9.30 <u>in</u> the evening

b Learners cover the table in **3a** and add *in, on* or *at*.

> 1 on Friday   2 on Friday morning   3 in the morning
> 4 on Tuesday evening   5 at 4 o'clock   6 in the evening
> 7 on Saturday afternoon   8 at 3.30

Alternative: Practice with books closed
Say the words in **3b** (or others of your own) but don't say the preposition. Learners add *in, on* or *at*.

SPEAKING

4 👥 Give each learner a letter, A or B. A learners look at their diary page on p89. B learners look at their diary page on p95. They ask questions to find out when they are both free.

Round-up. Ask pairs when they are both free (on Monday afternoon).

Target activity: Arrange to meet people

Goal: Arrange to meet people
Core language:

TASK VOCABULARY	Suggestions
3.1 VOCABULARY	Places in towns
3.2 VOCABULARY	The time
3.3 VOCABULARY	*in, on, at*

TASK VOCABULARY *Let's meet ...*

1 a Read the notes, then play recording **1.58**. Ask which note is correct.

> Friday, 12.30
> Café Metro

b Look at what Ling says. Use this to focus on:
– *Let's meet ...* (demonstrate or use gestures to show the meaning of *meet*).
– *How about ...?* (= *Is ... OK?*).

If necessary, give other examples to make the meaning clear.

Note
If you can use the learners' own language, you could tell them that these are useful ways to make a *suggestion*.

👤 / 👥 Learners add Clare's replies. Go through the answers together by listening to recording **1.58**.

> 1 Tomorrow – no, I'm busy tomorrow. Friday I'm free.
> 2 Café Metro – where's that?
> 3 Oh, I know, yes. OK, fine. What time?
> 4 Great. See you then.

2 Read through the expressions together and practise saying them. Focus on the stress pattern and the /ə/ sound in /ət/, /təmɒrəʊ/.

To demonstrate, have a few short conversations with two or three learners, as in the examples.

👥 Learners have short conversations, taking it in turns to start.

TASK

3 *Preparation for exercise 4.* To show what to do, tell the class that you want to meet someone. Write a possible time and place on the board, e.g.
bus station – Saturday afternoon

Learners note down a place and time of their own on a piece of paper.

4 a *Speaking.* To demonstrate the pair work, choose one learner and have a conversation:
– find out if he's / she's free.
– suggest a place and say where it is.
– arrange a different day or time if necessary.

Alternatively, two strong learners improvise a conversation in front of the class.

👥 Learners have conversations. They could have a second conversation with a different partner.

b *Round-up.* A few learners tell you where they will meet and when.

Keyword *at*

Goals: say where people are
read text messages

Core language:

at the + place
at home, at work, at school

1 a Learners look at A–F and say where the people are.

> A *at the airport*   B *at work*   C *at the shops*
> D *at the cinema*   E *at school*   F *at home*

b Learners write the expressions.

at the + noun	*at* + noun
at the airport	*at school*
at the shops	*at work*
at the cinema	*at home*

Point out that:
– to talk about places we know in a town, we usually say *at the ...* . You could also give other examples: *at the swimming pool, at the station, at the bus station, at the theatre.*
– *at school, at work, at home* are fixed expressions – we don't use *the*.

2 *Writing.* Give a few examples about yourself, e.g.
– *My son is at school just now.*
– *My friend works in an office, so she's at work now.*

Learners write one or two sentences about their friends or family. Then they read out their sentences.

3 *Writing.* Look at the text messages on p95. Use them to teach the words *text* or *text message* (or *SMS*) and *mobile phone*. Point out that in texts, people often leave out small words like *at, in, the*.

Look at text messages A–D and ask learners to add words to make them complete sentences. Write them on the board.

> A *Meet me at the airport at 7.00.*
> B *Are you at home tomorrow?*
> C *See you at school on Wednesday!*
> D *Let's meet at (the) Cinema Rex on Saturday at 7.30.*

3.4 Explore speaking

Goals: respond to questions
say you're not sure

Core language:

be short answers; *I don't know.; I'm not sure.*

1 a *Short answers (verb 'be'); 'I don't know'; 'I'm not sure'.* Look at the pictures and ask learners what answers are possible.

> 1 *Yes, it is.; No, it's not.; I don't know.; I'm not sure.*
> 2 *Yes, I am.; No, I'm not.; I don't know.; I'm not sure.*
> 3 *Yes, he is.; No, he's not.; I don't know.; I'm not sure.*

Point out that:
– in the answer, we say *yes* or *no*, then repeat the form of the verb *be*: *Is he ...?* → *Yes, he is.*
– in negative answers, we add *not.*

Present *I don't know* and *I'm not sure*, using gestures to make the meaning clear.

Practise saying the short answers, checking that learners pronounce them with the correct stress: *Yés, I ám. Nó, I'm nót*, etc.

b Play recording **1.59**, pausing after each conversation to check the answers.

> 1 *Yes, it is. / No, It's not.*
> 2 *Yes, I am. / I don't know. No, I'm not.*
> 3 *I'm not sure. Yes, he is. / No, he's not.*

c To practise, ask each question to one or two learners and get a variety of answers.

Alternatively, learners could ask and answer the questions in pairs.

2 a *Practice of short answers.* Look at each question in turn and ask learners what answers are possible.

> 1 *Yes, it is. / No, it's not. / I don't know. / I'm not sure.*
> 2 *Yes, I am. / No, I'm not.*
> 3 *Yes, they are. / No, they're not. / I don't know. / I'm not sure.*
> 4 *Yes, she is. / No, she's not. / I don't know. / I'm not sure.*
> 5 *Yes, it is. / No, it's not. / I don't know. / I'm not sure.*
> 6 *Yes, it is. / I don't know. / I'm not sure.*

b Learners ask and answer the questions.

3 a *Practice.* Look at **1**. Elicit possible questions:
– *Are you from the USA?*
– *Is Hilary Clinton from the USA?*

Learners write questions. Go round and check.

b In turn, learners read out their questions. Other learners answer them.

You could use photocopiable activity 3B on the Teacher's DVD-ROM at this point.

Across cultures: Shops

Goals: to give practice in reading short texts
to sensitise learners to customs in different
countries and cultures

Core language:
Adjectives: *open, closed*
Countries: *Egypt, Japan, Greece*

1 a *Reading for factual information.* Give time for
learners to read the texts. First they should try to guess
the unknown words, then let them use a dictionary.

b Learners write the country or countries next to the
sentences. If they finish early, pairs could check their
answers together.

> 2 Greece   3 Egypt, Greece   4 Egypt
> 5 Egypt, Greece, Japan   6 Japan

2 *Writing.* To prepare for the writing, draw attention to
these expressions, and write them on the board:
– *Most shops ...*
– *Some shops ...*
– *Many people ...*

In single nationality classes, ask learners to suggest a
few things they might say.

Learners write a few sentences about their own
country. As they do this, go round and check.

A few learners read out their sentences. Ask other
learners if they agree.

> **Alternatives**
>
> 1 Mixed nationality classes
>   Learners from the same country could work together
>   in pairs or groups. At the end, read out what they have
>   written and see if other learners can guess the country.
> 2 Learners from Egypt, Greece or Japan
>   Learners could either write about another country they
>   know, or about cafés and restaurants in their country.

Look again

VOCABULARY

1 *Similar words.* To show what to do, ask learners to
find another word that goes with *café.* Write it on the
board (*restaurant*).

👥 Learners find other pairs of words and write them.

station – airport	quiet – busy
near – in	open – closed
car – taxi	school – university
church – mosque	day – night
afternoon – morning	

2 a *Sentences.* Working alone, learners write sentences.
Possible answers:

> 1 There's a café near the station.
> 2 I live near the school.
> 3 The supermarket is closed in the afternoon.

b Learners read out their sentences.

3 *Places.* Learners decide what places the signs show.

> A station   B airport   C restaurant   D café
> E hotel   F church   G mosque   H bus station

4 *Prepositions.* Learners add prepositions to the table.

> 1 at   2 at   3 in   4 near   5 next   6 to   7 at   8 in   9 on

SPELLING

5 *Vowels.* Check that learners understand what vowels
are (a, e, i, o, u). Learners add the vowels. Write the
answers on the board.

> 1 Let's meet at the cinema.
> 2 My brother is nearly thirteen.
> 3 There's a very good café near the station.

CAN YOU REMEMBER? Unit 2

6 *Nouns.* Ask learners to suggest possible nouns to
replace the highlighted words. Possible answers:

> 1 sister, mother, father, friend, husband, son, daughter ...
> 2 café, restaurant, supermarket, hotel ...
> 3 teacher, student, manager ...
> 4 sons, daughters, boys, girls

7 To demonstrate, choose someone from your family
and say three things about them. The class guesses
who it is.

Learners choose someone in their family and write
sentences.

👥 In turn, they read out their sentences and try to
guess the person.

Round-up. A few learners read out their sentences.
The others guess who the person is.

GRAMMAR

there's / there are. Read through the table.

> **Alternative: Presentation with books closed**
>
> Write on the board:
> _____ a café.   _____ two cafés.
> _____ a shop.   _____ lots of shops.
> Ask learners to complete the gaps with *There's* or *There are.*

8 Learners correct the mistakes.

> 1 There are two restaurants in our street.
> 2 There is (There's) a good café in this street.
> 3 There are lots of taxis at the airport.
> 4 Is there a mosque near the university?

Self-assessment

To help focus learners on the self-assessment, you could
read it through, giving a few more examples of the language
they have learned in each section (or asking learners to tell
you). Then they circle a number on each line.

Unit 3 Extra activities on the Teacher's DVD-ROM

Printable worksheets, activity instructions and answer keys are on your Teacher's DVD-ROM.

3A Street scenes

Activity type: Speaking – Spot the difference – Pairs

Aim: To practise describing a street

Language: Streets; *there's / there are* – Coursebook p22 – Vocabulary and Grammar

Preparation: Make one copy of the worksheet for each pair of learners and cut it into A and B pictures along the dotted line.

Time: 15 minutes

3B Short-answer snap

Activity type: Speaking – Snap – Pairs

Aims:

To practise responding to questions with short answers

Language: Responding to questions – Coursebook p28

Preparation: Make one copy of the worksheet for each pair of learners. Cut along the dotted lines into a set of 32 cards.

Time: 15 minutes

Unit 3 Self-study Pack

In the Workbook

Unit 3 of the *English Unlimited Starter Workbook* offers additional ways to practise the vocabulary and grammar taught in the Coursebook. There are also activities which build reading and writing skills, and a whole page of tasks to use with the DVD-ROM video, giving your learners the opportunity to hear and react to spoken English.

- **Vocabulary:** Streets; Places in towns; Clock times; Days; *in, on, at*; *Let's meet …*
- **Grammar:** *there's / there are*
- **Time out:** Streets puzzle
- **Explore writing:** Joining ideas: *he, she, it, they, there*
- **DVD-ROM Extra:** *Let's meet for coffee.*

On the DVD-ROM

Unit 3 of the *English Unlimited Starter Self-study Pack DVD-ROM* contains interactive games and activities for your learners to practise and improve their vocabulary, grammar and pronunciation, and also their speaking and listening. It also contains video material (with the possibility for learners to record themselves) to use with the *Workbook*.

- **Vocabulary and Grammar:** Extra practice of Coursebook language and Keyword
- **Classroom language:** Your book
- **Sounds and spelling:** The letter *a*
- **Explore speaking:** Respond to questions
- **Video:** *Let's meet for coffee.*

4 About you

4.1

Goals: **say how you spend your time**
talk about things you often do
say what you like and don't like

Core language:

VOCABULARY	Activity verbs: *play football / basketball, play the piano / guitar, read a book / magazine, listen to music / the radio, watch TV / a DVD, speak English, go to school*
GRAMMAR	Present simple – positive: *I like, I play* Present simple – negative: *I don't like, I don't play*

Verbs and nouns

VOCABULARY Activity verbs

1 a Look at the photos and play recording **1.60** once through. Ask what the verbs are. If necessary, play the recording again, pausing after each remark.

> 1 go to school   2 speak Spanish   3 play the guitar
> 4 read magazines   5 listen to music   6 watch DVDs

Practise saying 1–6, focusing especially on the sound of *listen* and *watch*.

Alternative

Look at each photo in turn. Ask learners to guess what verb goes in 1–6. Then play recording **1.60** to check.

---

b *Listening for detail.* Play recording **1.60** again, pausing after each remark. Ask learners to identify the expressions and to give the whole sentence each time (e.g. *1 in a band: He says "I play music in a band."*).

> 1 I play music in a band.
> 2 I read magazines about music.
> 3 I listen to music on my MP3 player.
> 4 I speak Spanish a bit.
> 5 I watch DVDs on my laptop.
> 6 I go to school in Kingston – it's a town near London.

2 a Learners match the words and the pictures.

> A football   B book   C basketball   D tennis
> E newspaper   F TV   G radio   H piano

Play recording **1.61** to check, and practise saying the words. Focus on the pronunciation of *radio*.

b Learners add verbs from **1a** to the expressions.

> 1 play football   2 read a book   3 play basketball
> 4 play tennis   5 read the newspaper   6 watch TV
> 7 listen to the radio   8 play the piano

Language note

1 With music, we say *play the ...*: *play the piano*, *play the guitar*. With sport, we say *play* (without *the*): *play football*, *play basketball*.
2 We say *listen to the radio*, but *watch TV* (without *the*).
3 We can say *read the newspaper* or *read the paper*. Point this out as you present the items.

---

c *Verbs and nouns.* To show the difference between verbs and nouns, write a few verbs and nouns in two columns on the board. If necessary, tell the class that:
– verbs come after *I ...* (give a few examples: *I play, I am, I live ...*).
– nouns are the 'names' of things.

In single nationality classes, you could ask learners to give examples of nouns and verbs in their own language.

Learners find other examples of nouns and verbs from p30. Then go through this together, adding them to the two columns on the board.

d *Practice of activity verbs.* Learners cover the page. To demonstrate, say a noun, e.g. *music*. Learners add a verb to make an expression, e.g. *listen to music*.

Learners test each other.

I like ..., I don't like ...

GRAMMAR I don't (like) ...

1 a *Negative forms.* Read the sentences in **1a**. Use this to present the negative form of verbs:

> – *I like* → *I don't like*

Learners could look at the photos of André and Emma and guess who says each sentence.

Alternative: Presentation with books closed

Remind learners of how to form the negative of *I'm* – we simply add *not*:
I'm a learner. → *I'm not a learner.*
Then show how we form the negative with most verbs – we use an extra (auxiliary) verb *do + not*:
I like football. → *I do not like football.*
Show how we can make this shorter:
I don't like football.
Then open books and read the sentences.

Listening. Play recording **1.62**. Learners listen and write A (André) or E (Emma) beside the sentences.

> <u>André:</u>
> 1 I don't like sport.
> 2 I don't play football.
> 3 I don't watch football.
> 4 I don't go to football matches.
> <u>Emma:</u>
> 1 I like sport.
> 2 I don't play football.
> 3 I watch football.
> 4 I go to football matches.

b *Pronunciation.* Read the positive and negative forms, or play recording **1.63**. Learners repeat. Show how *don't like* and *don't watch* are run together: /dəʊn(t)‿laɪk/, /dəʊn(t)‿wɒtʃ/.

WRITING

2 To demonstrate, write *I like cats.* on the board. Ask a few learners if this sentence is true for them. If a learner says *Yes*, write *Yes* on the board. If a learner says *No*, ask him / her to make the sentence negative (*I don't like cats.*). Write this on the board.

Learners write *Yes* or a negative form beside each sentence.

Round-up. Go through the items and ask a few learners what they wrote.

LISTENING and SPEAKING

3 a *Me too, me neither.* Play recording **1.64**. Learners listen and complete conversations 1–3. Pause after each one and check the answers.

> 1 don't   2 me too   3 me neither

Check that learners understand when we use *me too* and *me neither*:
– yes + yes = me too
– no + no = me neither

Language note

In expressions like this without a verb, we use *me*, not *I*.
– Who's that?
– Me.
(*me* is an *emphatic pronoun*).

---

b Do some quick practice round the class. Say positive or negative sentences from **1** and **2** (or add other examples of your own). Learners respond with a sentence or with *Me too* or *Me neither*.

👥 / 👥👥 Learners take it in turns to say sentences from **2**. The other learner responds as in the examples.

Classroom language: Noun, verb, adjective

Goal: to identify nouns, verbs and adjectives

Core language:
noun, verb, adjective

1 Read the words and learners say which are nouns, verbs and adjectives. If necessary, show what adjectives are by giving a few examples:
– *It's a good book.*
– *This book is very good.*

> 1 noun   2 adjective   3 noun   4 verb   5 adjective
> 6 adjective   7 verb   8 verb   9 noun   10 noun

2 👤 / 👥 Learners look at p23 and find one word of each type. They tell you the words they found. Write them on the board in three lists.

4.2

Goals: say how you spend your time
say what you eat and drink
ask for a drink in a café
describe a restaurant or a café

Core language:

VOCABULARY   Food and drink: *meat, fish, fruit, vegetables, pasta, rice, bread, salad, tea, coffee, cola, lemonade, orange juice, water* (+ other items from learners)
eat, drink
Frequency: *often, sometimes, never, every day*
Countries and nationalities: *China, Chinese; Italy, Italian; the USA, American; India, Indian; Japan, Japanese*

Food

VOCABULARY Food

1 a *Food vocabulary.* Look at the pictures and establish what food they show. Play recording **1.65** to check.

Practise saying the words. Focus especially on the pronunciation of *fruit*, *vegetables* and *bread*.

Quickly check the words round the class by asking learners: *What do you have at home? Do you have meat? Do you have salad?*

Option: Stronger classes

Present words for common kinds of fruit and vegetables, e.g. *potato, tomato, cabbage, aubergine, onion, melon, grapes, orange, apple, banana,* etc.
You could use the pictures in the book for this, or bring pictures (or real fruit and vegetables!) into the class.

---

b *Listening.* Play recording **1.66**. Pause after each person and ask what they eat.

> Emma – meat, pasta, vegetables
> André – meat, fruit, pasta

c *Speaking.* To demonstrate the game, start to draw one of the kinds of food on the board. See how quickly learners can say what it is.

👥 Learners take it in turns to draw a kind of food. Their partner guesses what it is.

VOCABULARY *often, sometimes ...*

2 a *Frequency words.* Read the sentences or play recording **1.67** and show the words in a scale on the board:

↑ *every day*
often
sometimes
never

You could show meaning by referring to days, e.g.
– *I eat meat on Monday, Tuesday, Wednesday, Thursday ...* = every day
– *I eat meat on Monday, then maybe on Friday, then maybe again on Wednesday ...* = sometimes

(Show *never* with hand gestures.)

Learners round the class say which sentence is true of them.

b 👥 / 👥👥 *Practice of frequency words.* Learners make
true sentences about each of the kinds of food in **1a**.
Alternatively, they could write the sentences.

Round-up. A few learners say two or three of their
sentences.

3 👤 / 👥 *Extension.* Learners think of three other kinds
of food they often eat. They could use a dictionary
for this, or (in a single nationality class) they could
write words in their own language for you to translate.
Encourage them to think of common foods they eat
almost every day (e.g. *sugar, eggs, oil, potatoes* ...).

Go through the words together. Learners give a
sentence with their words like those in **2a**.

Drinks

VOCABULARY Drinks

1 a Look at the picture and ask learners to say what the
drinks are.

Point out the difference between *coffee* /ˈkɒfi/ (a
drink) and a *café* /ˈkæfeɪ/ (a place). Focus on the
pronunciation of *juice* /dʒuːs/.

b *Listening.* Play the three conversations in recording
1.68 to check.

> 1 coffee (espresso), cola
> 2 orange juice, tea
> 3 lemonade, bottle of water

2 a *Asking for a drink (I'll have ..., Can I have ...?).* Play
recording **1.68** again. Learners write the words they hear.

> 1 I'll have
> 2 Can I have
> 3 I'll have

Point out that *I'll have* ... and *Can I have* ... ? mean
roughly the same – they are both ways to ask for
things in a café or restaurant.

Practise saying sentences 1–3 round the class. Focus
on the main sentence stress:
– *I'll have a cȯffee, please.*
– *Can I have an ȯrange juice, please?*
– *I'll just have wȧter, please.*

b *Role play.* To demonstrate the role play, tell learners
they are in a café and you are the waiter. Two
learners order drinks, using the expressions they have
practised. Write down the order, then repeat it back to
them to check.

👥👥 Put learners in groups of three or four. One
learner is the waiter, the others order drinks.

Round-up. Some of the 'waiters' read out their orders.

3 a *Speaking.* To introduce the activity, tell the class
which drinks on the menu in **1** you like, often drink,
don't like, never drink, etc.

👥 Learners tell each other which drinks they like,
don't like and which they often drink.

Round-up. Go through the list of drinks and find out
which is the most (and least) popular drink.

b 👤 / 👥 *Extension: other drinks.* Working alone or in
pairs, learners think of two other drinks and write
them down.

Go through the words together and find out how many
learners like each drink and how often they drink it.
Depending on your class, you could introduce words
for alcoholic drinks (e.g. *wine, beer*) at this point.

Restaurants

READING

1 a 👤 / 👥 *Reading for main idea.* Learners read the guide
and add the names of the restaurants.

> 1 Pizzeria Bella Roma   2 Tokyo Restaurant
> 3 Taj Mahal Restaurant   4 The Burger House
> 5 Shanghai Restaurant

b *Nationalities.* Learners complete the table, finding
the words in the restaurant guide. Go through the
answers together by building up a list of countries and
nationalities on the board.

> Italy – Italian
> the USA – American
> India – Indian
> Japan – Japanese

Play recording **1.69** and practise saying the words.
Focus especially on the reduced /ən/ sound in
American, Italian, Indian.

Focus on 'a' and 'an'. Look at the examples with *a*
and *an* in the margin. Learners say them. Focus on the
pronunciation of /ə/ and /ən/. Point out that:
– we say *a* if the next word starts with a consonant
  (*Chinese, small*).
– we say *an* if the next word starts with a vowel (*Indian*).

You could give other examples with *an*, e.g.
an apartment, an old house, an adjective,
an orange juice, an English book.

c *Practice.* Learners make sentences about each
restaurant, e.g.
– *The Bella Roma is an Italian restaurant.*
– *They have Italian food: pizzas, pasta and fish.*
– *It's a small restaurant and it's not too expensive.*

If possible, they should try to do this without looking
at the guide.

Optional extra

👥 Learner A covers the guide. Learner B chooses a
restaurant. Learner A tells him / her about it.

WRITING

2 a To demonstrate, choose a restaurant or café in your
town that everyone knows. Say a few sentences about
it, but without mentioning its name. See if learners
can guess which restaurant / café it is.

👤 / 👥 Learners choose a restaurant or café and write a
few sentences about it.

b Learners read out their sentences. Other learners guess
which restaurant / café it is.

Sounds and spelling: *e, ee, ea*

Goals: to pronounce the letter *e* with the sounds /e/ and /iː/
to pronounce the letters *ee* and *ea* with the sound /iː/

Core language:
Words from Units 1–4 with the letters *e, ee* and *ea*

---

1 */e/ and /iː/.* Say the words or play recording **1.70**.
Focus on the /e/ and /iː/ sounds:
– /e/ is a short sound, with the lips loosely open.
– /iː/ is a longer sound, with the lips spread.

Point out that:
– we say *ea* and *ee* as /iː/.
– we say *e* + consonant + *e* as /iː/ (*Chinese*).

2 *Practice of /e/ and /iː/.* Play recording **1.72**. Learners
put the words in the correct group.

/e/	/iː/		
yes hello	Japanese	thirteen	meat please

3 a *Dictation.* Play recording **1.72**. Learners listen to each
sentence and write it down. Check what learners have
written (learners could write the sentences on the
board). Check that they spell words with *ea* and *ee*
correctly.

b Learners read out the sentences, checking that they
are pronouncing the /e/ and /iː/ sounds correctly.

4.3

Goals: say how you spend your time
ask how people spend their time
ask what people like

Core language:
GRAMMAR   Present simple – questions: *Do you ...?*

Do you ...?

GRAMMAR *Do you ...?*

1 a *Listening.* Look at the picture and ask where the
people are (In a café). Point out that the bubbles are
answers to questions. You could ask learners what
they think each conversation is about.

Play recording **1.73**, pausing after each conversation.
Ask learners what the questions are. Write them on
the board.

1 *Do you watch football?*
2 *Do you speak Spanish?*
3 *Do you live near here?*
4 *Do you have children?*

Show how we add *Do you ...* to make questions:

I watch football. → *Do you watch football?*

Pronunciation. Read the examples in the box
and practise saying the questions. Focus on the
pronunciation of *Do you live ...?* /djʊ lɪv/.

b *Practice of 'Do you...?'.* Get learners to ask you the
questions. Give answers yourself, e.g.
– *Do you watch TV?*
– *Yes, sometimes.*

1 *Do you watch TV?*
2 *Do you live in London?*
3 *Do you like Italian food?*
4 *Do you work in a bank?*
5 *Do you go to school?*
6 *Do you have a mobile phone?*
7 *Do you like tea?*
8 *Do you play the piano?*
9 *Do you like Mozart?*

Optional extra

Show learners how to answer the questions using short
answers: *Yes, I do. No, I don't.*
👥 Learners ask and answer the questions.

SPEAKING

2 a Learners read the conversation and listen to recording
1.74 as far as the pause. Ask which person it is. Then
play the last part to check. (Marie)

b Demonstrate the game. Choose a person and get
learners to guess by asking you questions.

👥 / 👥👥 Learners take it in turns to choose a person.
The others guess by asking questions.

Alternative

Play the game with the whole class together. Learners could
take it in turns to come to the front.

Target activity: Say how you spend your time

Goal: say how you spend your time

Core language:

4.1 VOCABULARY	Activity verbs
4.3 GRAMMAR	*Do you ... ?*

TASK READING

1 Read through the sentences and check that learners understand *poetry*, *fast food* and *classical music*.

👤 Learners write *Yes* or *No* in column A.

TASK

2 *Preparation for the task.* To introduce the activity, look at the sentences and ask learners what questions they will ask (e.g. *Do you read a lot of books?*). You could get learners to ask you a few of the questions.

Speaking. 👥 Learners ask each other the questions and write *Yes* or *No* in column B.

3 *'both'.* To present *both*, tell the class *I read a lot of books*. Then ask one or two learners
Do you read a lot of books?. If a learner says *Yes*, write on the board:
– *We both read a lot of books.*

Show the meaning of *both*:
– *he reads and I read = we both read.*

Round-up. Learners tell you a few things that they and their partner both do, or both like.

 You could use photocopiable activity 4A on the Teacher's DVD-ROM at this point.

Keyword *go*

Goal: use expressions with *go* to talk about habitual actions

Core language:

go + to: *go to university, go to a café ...*
other expressions with *go*: *go shopping, go out*

1 *Noticing task.* Learners read the Fact File and write expressions with *go* in the two lists. Then go through this together by writing the expressions on the board. Check that learners understand what they mean.

go to ...	go ...
go to university	*go shopping*
go to college	*go out*
go to bed	
go to a café	
go to a bar	
go to a club	
go to the cinema	
go to church	
go to a mosque	

Language note

We say:
– *go to a café, a restaurant, a bar, a club ... .*
– *go to the cinema.*
– *go to school, university, college, church, bed* (no article).

Option: Stronger classes

Teach a few other expressions with *go + -ing*:
go swimming, go walking, go skiing.

2 *Writing.* To introduce the activity, say a sentence about yourself and write it on the board (e.g. *I often go to the cinema on Saturday evening.*).

Learners write three sentences using expressions with *go*. Learners read out their sentences.

Alternative: Mingling activity

Learners move freely round the class. They tell other learners their sentences and ask *What about you?*.

4.4 Explore writing

Goals: write a description
join ideas using *and / but*

Core language:

and, but

1 *'and, but'.* Look at the pictures and ask learners what they show.

A a big flat with a balcony	B a small flat

Read the sentences under A and B. Ask which word goes in each gap: *and* or *but*.

A and	B but

Check that learners understand the meaning of *and* and *but*. If necessary, give a few other simple examples, e.g.
– *The restaurant is good and it's cheap.*
  (= both good things)
– *The restaurant is good but it's expensive.*
  (= a contrast – one good and one bad thing)

Alternative: Classes with a different writing system

Point out that *and* and *but* join sentences, so two sentences become one. Show this on the board:
– *The rooms are big. It has a big balcony.* (two sentences: each has a capital letter and a full stop)
– *The rooms are big and it has a big balcony.* (one sentence)

2 *Writing.* Look at **1** together and ask learners how it might continue. Write sentences on the board, getting learners to tell you what to write:

> *1 It's a very small village. There's no school and there are only two shops.*

👤 / 👥 Learners write sentences. Go round and check.

> *2 The hotel is OK. Our room is very nice, but it's quite noisy at night.*
> *3 They're a big family. They have five children, but only one lives at home.*
> *4 It's a good café. The coffee is very good and they have very good ice cream.*

3 To show what to do, choose one of the topics and learners suggest the first sentence, e.g.
– *Paris is a big city.*

Then learners suggest two more ideas, joining them with *and* or *but*, e.g.
– *There are lots of restaurants, but they are very expensive.*

Learners choose two or three of the topics and write sentences. As they do this, go round and check.

> **Note**
>
> Their sentences don't have to follow exactly the same pattern as the examples (e.g. they could write two sentences, each joined with *and*), but check that they are using punctuation correctly and using *and* and *but* where appropriate.

Across cultures: Tea

Goals: to give practice in reading short texts
to sensitise learners to customs in different countries and cultures

Core language:
tea, coffee; cup, glass, teapot; weak, strong; with milk / sugar

1 *Vocabulary.* Use the photos to present *teapot, cup* and *glass.*

2 a *Reading for general idea.* Learners read the texts and match them with the photos.

> *A Britain   B Japan   C Turkey*

b *Reading for detail.* Read through the questions in **2** and check that learners know *milk, green, strong* (= a lot of tea) and *weak* (= not strong). Learners read the texts and complete the answers.

> *1 Britain, Japan   2 Britain   3 Turkey   4 Japan*
> *5 Japan   6 Britain*

3 👥 / 👥👥 *Discussion.* Learners discuss the questions together. Then talk about them with the whole class.

Look again

VOCABULARY

1 *Verb and noun collocations.* Do the exercise with the whole class, or learners do it in pairs and then go through the answers together.

> | | |
> |---|---|
> | *eat meat* | *speak English* |
> | *watch television* | *go to the cinema* |
> | *play the guitar* | *drink water* |
> | *listen to the radio* | *read a book* |

2 a *Similar words.* Learners find two other words that go with *tennis.* Write them on the board (*football, basketball*). Ask them why (They're sports).

👥 Learners find other groups and write them down.

> *TV, radio, MP3 player (they all play music)*
> *Italian, Chinese, Japanese (nationalities)*
> *newspaper, magazine, book (you read them)*
> *speak, read, listen (verbs)*
> *often, sometimes, never (frequency words)*
> *cheap, expensive, good (adjectives)*

b Learners write sentences. Possible answers:

> *There's a newspaper on the table.*
> *There's a television in the room.*
> *In the evening, I watch television.*
> *In the evening, we sometimes go to the cinema.*
> *Do you speak Chinese?*
> *Do you often read a newspaper?*

3 a *Countries and nationalities.* Learners write the missing words.

> | | |
> |---|---|
> | *the USA – American* | *India – Indian* |
> | *Japan – Japanese* | *Russia – Russian* |
> | *Italy – Italian* | |

b 👥 Learners write three more countries. Build up a list of countries and nationalities on the board.

CAN YOU REMEMBER? Unit 3

4 a Discuss what words could be used.

> *1 Monday, Saturday, Friday evening ...*
> *2 drink, meal, coffee*
> *3 8.30, 6 o'clock ...*
> *4 Café Costa, bus station, town centre ...*

b 👤 / 👥👥 *Writing.* Learners write an email. They 'send' it to another learner or pair, who write a reply.

GRAMMAR

Present simple. Read through the table.

> **Alternative: Presentation with books closed**
>
> Write on the board:
> – *I like coffee.*
> Then write the negative and question forms with gaps:
> – *I _____ coffee.*
> – *_____ you _____ coffee?*
> Learners complete the gaps.

5 Learners correct the mistakes.

> | | |
> |---|---|
> | *1 I don't speak English.* | *4 I don't like cola.* |
> | *2 Do you eat meat?* | *5 Do you like football?* |
> | *3 We often listen to the radio.* | |

Frequency. Read through the table.

> **Alternative: Presentation with books closed**
>
> Write on the board: *I eat fish.*
> Write these expressions on the board in a box:
> *every day   often   never   sometimes*
> Learners add expressions to *I eat fish* to make true sentences.

6 Learners write the sentences in the correct order.

> *1 I watch TV every day.*
> *2 I often play football with my friends.*
> *3 They never eat meat.*
> *4 Do you sometimes go to the cinema?*

 You could use photocopiable activity 4B on the Teacher's DVD-ROM at this point.

Self-assessment

To help focus learners on the self-assessment, you could read it through, giving a few more examples of the language they have learned in each section (or asking learners to tell you). Then they circle a number on each line.

Unit 4 Extra activities on the Teacher's DVD-ROM

Printable worksheets, activity instructions and answer keys are on your Teacher's DVD-ROM.

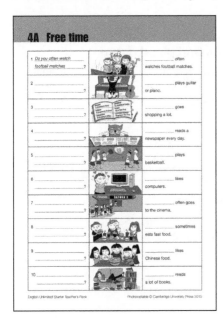

4B Odd one out			
Italian	glass	tennis	newspaper
play	cheap	water	DVD
magazine	radio	Indian	teapot
TV	listen	music	orange juice
cup	coffee	bread	films
book	MP3 player	like	basketball
speak	strong	read	watch
nice	expensive	pasta	football
rice	Japanese	weak	good

4A Free time

Activity type:
Speaking – Find someone who – Whole group

Aim: To practise asking and answering questions about free-time habits

Language: Say how you spend your time – Coursebook p35

Preparation:
Make one copy of the worksheet for each learner.

Time: 15–20 minutes

4B Odd one out

Activity type:
Speaking – Odd one out – Pairs / Groups of four

Aim: To review nouns, verbs and adjectives

Language: Review of vocabulary – Coursebook, Unit 4

Preparation: Make one copy of the worksheet for each pair of learners. Cut along the dotted lines into a set of 36 cards.

Time: 20–25 minutes

Unit 4 Self-study Pack

In the Workbook

Unit 4 of the *English Unlimited Starter Workbook* offers additional ways to practise the vocabulary and grammar taught in the Coursebook. There are also activities which build reading and writing skills, and a whole page of tasks to use with the DVD-ROM video, giving your learners the opportunity to hear and react to spoken English.

- **Vocabulary:** Activity verbs; Food and drink; *often, sometimes*; Countries and nationalities; Adjectives
- **Grammar:** *I don't ...*; *Do you ... ?*
- **Explore reading:** Advertisements
- **DVD-ROM Extra:** *Do you like football?*

On the DVD-ROM

Unit 4 of the *English Unlimited Starter Self-study Pack DVD-ROM* contains interactive games and activities for your learners to practise and improve their vocabulary, grammar and pronunciation, and also their speaking and listening. It also contains video material (with the possibility for learners to record themselves) to use with the *Workbook*.

- **Vocabulary and Grammar:** Extra practice of Coursebook language and Keyword
- **Classroom language:** Noun, verb, adjective
- **Sounds and spelling:** *e*, *ee* and *ea*
- **Explore writing:** Join ideas using *and* / *but*
- **Video:** *Do you like football?*

5 Things to buy

Unit goal: choose and buy things

5.1

Goals: choose and buy things
identify common objects
ask about things in shops
say how much things are

Core language:

VOCABULARY Common objects: *pen, watch, stamp, glasses, sunglasses, sandwich, postcard, newspaper, magazine, bottle, glass*
Asking about things: *Do you sell ...?; Do you have ...?*
Numbers, prices: *10, 20, 30 ... 100; euros, pounds, dollars*
Asking for food and drink: *Can I have ...?*
GRAMMAR Singular and plural nouns: *pens, glasses ...*

Everyday things

VOCABULARY Common objects

1 a Look at the picture and use this to teach the word *things*. Give time for learners to look at the words in the box and mark those they know.

Optional extra

Learners underline words they don't know and find out what they mean in a dictionary.

Go through the words together and ask learners to identify them in the picture.

b Go through the answers by playing recording **1.75**.

---
1 a newspaper   2 a magazine   3 a postcard   4 a pen
5 a stamp   6 a bottle   7 a glass   8 a sandwich
9 sunglasses   10 glasses   11 a watch

Practise saying the words. Focus on the pronunciation of *watch* and *sandwich*.

Point out the difference between:
– *a glass* (plural *glasses*).
– *glasses, sunglasses* (plural only).

c To introduce the practice, say *1* and elicit *It's a newspaper*. Then say *10* and elicit *They're glasses*. Write on the board:

– *It's a ...   They're ... .*

👥 Learners cover the words and practise.

2 To introduce the game, choose one of the objects and begin a simple drawing of it (just a single line). Then pause and learners guess what it is, then add another line, and so on until learners guess correctly. Check that learners guess by asking *Is it a ...?* or *Are they ...?*

👥 Learners take it in turns to draw and guess.

A few learners could come to the front of the class one at a time and try out one of their drawings with the whole class.

Street kiosk

GRAMMAR Singular and plural nouns

1 a *Plurals.* Write two headings on the board: + *-s* and + *-es*. Add words from the box, getting learners to tell you where to write them.

+ -s	+ -es
pens	glasses
stamps	sunglasses
postcards	sandwiches
magazines	
newspapers	

b Ask the questions and establish that:
– most words add *-s* in the plural.
– words that end in *-s, -ch* or *-sh* add *-es*.

Alternative: Presentation with books closed

Write on the board:
– *a pen*
– *a magazine*
– *a glass*
To elicit the plural forms, ask: *We say 'a pen', but we say 'two ...' ?*. Add the plural forms on the board:
(*pens, magazines, glasses*)
Use this to establish the two kinds of plural ending.

Optional extra

Bring in two or three pens, magazines and (drinking) glasses. Use these to present singular and plural forms.

---

c *Pronunciation: /s/, /z/ and /ɪz/ endings.* Play recording **1.76** or say the words and ask learners to repeat. Point out that:

– in many words, the *-s* ending sounds more like /z/: /ˈnjuːzpeipəz/, /ˈpəʊskɑːdz/, /penz/.

– *-es* is pronounced /ɪz/ (this is because it is almost impossible to say, e.g. *sandwichs*!)

Language note

The *-s* ending is pronounced /s/ after voiced consonant sounds (t, p, k, f) and more like /z/ after unvoiced consonant sounds (d, b, g, v) and vowel sounds, though the difference is slight. Encourage learners to say e.g. /penz/ rather than /pens/, but don't waste too much time over this.

LISTENING

2 a Look at the photo of the kiosk and ask learners what they think they sell. Get them to suggest five items and build them up on the board.

b *Listening.* Play recording **1.77**. See which of the items learners suggested were correct.

---
newspapers, magazines, postcards, pens, stamps, sunglasses

Ask if they sell food (No) and if they sell drinks (Yes – bottles of water and soft drinks). (soft drinks = drinks without alcohol)

3 a *Do you have / sell ...?* Play recording **1.78** and establish what the questions are.
 – *Do you sell stamps?*
 – *Do you have Newsweek?*

 b *Practice of the questions.* Focus on the stress pattern:
 – *Do you sell ståmps?*
 – *Do you have Nèwsweek?*

 👥 Learners cover the conversations and practise them. They could also have further conversations, asking about other items.

SPEAKING

4 *Preparation for the role play.* Give learners letters, A or B. A looks on p90. B looks on p95. They read their role card for Conversation 1.

To demonstrate the role play, ask B a question (e.g. *Do you sell pens?*). B should answer according to what is on his / her card.

👥 *Role play.* Learners form pairs, one A and one B. Learner A asks for things at the kiosk and B replies.

A and B change roles and have a second conversation (Conversation 2 on their role cards). They could form new pairs for Conversation 2.

Prices

VOCABULARY Numbers, prices

1 *Review of numbers 10 – 50.* Books closed. Write numbers 10, 20, 30, 40, 50 on the board and ask learners to say them. Check that they can spell them (this is a good opportunity to practise the alphabet) and write them as words on the board.

Numbers 60 – 100. Books open. Look at the numbers 60, 70, 80, 90, 100 and ask learners to say them. Play recording **1.79** or say them yourself and get learners to repeat.

Focus on the difference between:
 – 13, 14, 15, 16, etc. Both syllables are more or less equally stressed and the *-teen* is long: /θɜːtiːn/, /fɔːtiːn/, /fɪftiːn/
 – 30, 40, 50, 60, etc. The stress is clearly on the first syllable, and the second syllable is short: /ˈθɜːti/, /ˈfɔːti/, /ˈfɪfti/

To practise, write pairs of numbers on the board, e.g. 13 / 30, 16 / 60, 18 / 80. Point to a number and learners say it.

2 *Prices.* Learners read the prices aloud.

> A four pounds seventy-five
> B one dollar sixty
> C two euros seventy; one euro thirty
> D eighteen dollars ninety-five
> E three pounds eighty
> F seventy-five; forty-five euros

Teach the words for currencies:
 – $1 = one dollar   – $4 = four dollars
 – €1 = one euro   – €5 = five euros
 – £1 = one pound   – £18 = eighteen pounds

Point out that:
 – we say *four sixty* or *four dollars sixty* (without *and*)
 – we say *euro* as /ˈjuːrəʊ/.

Language note

Most world currencies add a plural *-s* in English: *dollars, pounds, euros, rials, dinars, roubles, rupees, pesos, cents.* A few stay the same: *yen, yuan, krone.*

You could give more practice by writing prices on the board and asking learners to say them.

3 *Listening.* Look at the picture and ask what it shows (a restaurant or café, maybe at an airport or a station). Look at the list and ask learners to read the items and prices aloud.

Play recording **1.80**. Learners listen and complete the sentences. Pause after each conversation and go through the answers.

> 1 She wants two coffees and a mineral water. It's 2.90.
> 2 He wants a small salad and a cola. It's 2.50.

4 *Role play.* To demonstrate the activity, choose something to eat and drink from the price list. Ask the class how much it is. Then change roles: a learner chooses something to eat and drink and you say how much it is.

👥 Learners take turns to choose something to eat and drink. The other learner says how much it is.

Round-up. A few learners say what they want to eat and drink and how much it costs.

Conversation practice

You could do the conversation practice exercises on p117 at this point.

Classroom language: Instructions (1)

Goal: to understand simple classroom instructions
Core language:
say, again, (all) together, everyone, (in) pairs, (with a) partner

1 *Listening.* Read through the expressions for Teacher 1, then play recording **1.81**. Learners put them in order.

> 2 Say sandwich.   3 All together.   4 Again. Sandwich.
> 5 Very good.

Check that learners understand what the expressions mean. If necessary, use gestures and mime to show the meaning. Repeat the procedure for Teacher 2.

> 2 In pairs.   3 Work with a partner.   4 That's right.
> 5 Ask your partner questions.

2 Learners write the words in their own language. In a single nationality class, check what they are writing, or they can check with each other.

5.2

Clothes

VOCABULARY Clothes

1 a Read the words in the box, and check that learners can say them. They identify each word in the pictures. Play recording **1.82** to check.

Alternatives

1 Group matching / dictionary task
👥 / 👥 Learners look at the words in the box and see how many they can match to the pictures. They could also use dictionaries to look up new words. Then go through the answers, playing recording **1.82** to check and focus on pronunciation.

2 Use magazine photos
Books closed. Bring in photos from magazines and use them to present the words. Then use the exercise in the Coursebook as practice.

Point out that:
– *trousers* and *jeans* are plural in English, so we say: *His jeans are new. The trousers are €100.* (not *His jeans is new.*)
– We can't say *a trouser* or *a jeans*, but we can say *a pair of trousers, a pair of jeans.*

b *'Men, women'.* Write on the board: *man, woman*. Then ask learners to say the plural forms. Add them on the board: *men, women*. Practise saying the words: make sure learners pronounce /ˈwʊmən/ and /ˈwɪmɪn/ correctly.

Practice of clothes vocabulary. Ask which clothes men wear, which women wear, and which men or women wear.

Alternatively, give time for learners to do this on their own, writing *M, W* or *M / W* beside each word. Then go through the answers together. Expected answers:

---
1 *suit, tie*   2 *blouse, dress, skirt*   3 *the others*

Language note

Women can also wear a *suit*, but it would normally be a matching jacket and skirt. Matching jacket and trousers for women are usually called a *trouser suit*.

---

2 a *Writing.* To introduce the activity, tell the class a few clothes that you often, sometimes and never wear.

👤 Working alone, learners write the clothes in three lists. As they do this, go round and check that they are spelling the words correctly.

b *Speaking.* To introduce the pairwork phase, tell the class what you wear at home, at work and at a party. Check that learners have understood by asking them what you said.

👥 / 👥 Learners tell each other what they wear at home, at school, or at a party.

Alternative: Mingling activity

Learners move freely round the class, telling two or three different learners what they wear, and asking: *What about you?*.

Round-up. A few learners tell you one interesting thing they heard from their partner. They should say *He / She wears ...* (you could write this on the board as a model).

How much ...?

GRAMMAR *How much ...?*

1 a *'How much is / are ...?'*. Ask learners to look at the pictures of clothes. Write on the board:
– *How much ...?*

Ask what question you can ask about the skirt (*How much is the skirt?*). Then ask what question you can ask about the trousers (*How much are the trousers?*). Write the two questions on the board:
– *How much is the skirt?*
– *How much are the trousers?*

Ask why the second question has *are* (because trousers are plural). Read the questions and answers, and ask what words go in the gaps.

---
1 *is*   2 *It's*   3 *are*   4 *They're*

---

b Look at the clothes together. Learners say the prices. Check that they can say numbers like *twenty-six* and *forty-two* (this shouldn't be a problem).

c Give a few prompts for learners to practise asking questions, e.g.
– *shirt: How much is the shirt?*
– *jeans: How much are the jeans?*
👥 Learners ask and answer the questions.

2 *Listening.* Play recording **1.83** and ask what the question is. Write it on the board:
– *How much is a cheap suit in Germany?*

Then ask what the answers are (150 euros, 200 euros, 80 euros, 100 euros, 50 euros).

Large numbers. Ask round the class: *How much is a cheap suit in your country?* Write possible answers on the board.

Point out that:
– 100 = *a hundred* or *one hundred*
– 150 = *a hundred and fifty* (not *a hundred fifty*)
– 200 = *two hundred* (not *two hundreds*)

3 Put learners in groups of three or four. Together, they discuss how much the clothes in the list are in their country.

Round-up. Go through the answers and see if all the groups agree.

Alternatives

1 Mixed nationality classes

Learners work in pairs or groups, and compare prices in different countries. Obviously, they will need to 'translate' the prices into the currency of the country where you are.

2 Mingling activity

Give each learner a different item to ask about (you could write these on pieces of paper and give one to each learner). Learners move freely round the class, asking their question to two or three other learners.

Round-up. Ask a few learners what different answers they had to their question.

Colours

VOCABULARY Colours

1 a Learners look at the photos and see how many colours they can match with the pictures.

---

1 grey   2 white   3 green   4 black
5 blue   6 brown   7 yellow   8 red

Then play recording **1.84** to check (or say the colours yourself) and practise saying the words. Focus on the words with double consonant sounds:
brown, grey, green, black, blue.

Language note

All adjectives, including colours, come before the noun in English, so we can say:
– *My T-shirt is* **black**.
– *I have a* **black** *T-shirt.* (not *I have a T-shirt black.*)
If necessary, point this out to the class.

Optional extra

Point to things in the class or learners' clothes. Learners say what colour they are.

---

b *Practice of colours.* Use the photos on page 40 (Clothes) as a memory test. Learners cover the page and see if they can remember the colours.
(Ask: *There's a woman with trousers. What colour are they? What about her coat? The man has a T-shirt. What colour is it?* etc.)

Alternative: Pair work

One learner covers a picture and the other tests him / her on it. You could write a model question on the board:
What colour is ...?

---

2 *Speaking.* To introduce the activity, ask one or two of the questions round the class. Then get learners to ask you the questions, and give true answers.

Learners ask each other questions.

Round-up. A few learners to tell you which of the clothes their partner has (e.g. *She has a pair of red shoes and she has four white T-shirts*).

I wear ...

LISTENING

1 *Listening for main points.* Play recording **1.85** straight through. Learners listen and write the O, B or D beside the colours.

Go through the answers by playing the recording again to check, pausing after each speaker.

---

1 O   2 D   3 O   4 B   5 B   6 O, B, D   7 O, D   8 B, D

GRAMMAR *He / she doesn't* + verb

2 a Play recording **1.86** or read the sentences aloud. Point out that:
– after *He / she*, we add an *-s* to the verb
  (*like → likes*), so *don't* changes to *doesn't*.
– we don't add an *-s* to the *main verb*
  (so we don't say *doesn't likes*).

Practise saying the sentences. Check that learners pronounce /dʌznt/ correctly.

Alternative: Presentation with books closed

Write on the board:
– *I like black clothes.*
– *He / She likes black clothes.*
Remind learners that after *He / She* we add *-s* to the verb.
Now write: *I don't like black clothes.*
Remind learners that in the negative, we use the verb *don't* (= do not).
Then write: *He/ She doesn't like black clothes.*
Then open books and play recording **1.86**.

---

b Do the exercise round the class, or let learners do it in pairs, then go through the answers together.

---

1 I don't like red.
2 He doesn't like green.
3 My mother doesn't wear black.
4 She doesn't wear blue jeans.
5 I don't wear a hat.
6 My father doesn't wear a tie at work.

---

c Learners write *True* or change the sentence into the negative. Then go through the answers and play recording **1.86** again to check.

---

1 True; 2 She doesn't like brown clothes; 3 She likes red.
4 True;   5 He doesn't wear red clothes.;
6 He doesn't like yellow.

SPEAKING

3 a To introduce the activity, tell the class what colours you like, don't like, often wear, etc.

Learners say what colours they like and don't like.

b *Round-up.* In turn, learners tell the class one colour their partner likes or wears and one colour he / she doesn't like or doesn't wear.

Alternative: Writing sentences

Learners write two sentences about their partner, one beginning *He / She likes ...* or *He / She wears ...*, the other beginning *He / She doesn't like ...* or *He / She doesn't wear... .*
Go round and check.
Collect the sentences and read them out. The class guesses which learner they are about.

Sounds and spelling: The sound /ə/

Goal: to recognise and pronounce the sound /ə/ in words with *a*, *e* and *er*

Core language:
Words from Units 1–5 with the sound /ə/

1   Play recording **1.87**. Focus on the /ə/ sound. Point out that we often say /ə/ in unstressed syllables (demonstrate this by showing which part of the words is stressed – use gestures to make this clear).

2   **a** Learners circle the /ə/ sounds.

    b Play recording **1.88** to check, and practise saying the words.

words with 'a'	words with 'e'	words with 'er'
hospit**a**l	sent**e**nces	wait**er**
about	list**e**n	nev**er**
col**a**	par**e**nts	numb**er**
		fath**er**

5.3

Goals: choose and buy things
        look at things in shops
        ask about price and size

Core language:

VOCABULARY	Household objects: *lamp, bag, carpet, plate*
	Questions: *How much is / are … ?*; *What size is …?*
	Answers: *large, medium, small*; *size (44)*; *(10 Euros) each*
GRAMMAR	*this, these*

this, these

GRAMMAR *this, these*

1   To introduce the topic, look at the pictures and ask where they are (a big shop or store). Ask learners if they go to shops like this and if so, where.

Ask learners what they can see in the pictures and use this to present the key vocabulary: *lamp, carpet, plates, bags*.

Listening. Play recording **1.89**. After each conversation, pause and ask:
– *Which picture is it? What do they want to buy?*
– *Do they say 'this' or 'these'?*

As you play the recording, present *this* and *these* on the board:

Singular	*Plural*
this lamp	*these* plates
this carpet	*these* bags

Pronunciation. Point out that:
– /ðɪs/ has a short /ɪ/ sound and ends in a /s/ sound.
– /ðiːz/ has a longer /iː/ sound and ends in a /z/ sound.

To practise, get learners to say expressions (e.g. *this bag, these bags*) round the class.

2   Practise the sentences round the class. Then learners practise them in pairs. Alternatively, learners could write the sentences.

Questions and answers

SPEAKING

1   *'How much …?, What size…?'*. Learners match the questions and answers.

> *1 c   2 a   3 b*

Use the examples to focus on:
– the question *What size is …?* (= Is it big, small?).
– ways of talking about size: *large* (= big), *medium*, *small*. (Learners will probably know L, M, S from clothes labels.)
– the expression *They are 10 euros each*. (= one is 10 euros). If necessary, give a few other examples e.g. *coats $100 = they are $100 dollars each*.

2   👤/👥 Learners complete the questions and answers.

> 1 A How much are these pens?
>   B They're 3.50 each.
> 2 A What size is this jumper?
>   B I think it's medium.
> 3 A What size are these shoes?
>   B They're size 44.
> 4 A How much is this lamp?
>   B It's 55 euros.

3   *Role play.* 👥 Learners ask and answer questions. If possible they should try to do this without reading from the Coursebook.

> **Conversation practice**
> You could do the conversation practice exercises on p118 at this point.

Target activity: Choose and buy things

Goal: choose and buy things

Core language:

5.1 VOCABULARY	Numbers, prices
5.2 VOCABULARY	Clothes, colours

PREPARATION

1   *Vocabulary.* Look at the picture of the two market stalls and ask what you can see in them.

> A cups, glasses, plates, books, magazines, a lamp, a clock
> B jeans, a coat (or shirt), T-shirts, shoes, bags, sunglasses

Set the situation: you are at the market and you want to buy a T-shirt. Ask learners what questions they could ask. Build up the basic questions on the board:
– *How much is this T-shirt?*
– *How much are these T-shirts?*
– *What size is it?*
If necessary, add other questions:
– *Can I try it on?*
– *Do you have green T-shirts?*

To demonstrate the activity, take the role of the stall holder and learners buy a T-shirt from you. Improvise a conversation, giving realistic answers to their questions.

TASK

2 *Role play 1.* Give learners a letter, A or B.

Read through the instructions. Emphasise that A has only $20. B should follow the Price Guide on p90, but can sell things for more or for less (give an example to make this clear).

👥 Learners have conversations.

3 *Role play 2.* Learners change roles and have a second conversation. A looks at the Price Guide on p97.

Round-up. Ask a few learners to tell you what they now have (i.e. what they bought at the market stall). Try to talk about this without using the past tense.

 You could use photocopiable activity 5A on the Teacher's DVD-ROM at this point.

Keyword *in, on*

Goal: say where things are

Core language:
in + place
on + place
Places in rooms: *table, wall, floor, shelf, cupboard, bag*

1 *'in', 'on'.* Look at the pictures and establish what and where the objects are.

> A cups – *in the cupboard* D books – *in the bag*
> B a glass – *on the table* E newspapers – *on the floor*
> C a clock – *on the wall* F a bottle – *on the shelf*

Language note

We use *on* for horizontal surfaces e.g. *on the table, on the floor,* and also for vertical surfaces e.g. *on the wall, on the door.*

2 *Practice of 'in' and 'on'.* Ask learners to make questions with *Where's ...?* or *Where are ...?* and find the answers in the picture.

> – *Where are my glasses? (They're on the shelf.)*
> – *Where's my mobile? (It's on the table.)*
> – *Where's my pen? (It's on the table.)*
> – *Where's my guitar? (It's in the cupboard.)*
> – *Where are my keys? (They're on the floor.)*
> – *Where are my books? (They're on the chair.)*

👥 Learners ask and answer the questions.

3 *Speaking.* To introduce the activity, tell learners where some of the things are in your house / flat.

👥 / 👥👥 Learners talk about where things are in their house / flat.

Round-up. A few learners tell you something surprising or interesting they heard from their partner.

Language note

We often use the word *keep* in this context:
– *We keep cups in a cupboard.*
– *We keep coffee on a shelf in the kitchen.*
You could introduce *keep* at this point.

5.4 Explore speaking

Goals: use *sorry* and *excuse me* to apologise, attract attention and start a conversation

Core language:
sorry, excuse me

1 a *Listening.* Look at the pictures and play recording **1.90**, pausing after each conversation. Ask whether the person said *Sorry* or *Excuse me*.

> 1 Sorry
> 2 Excuse me; Sorry
> 3 Excuse me

Point out that:
– we say *sorry* if we do something bad.
– we say *excuse me* if we want someone to listen to us.
– we say *excuse me* when we start talking.

Single nationality classes

You could ask learners what they say in their own language. This will help to give insight into any differences between their own language and English.

b *Pronunciation.* Practise saying *Sorry* and *Excuse me.* Point out that when we say *Excuse me* our voice often goes up (= this isn't the end of the sentence – I want to say something else).

2 a 👤 / 👥 Learners add *sorry* or *excuse me* to the bubbles.

b Play recording **1.91**, pausing after each conversation to check.

> 4 Sorry
> 5 Excuse me
> 6 Excuse me; Sorry
> 7 Excuse me

Ask what the answers were. Learners could also suggest other possible answers (given in brackets).

> 4 That's OK. (Why are you late; No problem.)
> 5 Yes, I am. (No, I'm not.; Yes, why?; What's the problem?)
> 6 Sorry, I don't know. (It's there.; It's down this road.)
> 7 Oh yes, thank you. (No, it's not my bag.)

3 *Speaking.* Practise each conversation with the class. First take the role of the first speaker yourself and get learners to respond. Then choose pairs of learners to have each conversation.

👥👥 Learners choose a picture and practise the conversation. If possible, they should do this without reading from the Coursebook.

Across cultures: Office clothes

Goals: to give practice in reading short texts
to sensitise learners to customs in different
countries and cultures

Core language:
formal, casual; clothes (review)

1 *Reading for general idea.* Use photos B and C to teach the words *casual* and *formal*. You could ask learners if they like to wear formal or casual clothes.

Learners read the texts and match them with the photos.

> *A India   B Germany   C Britain*

To review clothes vocabulary, you could ask learners what clothes they can see in the photos.

2 a *Reading for main idea.* Learners read the quotes again and complete the answers.

> *2 Britain   3 India   4 Germany; India   5 Germany*

b Discuss what the highlighted words mean. Focus on *formal* and *casual* at this point if you didn't introduce them earlier.

3 *Writing.* Learners write sentences. Then they read out their sentences and find out what differences there are.

Look again

VOCABULARY

1 *Expressions with 'of'.* Do the exercise with the whole class, or learners do it in pairs and then go through the answers together.

> *a bottle of lemonade*
> *a pair of jeans / sunglasses*
> *a glass of lemonade*
> *a cup of coffee*

2 a *Similar words.* To show what to do, ask learners to find two other words that go with *twenty*. Write them on the board (*twelve, eighty*). Ask them why (They're numbers).

Learners find other groups and write them down.

> *– sunglasses, glasses, watch (you wear them)*
> *– yellow, red, green (colours)*
> *– shirt, suit, pullover (clothes)*
> *– postcard, stamp, pen (you buy them at a kiosk; you need them to write a postcard)*
> *– pizza, burger, sandwich (food)*

b Learners write sentences. Then they read out their sentences. Possible answers:

> *• He often wears a pullover / sunglasses / a red shirt ...*
> *• How much is this shirt / this watch / a sandwich? ...*
> *• Do you sell sunglasses / postcards / burgers? ...*

3 *Numbers.* Learners write the numbers.

> *b twenty   c seventeen   d thirty-three   e fifty-five*
> *f eighty-two   g twelve   h twenty-eight*

SPELLING

4 Ask learners to spell the words correctly. Write them on the board.

> *1 jacket   2 shoes   3 watch*
> *4 sandwich   5 magazine   6 fruit*

CAN YOU REMEMBER? Unit 4

5 👤/👥 *Focus on common verbs.* Learners continue the expressions. Then discuss these with the whole class and build up expressions on the board.

> **Optional extra**
> Gve one point for each correct answer and two points for an answer no one else thought of.

6 a *Writing.* To demonstrate, choose a learner and say a few things you think you know about him / her. Ask questions to check if you are correct.

👤/👥 Learners choose another learner and write sentences. You could tell learners which person to write about (write names on pieces of paper and give them out at random). Go round and check.

b Learners ask questions to check.

> **Alternative: Checking in pairs**
> Learners write sentences about the person next to them. Then they form pairs to check if they are correct.

GRAMMAR

Present simple. Read through the table.

> **Alternative: Presentation with books closed**
> Write on the board:
> – I like coffee.
> – She likes coffee.
> Then write the negative and question forms with gaps:
> – I _____ coffee.   _____ coffee?
> – She _____ coffee.   _____ coffee?
> Ask learners to complete the gaps.

7 Learners change the sentences to the negative.

> *1 I don't live in Italy.   2 He doesn't like books.*
> *3 Paula doesn't work in Paris.*
> *4 They don't have a son.   5 He doesn't wear glasses.*

8 Learners write the sentences in the correct order.

> *1 Do you sell stamps?   2 How much is this coat?*
> *3 I often wear black clothes.*
> *4 What size are these shoes?*

9 Learners write the plural forms.

> *2 watches 3 postcards 4 glasses 5 women 6 shoes*
> *7 dresses 8 sandwiches 9 these*

 You could use photocopiable activity 5B on the Teacher's DVD-ROM at this point.

Self-assessment

To help focus learners on the self-assessment, you could read it through, giving a few more examples of the language they have learned in each section (or asking learners to tell you). Then they circle a number on each line.

Unit 5 Extra activities on the Teacher's DVD-ROM

Printable worksheets, activity instructions and answer keys are on your Teacher's DVD-ROM.

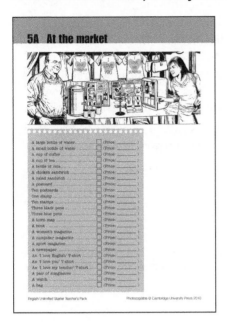

5A At the market

Activity type:
Speaking – Role play – Groups of four or six / Whole group

Aim: To practise language used for shopping

Language: Choose and buy things – Coursebook p43

Preparation:
Make a copy of one worksheet for every learner.

Time: 25 minutes

5B Bingo!

Activity type: Listening – Bingo game – Whole group

Aim: To practise listening comprehension of similar sounding words and plural forms

Language: Review of vocabulary – Coursebook, Unit 5

Procedure: Make one copy of the worksheet for every four learners. Cut the worksheet along the dotted lines to make four bingo cards.

Time: 20 minutes

Unit 5 Self-study Pack

In the Workbook

Unit 5 of the *English Unlimited Starter Workbook* offers additional ways to practise the vocabulary and grammar taught in the Coursebook. There are also activities which build reading and writing skills, and a whole page of tasks to use with the DVD-ROM video, giving your learners the opportunity to hear and react to spoken English.

- **Vocabulary:** Common objects; Clothes; Numbers, prices; Colours
- **Grammar:** Singular and plural nouns; Present simple – negative
- **Time out:** Market stall puzzle
- **Explore writing:** *and, but, or*
- **DVD-ROM Extra:** In a clothes shop

On the DVD-ROM

Unit 5 of the *English Unlimited Starter Self-study Pack DVD-ROM* contains interactive games and activities for your learners to practise and improve their vocabulary, grammar and pronunciation, and also their speaking and listening. It also contains video material (with the possibility for learners to record themselves) to use with the *Workbook*.

- **Vocabulary and Grammar:** Extra practice of Coursebook language and Keyword
- **Classroom language:** Instructions (1)
- **Sounds and spelling:** The sound /ə/
- **Explore speaking:** Use *sorry* and *excuse me* in conversations
- **Video:** In a clothes shop

6 Every day

6.1

Goals: **talk about things you do every day**
talk about your daily routine
say where and when you have meals

Core language:

VOCABULARY	Daily routine: *wake up, get up, read the paper, have tea / coffee, have breakfast, have a shower, go to school / work, watch TV, listen to the radio, go to bed; start work, finish work* Frequency: *always, usually, sometimes, never*
GRAMMAR	Present simple: *-s / -es* endings

In the morning

VOCABULARY Morning activities

1 a Read the expressions with the class or play recording **2.1** and make sure learners can say them. Focus especially on the rhythm of the expressions:
– have a shower
– listen to the radio
– go to school.

Point out:
– the difference between *wake up* and *get up* (show this by miming).
– that we usually say *have* (not ~~drink~~) *tea / coffee*, *have* (not ~~eat~~) *breakfast, have a shower.*

b Learners look at the expressions and write down those they do in the morning. To demonstrate this, you could go through the expressions yourself, saying which things you do.

c *Sequence words (first, then, and).* To present *First ..., then ...,* tell the class what you do in the morning (e.g. *First I wake up, then I get up, then I read the paper and listen to the radio ...*). The class tells you what you said. Write the expressions on the board:
– *First I wake up.*
– *Then I get up.*

Point out that if you do two things at the same time, you can use *and*. Write an example on the board:
– *I read the paper. I listen to the radio.*
  → *I read the paper and listen to the radio.*

Ask learners to look at the expressions they wrote down and to put them in order (writing numbers 1, 2, 3 ...).

d 👥 Learners tell their partner what they do in the morning.
Round-up. One or two learners tell you what they do.

2 a *Preparation for the listening.* Look at the photo and ask the class what they think Emma's job is and whether she gets up early or late.

b Play recording **2.2**. Learners listen and write numbers beside the expressions. Then go through the answers together by playing the recording again to check.

> 1 *get up*   2 *have a shower*   3 *have a cup of coffee*
> 4 *go to work*   5 *have breakfast*   6 *read the paper*

3 a *Review of third-person verb forms.* Learners complete the table.

> *gets*
> *has*

You could do some quick practice round the class. Say a verb with *I* and ask learners to say it with *He* or *She*:
I get up → *She gets up*
I have → *He has*
I read → *She reads*

> **Note**
> There is no need to go into spelling (of *-s* and *-es* endings) at this point. This is focused on in the next section (Daily routine).

b Ask learners if they can remember what their partner does in the morning.

Daily routine

READING

1 a To introduce the topic, look at the photos and establish that the people work in a 24-hour supermarket (= it's open 24 hours, day and night). Ask learners if there are supermarkets like this in their own country and when most supermarkets open and close.

👤 / 👥 *Reading and speaking.* Learners read the texts and answer the questions.

> 1 *Carla*   2 *Carla, Salman*   3 *Salman*
> 4 *They're both at work from two to three in the afternoon.*

b *'Daily routine' expressions.* Learners find pairs of expressions in the texts. Write them on the board:

> *get up – go to bed*
> *go to work – come home*
> *start work – finish work*

Check that learners understand:
– *go* and *come* (show this by gestures – *go* = from here to there; *come* = from there to here).
– *start* and *finish* (give examples: say when the lesson starts and finishes).

To activate these expressions, ask learners round the class: *When do you go to work? When do you start work? When do you come home?* etc.

GRAMMAR Present simple: -s / -es endings

2 a Learners read the sentences about Salman and complete the table.

Go through the answers together by writing the verbs on the board.

> get up – gets up
> start – starts
> come – comes
> go – goes
> finish – finishes
> watch – watches

b *-s and -es endings.* Establish that most verbs add *-s* in the third person (after *He / She ..., Salman ..., Carla ...*).

Point out that some verbs add *-es.* These are:
– verbs that end in *-o* (*go* → *goes*, also *do* → *does*).
– verbs that end in *-ch, -sh, -s* (*finishes, watches*).

Practise saying the verbs. Focus on the /z/ and /ɪz/ endings.

c *Practice in writing sentences.* Learners write sentences about Carla.

> She gets up at five in the morning.
> She goes to work at about six.
> She starts work at seven.
> She finishes work at three in the afternoon.
> She comes home and has lunch.

Optional extra

👥 Learners ask each other about their routine (write a model question structure on the board: *When do you ...?*).
Then learners tell you about their partner's routine, using the verbs they have practised in **2**.

Meals

VOCABULARY Frequency

1 a Introduce the words *meal* and *lunch* by saying: *Breakfast is a meal. Tell me another meal. What do I have at one o'clock?* (You could also introduce *dinner* in the same way.)

Listening. Read the sentences. Then play recording **2.3** without pausing. Learners listen and write numbers by the sentences.

> lunch in a restaurant 3, 2
> lunch at home 2
> lunch in a café 1
> a bar of chocolate 4
> a sandwich 1
> a cup of coffee 1

Play the recording again to check, pausing after each speaker, and ask what else they say:

> 1 There's a café near my office.
> 2 I sometimes go to a restaurant, but it's expensive.
> 3 It's a really good restaurant, so we all eat there.
> 4 I don't have time for lunch.

b *Frequency adverbs.* Learners complete the sentences.

> 1 usually   2 sometimes   3 always   4 never

If necessary, play recording **2.3** again, or let learners listen and check the script on page 124.

c Draw the scale on the board and ask learners where to add the words.

> 0% ◄─────────────────────► 100%
> never   sometimes   usually   always

If necessary, give other examples to make the meaning clear (learners should know *sometimes* and *never* from Unit 4.2).

2 a *Writing.* To show what to do, look at sentence 1 together. Change it so it is true for you. Then ask three or four learners *What about you?*.

Learners write true sentences, adding a frequency word. As they do this, go round and check.

👥 *Speaking.* Learners read their sentences to each other.

Round-up. Learners tell you one thing about their partner (e.g. *She never has coffee with breakfast.*).

Language note

Always and *never* must come before the main verb. *Sometimes* and *usually* can come before the main verb, or at the beginning or end of the sentence:
– I *sometimes* have a big breakfast.
– *Sometimes* I have a big breakfast.
– I have a big breakfast *sometimes*.
These words can't come after the verb, so we can't say:
~~I have sometimes a big breakfast.~~

Classroom language:
Let's ... , Could you ... ?

Goal: to understand simple requests and instructions from the teacher

Core language:
Let's ..., Could you ...?
Verbs: *open / close (the door); play (a game); start, finish*

1 a Books closed. To remind learners of *Let's ...* (Unit 3.3), make suggestions to a few learners, e.g. *Let's meet on Saturday* or *Let's go to the cinema* and check what this means (= *I want to meet; I want to go with you*).

Then ask a few questions with *Could you ...?*, e.g. *Could you open the door?* and check what it means (= *Please open the door*).

Write *Let's ...* and *Could you ...?* on the board.

👤 / 👥 *Open books.* Learners add verbs to the remarks.

b *Listening.* Play recording **2.4** to check, pausing after each remark.

> 1 close   2 start   3 open   4 play   5 finish

Ask a few further questions, e.g.
1 *What does she say next?* (Come in.)
  Why? (Another learner comes.)
2 *What does she say next?* (Look at this picture.)
3 *Why do they want to open the window?*
  (It's very hot.)
4 *What does she say about the time?*
  (They have 10 minutes.)
5 *When is the next class?* (Next Tuesday.)

2 Learners write the expressions in their own language. In a single nationality class, check what they are writing, or they can check with each other. You could ask learners to translate all five remarks into their first language.

Goals: **talk about things you do every day**
describe transport in towns
ask and say how to get to places
say how you go to work or school

Core language:

VOCABULARY Transport: *train, bus, tram, plane, underground (metro), boat, taxi*; *walk, cycle, drive*; *go by bike, go by car*
Adjectives: *cheap, expensive*; *fast, slow*; *good*
Questions: *How can I get to ...?*

Transport

VOCABULARY Transport

1 a Look at the small pictures. Learners match them with the words. Say the words or play recording **2.5** and ask learners to repeat them.

> *A boat   B tram   C taxi   D plane   E bus*
> *F underground   G train*

Language note

Instead of *underground* you can also say *metro*. In London, people usually talk about the *underground* or the *Tube*. North American English is *subway*.
Plane is short for *aeroplane* (or *airplane*).
We can use the word *boat* to talk about either a small boat or a larger *ferry* or *ship*.

b *Speaking*. Look on p90. Ask learners what they think photo A is (probably a boat).

Learners look at the other photos and decide what they are. You could ask learners to write the words down.

Turn to p98 and look at the larger photos to check the answers.

> *A a boat   B a bus   C a taxi   D a train   E a plane*
> *F a tram   G an underground (train)*

Two cities

LISTENING

1 a Introduce the topic by looking at the photos of London and Istanbul. Ask what the photos show.

> **London:**
> *a street with a bus and a taxi; an underground station.*
> **Istanbul:**
> *a boat (ferry); a mosque with a taxi.*

b *Preparation for the exercise*. Read the sentences. Use them to present *go by*. Point out that we say *go by taxi / car / bus* (not ~~go by the taxi~~).

To practise, quickly ask about transport in the town where you are (*You can go ...*).

c *Listening*. Play recording **2.6**, pausing after each speaker to check the sentences in **1a**.

> *1 London   2 Istanbul   3 Istanbul   4 London   5 London*

Don't go into any more detail about the listening at this stage. Learners will listen again in **3**.

2 a Play recording **2.7**. Read the sentences in the table and practise saying them. Focus on the sentence stress and on the reduced vowels in *there's a, there are, you can*.

Remind learners that we use *There's* with singular nouns (metro) and *There are* with plural nouns (taxis).

b ⚊/⚊⚊ Learners complete the sentences.

> *1 there are   2 you can   3 there are*
> *4 you can   5 there's   6 you can*

VOCABULARY Adjectives

3 *Listening for detail*. Play recording **2.6** again, pausing after each speaker, and ask learners to listen for the adjectives.

> *1 very fast, quite expensive*
> *2 very expensive   3 slow   4 not too expensive*
> *5 cheap, quite slow   6 very good, cheap*

As you go through the answers, present the adjectives, using gestures and simple examples. Teach the words *very* and *quite* (= not very).

To check, you could ask a few questions about transport in your area, e.g. *What about buses? Are they slow? Fast? Very slow or quite slow?*

4 a *Writing*. To help prepare for the writing activity, remind learners of the language taught in this section and write expressions on the board:

> *– go by ...*
> *– You can ...*
> *– There's a ... / There are ...*
> *– Adjectives: fast, expensive ....*

Learners write sentences about their own town. If learners come from the same town, they could do this in pairs. As they do this, go round and check.

b *Speaking*. In turn, learners read out their sentences. If other learners come from the same place, ask them if they agree.

Alternative: Pair or group work

Learners move into groups of four to read out their sentences, or form new pairs. In mixed nationality classes, they could form groups with learners from other countries.

Homework option: Internet research

As homework, name a few different cities. Learners find out about the transport there on the Internet (they could do this in their own language or in English). Learners then report back in the next lesson.
This would be a good alternative activity for learners who live in Istanbul.

How can I get to ...?

VOCABULARY *How can I get to ...?*

1 a *Listening.* Look at the picture and establish where it is. Play recording **2.8** and answer the questions.

> – the airport.   – go by train or by taxi.

Practise the question *How can I get to ...?*. Focus on the stress and the reduced *can*: /hǎʊ‿kən‿ǎɪ/.

👥 *Speaking.* Learners ask and answer the question. If possible, do this without reading from the book.

If your town has an airport, you could change the information so it is true of where you are.

b *Practice of questions and answers.* Look at the notes. Ask learners to give the questions and answers.

> 1 – How can I get to the town centre?
>   – You can go by tram, or by underground.
> 2 – How can I get to Oxford?
>   – You can go by train, or by taxi.
> 3 – How can I get to Paris?
>   – You can go by train, by plane, or by bus.
> 4 – How can I get to Malta?
>   – You can go by plane, or by boat.

2 a *Writing.* To prepare for the writing, learners think of places in the town where you are and build up a list on the board (e.g. famous buildings, hotels, restaurants, the bus station ...). Then build up a list of other towns they want to go to (ask them to suggest places in the same country and other countries).

Learners write two (or more) questions. As they do this, quickly go round and check.

b 👥 / 👥👥 *Speaking.* Learners ask each other questions.

Round-up. Ask a few learners what their questions were, and what answers they received.

Conversation practice

You could do the conversation practice exercises on p118 at this point.

 You could use photocopiable activity 6A on the Teacher's DVD-ROM at this point.

Work and school

LISTENING and SPEAKING

1 Learners match expressions with the photos.

> A walk
> B cycle / go by bike
> C drive / go by car

Point out that:
– *drive* and *go by car* mean the same.
– *cycle* and *go by bike* mean the same.

Check that learners understand the meaning of *walk* (demonstrate or show with your fingers).

Language note

The verb *go* has a general meaning in English. *I go to work* could mean *I walk, I drive, I cycle, ...*
If we want to say *I go on foot* (i.e. not in a car or a bus), we say *I walk*.

---

2 a Play recording **2.9**, pausing after each speaker. Learners underline the correct words.

> 1 cycles, goes by bus
> 2 walks, goes by bus
> 3 drives
> 4 walks, goes by train

b Discuss the questions. Then play recording **2.9** again to check.

> **Donna:** *In a big city, quite near her home (she cycles).*
> **Olga:** *In an office, near her home.*
> **Ben:** *In the next town.*
> **Emma:** *In the city.*

3 *Review of frequency adverbs.* To introduce the activity, tell the class how you go to work. Tell them what you usually, sometimes and never do. Then ask the class to tell you what you said. Use this to remind learners of frequency adverbs, and write examples on the board:

	always usually sometimes never	go by bus.
I		

👥 *Speaking.* Learners tell each other how they go to work, school or university.

Round-up. A few learners tell you how they go to work / school.

Alternative

Check that learners can say the following third-person forms. Write them on the board:
He / She usually goes ...
              walks ...
              drives ...
              cycles ...
A few learners tell you what they found out from their partner.

Sounds and spelling: *o, oa* and *oo*

Goals: to pronounce the letter *o* with the sounds /ɒ/, /əʊ/
and /ʌ/
to pronounce the letters *oa* with the sound /əʊ/
to pronounce the letters *oo* with the sound /ʊ/

Core language:
Words from Units 1–6 with the letters *o, oa* and *oo*

1 *Presentation of /ɒ/, /ʌ/, /əʊ/ and /ʊ/.* Say the words or play recording **2.10**. Focus on the four sounds:
– /ɒ/ is a short sound, with the lips loosely rounded (but wider open than the /o/ sound in many languages).
– /ʌ/ is a short sound, said with the mouth open (lips not rounded) – it is very similar to the /a/ sound in many languages.
– /əʊ/ is longer and has two sounds together: /ə/ and /ʊ/. To practise, get learners to say the two sounds separately, then run them together.
– /ʊ/ is a short sound, with the lips rounded.

2 a *Practice of the sounds.* Learners put the words in the correct group. Check answers by listening to recording **2.11**.

> /ɒ/ – hospital, mosque, sorry
> /əʊ/ – no, so; boat
> /ʌ/ – brother, Monday
> /ʊ/ – cook, look

b Play recording **2.12** or say the expressions yourself. Learners repeat them.

Learners write down as many as they can remember.

Learners read out the expressions. Then play the recording again to check.

6.3

Goals: talk about things you do every day
ask about daily routines
ask about weekends and holidays

Core language:

GRAMMAR   Present simple – questions

Questions

GRAMMAR Present simple questions

1 a *Listening.* Look at the photo and ask where they are (In the street). Establish that the woman asks the man questions.

Play recording **2.13**. Then ask what the questions were and write them on the board.

> – When do you finish work?
> – Where do you have lunch?
> – How do you go to work?

Focus on the pronunciation of *do you*: /wen‿djuː/, /weə‿djuː/, /haʊ‿djuː/.

b Ask what the man's answers are.

> 1 four o'clock   2 in a café   3 by train, then he walks

c Discuss the questions together. If necessary, play recording **2.13** again to check.

> 1 He finishes work at one or two.
> 2 It's near his office.
> 3 It's near the station.

2 a *Wh- questions.* Look at the questions in the box. Ask the questions round the class and get learners to suggest possible answers. Point out that we can ask two kinds of question:
– questions beginning *Do you ...?* (the answer is *Yes* or *No*).
– questions beginning with a question word (*Where*, *When*, *How* ...) (the answer is a sentence or an expression).

Emphasise that we use *do* in both kinds of question. Play recording **2.14** and ask learners to practise saying the questions.

b *Practice in making questions.* Look at **1** together and ask what the question is.

> 1 Where do you work?

🧍/👥 Learners write questions for the other items.

> 2 When do you start work?
> 3 Where do you have lunch?
> 4 When do you come home?
> 5 How do you go to work?

c 👥 *Speaking.* Learners ask and answer the questions.

What do you do?

SPEAKING

1 a Books closed. Ask the question *What do you do in the evening?* and see if learners can answer it.

> **Optional presentation**
>
> Point out that:
> 1 We use the verb *do* to talk in general. Give a few examples: *On Saturday, I play football, I go out, I read, I watch TV ...* = *I do* a lot.
> 2 We also use *do* to make questions:
> *I play ... → What do you play?*
> *I read ... → What do you read?*
> *I do ... → What do you do?*
> So in the question *What do you do?* we use *do* in both these ways.

b *Pronunciation.* Play recording **2.15**. Learners repeat round the class. Focus on the stress pattern in /wɒt djuː duː ɪn ðə iːvnɪŋ/. Then learners ask the question to the person next to them.

c 🧍/👥 Learners match the questions and answers.

> 1b 2a 3d 4c

Learners could ask each other the questions.

> **Language note**
>
> We can also ask *What do you do?* meaning *What's your job or occupation?* e.g.
> – *What do you do?*
> – *I'm a student.*
> (see Unit 2.2)

Target activity: Talk about things you do every day

Goal: talk about things you do every day

Core language:

6.1 VOCABULARY   Daily routine
6.3 GRAMMAR   Present simple – questions

PREPARATION

1 Explain that learners will ask questions to find out what most people in the class do.

👥 Go through the questions together. Choose one learner to ask each question and another learner to answer it.

2 To demonstrate how the survey will work, choose one group of questions. Ask the questions to several learners in turn and make a brief note of the answers on the board. Then establish what answers most people gave.

TASK

3   Divide the class into groups of five. In each group, give each learner a letter: A–E.

👥👥 Learners ask their questions to the others in the group and make a note of the results.

4   *Round-up.* Taking each number in turn, learners from each group say what most people in their group do, e.g.

A – Most people in my group get up at 8.00. They have a small breakfast with coffee. After breakfast they go to work.

Alternatives

1 Learners compare their answers
After the group work, learners form new groups (all the A learners together, all the B learners together, etc.). They compare their results and work out what most learners in the class do.
Round-up. One learner from each new group reports back their results.

2 Mingling activity
Give each learner one question to ask. They move freely round the class, asking their question to as many learners as possible and make brief notes of the replies.
Round-up. Ask each learner to say what most people in the class do.

 You could use photocopiable activity 6B on the Teacher's DVD-ROM at this point.

Keyword *have* (2)

Goals: use expressions with *have* / *don't have* to talk about everyday activities, food, drink and meals

Core language:
Have / don't have as an activity verb (= *eat*, *drink* or *take*)

1 **a** 👥 / 👥👥 *Reading.* Working together, learners read the sentences and choose the answers they think are correct.

    b Discuss the answers together. Then look on p98 to check.

      | 1a 2b 3b 4b 5b 6a 7a |

2   *Expressions with 'have'.* Point out that *have* is often used with the meaning *eat* or *drink*. Learners find expressions. Build up lists on the board.

have = eat	have = drink	others
have breakfast have lunch have a meal have a burger	have a cup of coffee have a cup of tea have a can of cola	have a shower

3   *Writing.* Learners write three true sentences about themselves. As they do this, go round and check.

    Round-up. A few learners read out their sentences.

6.4 Explore writing

Goal: join ideas using *so / because*
               give reasons and explanations

Core language:
so, because

1   Look at the photo and ask learners what it shows. (An Indian woman in a Sari.) Ask learners what they remember about saris (they're cotton, they're like a long dress, they're cool).

'so' and ' because'. Read the sentences. Ask which word goes in each gap: *so* or *because*.

> A so
> B because

2   *Writing.* Look at **1** together and ask learners how it might continue. Write sentences on the board, getting learners to tell you what to write:

> 1 Lots of students go to Dino's Café because the food is cheap.

👤 / 👥 Learners write sentences. As they do this, go round and check.

> 2 Their flat is near the station, so it's quite noisy.
> 3 I go to work at six, so I usually go to bed early.
> 4 The journey is about 2,000 kilometres, so it takes three or four days.
> 5 I don't see them very often because they live in Australia.

3 **a** *Writing.* To show what to do, choose one of the topics and learners suggest a beginning, e.g.
    I like my flat ...

    Then ask them to add an idea, using *because*, e.g.
    I like my flat because it's near the town centre.

    Learners choose two or three of the topics and write sentences. As they do this, go round and check.

    b Learners read out their sentences.

Optional extra

Give sentence beginnings on a worksheet for learners to choose from. This may make it easier for them to think of sentences with *so* or *because*.

Across cultures: Journeys

Goals: to give practice in reading short texts
                to give learners information about other parts of the world

Core language:
journey; leaves, arrives (in), takes (three hours)

1 **a** *Reading.* Introduce the word *journey* (give an example, e.g. *I go from London to New York – this is a journey*).

Learners read the texts and match them with the photos. They should try to do this without a dictionary and guess the meaning of any unknown words.

Discuss the answers together.

> 1 the Trans-Siberian railway in Russia (a train, forests, mountains)
> 2 a train station on the Trans-Siberian railway
> 3 a boat on the Amazon
> 4 the Amazon river, forest
> 5 hammocks on a boat

b Learners read again, checking words in the dictionary. Read through the texts together, and present any new words. Focus especially on: *through* (Siberia); *down* (the Amazon); *leave* (= start the journey); it *takes* six days (= the journey is six days).

2 *Writing.* To introduce this stage, say a few sentences about a journey that you know of, using the sentence beginnings. Then learners tell you what you said.

👤 / 👥👥 Learners write a few sentences about a journey in their country. As they do this, go round and check.

Round-up. Learners read out their sentences.

Look again

VOCABULARY

1 a *Similar words.* Do the exercise with the whole class, or learners do it in pairs.

lunch – breakfast	finish – start
station – airport	walk – drive
tram – bus	never – always

b Learners complete the sentences. Possible answers:

> 1 drive, walk ... 2 station, airport ... 3 finish, start ...
> 4 tram, bus ... 5 lunch, breakfast ...

2 Learners add verbs to the expressions, e.g.

> 1 have, start, finish ... 2 go, drive, walk, cycle ...
> 3 have ... 4 read, buy ... 5 listen ... 6 go ...

3 👤 / 👥👥 *Transport.* Learners either tell each other their answers, or (if they come from the same place) discuss the answers together.

Round-up. Take each question in turn and get answers from different pairs or groups.

SPELLING

4 Learners spell the words correctly. Write them on the board.

> 1 usually 2 lunch 3 breakfast
> 4 shower 5 expensive 6 sometimes

CAN YOU REMEMBER? Unit 5

5 a *Common objects and clothes.* Learners write the words in two lists.

> 1 a pair of sunglasses; a newspaper; a postcard; a sandwich; a pen
> 2 a suit; a skirt; a tie; a coat; a hat

b 👤 / 👥👥 Learners add three more words to each list.

Learners say what they wrote. Write the words on the board in two lists.

6 Get a learner to read sentence A. The next learner reads sentence B. The next learner reads sentence C and adds a new expression. Continue round the class, with each learner repeating what the others have said and adding a new expression.

GRAMMAR

Present simple -s endings. Read through the tables.

Present simple – questions. Read through the tables.

Can. Read through the tables.

7 Learners correct the mistakes.

> 1 She starts work at 9.00.
> 2 Where do you have lunch?
> 3 How can I get to the airport?
> 4 The children go to school by bike.
> 5 The film finishes at 10.30.

Self-assessment

To help focus learners on the self-assessment, you could read it through, giving a few more examples of the language they have learned in each section (or asking learners to tell you). Then they circle a number on each line.

Unit 6 Extra activities on the Teacher's DVD-ROM

Printable worksheets, activity instructions and answer keys are on your Teacher's DVD-ROM.

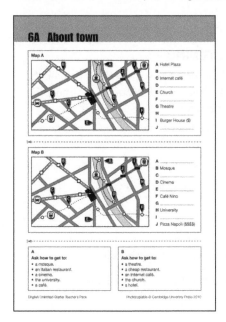

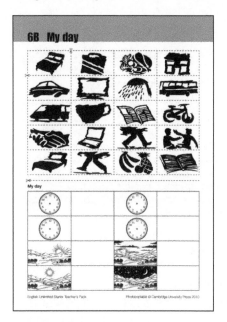

6A About town

Activity type: Speaking – Information gap and role play – Whole group / Groups of four or six

Aim: To practise asking how to get to places

Language: Transport – Coursebook p48; *How can I get to ...?* – Coursebook p49 – Vocabulary

Preparation: Make one copy of the worksheet for every pair of learners. Cut the worksheet along the dotted lines into two maps and two role cards.

Time: 20 minutes

6B My day

Activity type: Speaking – Information gap – Pairs

Aim: To practise asking and talking about routines

Language:
Talk about things you do every day – Coursebook p51

Procedure: Make one copy of the worksheet for every learner. Cut the worksheet along the dotted lines to make a set of 20 cards and one table for each learner.

Time: 20 minutes

Unit 6 Self-study Pack

In the Workbook

Unit 6 of the *English Unlimited Starter Workbook* offers additional ways to practise the vocabulary and grammar taught in the Coursebook. There are also activities which build reading and writing skills, and a whole page of tasks to use with the DVD-ROM video, giving your learners the opportunity to hear and react to spoken English.

- **Vocabulary:** Daily routine; Transport; *How can I get to ... ?*; Adjectives
- **Grammar:** Present simple – questions
- **Explore reading:** A travel information website
- **DVD-ROM Extra:** *How can I get to Haxby?*

On the DVD-ROM

Unit 6 of the *English Unlimited Starter Self-study Pack DVD-ROM* contains interactive games and activities for your learners to practise and improve their vocabulary, grammar and pronunciation, and also their speaking and listening. It also contains video material (with the possibility for learners to record themselves) to use with the *Workbook*.

- **Vocabulary and Grammar:** Extra practice of Coursebook language and Keyword
- **Classroom language:** *Let's ...*, *Could you ...?*
- **Sounds and spelling:** *o*, *oa* and *oo*
- **Explore writing:** Join ideas using *so* / *because*
- **Video:** *How can I get to Haxby?*

7 Last week

7.1

Goals: talk about things you did or saw
  say what you often do at the weekend
  say what you did last weekend

Core language:

VOCABULARY	Activities: *cook (meals), phone (friends), meet (friends), go shopping, go for a walk*
GRAMMAR	Past simple (regular forms): *stayed, listened, phoned, cooked, watched* Past simple (irregular forms): *got up, went, had, wrote, met*

At the weekend

VOCABULARY Activities

1 Read the sentences in green and blue and present *stay* and *go out* (use gestures to show the meaning). Ask learners what days are the weekend in their country and write *at the weekend* on the board.

Optional lead-in

Books closed. Say a few things about what you do at the weekend. Use this to present *stay, go out* and *at the weekend*.

To make it clear what the line shows, say a few things about yourself. Draw a line on the board and make a cross to show your position. Then ask learners to mark their own place on the line. Ask: *Who is in the green part? Who is in the blue part?*.

2 a *Reading.* Read the questions (or learners read them) and ask which expressions the pictures go with.

> 1 go for a walk   2 cook meals   3 phone friends or family

Make sure learners understand the verbs *cook* and *phone* and can say them correctly.

b *Quiz: asking and answering questions.* To demonstrate, ask a learner one or two of the questions and give him / her a score.

Alternative

Get learners to ask you the questions. As you answer, write scores for yourself on the board in two columns. Then add them up to see if your A or B answers have a higher score.

  In turn, learners ask the questions and write scores for their partner.

c Learners add up their partner's scores.

  Feedback. Ask learners if their partner has a higher score for the questions in A or in B. You could find out who has the highest and lowest scores for A and for B.

Last Saturday

READING and LISTENING

1 a To introduce *last Saturday,* write today's date on the board, then ask: *When was last Saturday?* Show the meaning with gestures.

  / 　Learners read what the people say and guess who the three people are.

b Play recording **2.16** and check the answers.

> A Olga   B Connie   C André

Ask what else each person says. If necessary, play the recording again.

> **Olga:** *It was my brother's birthday, he was 50.*
> **Connie:** *It was really nice. I was quite tired.*
> **André:** *I went to the cinema with my girlfriend.*

Point out that *was* is the past of *am* or *is* (this is introduced in 7.2).

GRAMMAR Past simple – positive

2 Learners find past forms of the verbs. Write them on the board in two columns: regular and irregular. Point out that:
  – regular verbs add *-ed*. If they already end in *-e*, they just add *-d* (show this from examples on the board).
  – many common verbs are irregular. You have to learn these.

Regular		Irregular	
Verb	**Past**	**Verb**	**Past**
stay	stayed	get up	got up
listen	listened	go	went
phone	phoned	have	had
cook	cooked	write	wrote
watch	watched	meet	met

Play recording **2.17** and practise saying the past forms. You could also give short sentences and get learners to repeat them (e.g. *I phoned a friend, I listened to the radio*). Check that learners don't insert an /e/ sound before the /d/ (/lɪsənd/, not /lɪsəned/).

Language note

After unvoiced consonants the *-d* ending tends to be pronounced as /t/ as in /kʊkt/ or /wɒtʃt/. You could point this out, but don't spend too much time on it.

3 a *Practice of past simple verbs.* Give out post-its, small cards or pieces of paper, or ask learners to take a sheet of paper and tear it into pieces. Learners write the verbs from **2** on one side and the past forms on the other side. As they do this, go round and check.

To show what to do, take a card and show the verb. Learners say the past form. Then turn it over and show the answer.

b 　Learners use the flashcards to test each other.

4 a / 👥 Learners add pronouns and past simple verbs to the sentences.

> 1 had   2 got; listened   3 met; went
> 4 went   5 stayed; watched   6 wrote

b To show what to do, tell the class the sentences (or parts of sentences) that are true of you (e.g. *Last Saturday I got up early. I went shopping ...*).

Learners underline the sentences that are true of them.

Round-up. Learners round the class read out the parts they underlined.

> 💿 You could use photocopiable activity 7A on the Teacher's DVD-ROM at this point.

Your weekend

WRITING and SPEAKING

1 *'He / she went', 'They went'.* Learners read the sentences and say who they are about.

> 1 André   2 Connie   3 Olga   4 André and his friend
> 5 André and his girlfriend   6 Olga

Look at the box and establish that the past simple is the same in all persons. You could give a few examples to demonstrate this.

2 a *Writing.* To demonstrate the activity, tell the class a few things you did last weekend. You could write these time expressions on the board:
– Last weekend ...
– In the morning ...
– On Saturday ...
– In the afternoon ...
– On Sunday ...
– In the evening ...
– Then ...

Working alone, learners write three things they did. As they do this, go round and check.

b 👥 *Speaking.* Learners tell each other what they did. They should do this without looking at their sentences.

c *Feedback.* Ask a few learners what their partner did at the weekend.

> **Alternative: Group work**
>
> 👥👥 Learners sit in groups of four or five and say in turn what they did at the weekend. In the feedback stage, one person from each group reports back on what the other people in the group did.

Classroom language: Instructions (2)

Goal: to understand simple instructions for doing exercises

Core language:
circle, underline, cross out, put a tick / cross (by)

1 / 👥 Learners match the instructions with the words. Present any words learners have difficulty with.

> 2 a   3 e   4 b   5 d

> **Alternative: Give instructions (books closed)**
>
> For each item, choose a word and give an instruction, e.g. *Write the word 'watched'. Now underline it.*

2 *Practice in following instructions.* Learners do the exercise alone or in pairs.

> 1 b <u>stayed</u>   2 b I went to the cinema ✗
> 3 (personal answer) ✓   4 b ⃝milk   5 c b̶u̶s̶y̶

7.2

Goals: talk about things you did or saw
ask and say where people were
say where you were

Core language:

VOCABULARY	*on holiday, busy, ill*
	Past time expressions: *last night, last week, yesterday*
	Place expressions: *at home, at work; at a meeting, at a party; in bed; in a café; on holiday; asleep*
GRAMMAR	*be* past: *was, were; wasn't, weren't; Were you ...?, Where were you?*

I was there

READING

1 Look at the photo of the meeting and ask what it shows (a meeting, in an office).

Read the email aloud. Ask: *Who are the people in the pictures?*

> At the meeting: Tom, Hassan, Paula
> Not at the meeting: A Boris, B Maria, C Peter

Use the photos to present *busy* (already known), *on holiday* and *ill.*

You could also use the photos to present other expressions: *at work, on the phone; on the beach, asleep; in bed, in hospital.*

> **Language note**
>
> In British English, we usually say *He / She is ill.*
> In US English, we say *He / She is sick.*

GRAMMAR *was, were*

2 a Learners complete the table. Write it on the board.

Singular	*Plural*
I was	*We were*
He / She was	*They were*

Point out that we use *was* for singular forms and *were* for plural forms.

b *Practice of 'was', 'were'.*
 / 👥 Learners add *was* or *were* to the sentences.

> 1 was   2 were   3 were   4 were   5 was   6 was

Practise saying the sentences, focusing on the pronunciation of *was* and *were*: /aɪ wəz/, /ðeɪ wə/ and the stress pattern of the sentences (*was* and *were* are not stressed).

3 *Listening.* Play recording **2.18** (this is an expanded version of the email in the previous section). Learners choose the words he says.

> *1 was 2 weren't 3 wasn't 4 wasn't*

As you go through the answers, learners say the sentences. Focus on the pronunciation of /wɒznt/ and /wɜːnt/ and the stress pattern of the sentences (*wasn't* and *weren't* are stressed).

On the board, show how we add *n't* (= *not*) to make the negative:

– *was + not → wasn't*
– *were + not → weren't*

Optional extra

Learners change the sentences in **2b** into the negative (e.g. *I wasn't in London on Monday*). Or give positive sentences of your own and ask learners to change them into the negative.

WRITING

4 a Introduce the topic by reading the email and establishing who wrote it (Boris).

b *Preparation for the exercise.* Look at the words in boxes A and B and ask what words (if any) go with them.

A	**B**
(at the) meeting	*(in) London*
last night	*(on) holiday*
(at the) English class	*ill*
yesterday	*busy*
(at the) party	
(on) Tuesday	

Writing. Learners write an email. As they do this, go round and check. Learners who finish quickly could write a second email.

Round-up. A few pairs read out their emails.

Optional extension

Learners 'send' their email to another learner, who writes a reply. You could prepare for this by teaching useful expressions, e.g.
– *Never mind.*
– *That's OK.*
– *What a pity.*
– *Thank you for your email.*

Questions

GRAMMAR *Were you ...?*

1 a Look at the photo and ask: *Who are the people?* (Hassan, Peter).

b *Listening.* Play recording **2.19**. Ask learners to correct the false sentences.

> *1 True 2 True 3 False – he was at home.*
> *4 False – he was tired.*

2 a Learners complete the questions.

b Play recording **2.19** to check and write the questions on the board.

> *Were you at the office party?*
> *What was it like?*
> *Where were you?*

Show how we change the word order to make a question:

1	2		2	1

You were (at home) → *Were you (at home)?*
Where were you?

Point out that we always use *were* with *you*, both for singular and plural.

Practice of questions. Act out the conversation with one learner.

Then learners act out the conversation in pairs.

3 a *Writing.* Look at **1** together and ask learners to say it in the correct order.

/ Learners write the other questions in the correct order.

> *1 Where were you on Saturday?*
> *2 Were you at home last night?*
> *3 Where were you yesterday afternoon?*
> *4 Were you here last week?*
> *5 Where were you at the weekend?*

---

b *Practice in asking and answering questions.*

Pair work. Learners ask and answer the questions.

Round-up. Learners tell you one thing they found out about their partner.

Alternative: Mingling activity

Give each learner one question to ask. They move freely round the class, asking their question to other learners.

 You could use photocopiable activity 7B on the Teacher's DVD-ROM at this point.

Where were you?

VOCABULARY Place expressions

1 Look at the photos and ask where the people are, using the expressions in the box. Present any that learners are not clear about.

> *A They're at a meeting / at work.   B He's on holiday.*
> *C He's in bed / asleep / at home.   D They're in a café.*
> *E She's at a party.*

SPEAKING

2 To demonstrate the game, choose a strong learner and ask questions:
– *I phoned you last night. Where were you?*
– *Where were you last Thursday?* etc.

The learner should think of a different place each time. Then change roles and get another learner to ask you questions.

Put learners into A/B pairs. A asks B questions and B replies. Then they change roles.

Sounds and spelling: /ɜː/ and /ɜʳ/

Goal: to recognise and pronounce the sound /ɜː/ or /ɜʳ/

Core language:
Words from Units 1–7 featuring -ir, -ur, -or and -er

1 *Presentation of* /ɜː/ *and* /ɜʳ/. Play recording **2.20**. Focus on the /ɜː/ sound and point out that:
– in standard British English, you don't hear the /r/
– in US English and some British dialects, the /r/ sound is pronounced.

2 Learners put the words in the correct group. Play recording **2.21** to check.

ir	ur	or	er
shirt skirt	Thursday	work	person

3 a *Dictation.* Play recording **2.22** or say the expressions yourself. Learners listen, then write them down.

b Learners read out the expressions, checking that they are pronouncing the /ɜː/ sound correctly (it doesn't matter whether they add the /r/ sound or not).

Check what learners have written (you could ask learners to write the sentences on the board).

7.3

Goals: talk about things you did or saw
talk about a film or a book
talk about a place you know

Core language:
VOCABULARY *A book / film called ...; A book / film by ...*
Adjectives: *good, bad; interesting, boring; cheap, expensive; short, long; wonderful, terrible*

Films, books, restaurants

VOCABULARY *A film called ..., a book by ...*

1 a Look at the pictures and ask what they are.

A a book B a film C a restaurant D a café

Look at the book and present:
– *It's by Paulo Coelho.* (= he wrote it)
– *It's called The Alchemist.* (= the name).

b *Listening for main idea.* Play recording **2.23**. Pause after each person and establish what they said.

1 We went to the cinema. We saw a film called Streets of New York.
2 I read a book by Paulo Coelho.
3 We went to a restaurant called Burger House.

Use this to present the past form *read* (pronounced /red/).

Optional extra

Give sentences and ask learners to add *by* or *called*, e.g.
– *I read a book – J. K. Rowling.*
– *I went to an Italian restaurant – Nino's.*
– *I saw a film – Batman 3.*

WRITING

2 Look on p91. To demonstrate, build up a sentence together on the board, getting learners to suggest what to write for each stage. First elicit a past time expression (*yesterday, last night, last week*), then a verb (*I saw, we went to, I read*) and so on.

Play the game. Learners write parts of a sentence and then pass their paper to the next learner to continue. Make sure learners only write a single word or expression at each stage.

Round-up. When the sentences are complete, learners read them out in turn. Check that the sentences are correct and make sense.

Good, bad ...

VOCABULARY Adjectives

1 a *Presentation of adjectives and nouns.* Look at each picture in turn and ask learners to say an expression using the words in the box.

A an interesting book B a boring book C a cheap book
D an expensive book E a long book F a short book

Use this to present the pairs *interesting / boring, good / bad, long / short* and *cheap / expensive*. Show meaning with gestures and facial expressions. Focus on the pronunciation of *interesting* /ɪntrəstɪŋ/ and *boring* /bɔːrɪŋ/.

2 a *Reading.* Look at the sentences. Ask learners what they are about.

A a book or film B a restaurant
C a book or film D a café

b *'very' and 'quite'.* Draw the table on the board and ask learners where to write the expressions.

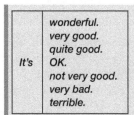

It's	wonderful. very good. quite good. OK. not very good. very bad. terrible.

c Play recording **2.24** to check and practise saying the expressions. Point out that:
– we say *quite good*, but we don't usually say *quite bad*. Instead, we say *not very good*.
– *wonderful* means *very very good*; *terrible* means *very very bad*.

SPEAKING

3 a Choose a well-known shop in your area. Ask learners what they think of it and present the question:
What do you think of ...? (= Do you think it's good?)
Encourage learners to use *quite* and *very*.

🧍 / 🧑‍🤝‍🧑 Learners choose other places and things and write them down.

b 🧑‍🤝‍🧑 Learners compare what they think of the places.

Round-up. Ask a few pairs to tell you about one of the things or places they talked about.

Target activity: Talk about things you did or saw

Goal: talk about things you did or saw

Core language:

7.1 GRAMMAR	Past simple – positive
7.2 GRAMMAR	*be* past
7.3 VOCABULARY	*A film called …, a book by …*
7.3 VOCABULARY	Adjectives

TASK LISTENING

1   *Preparation for the listening.* Read through the notes in 1 and the handwritten sentences. Ask what is in the sentences but not in the notes (the words in orange):
   – past simple verbs (*went, was*)
   – 'small words': *a, the, but, to, on*

> **Alternative: Books closed**
>
> Write the notes (the words in black) about the Japanese restaurant on the board and ask learners what words are missing. Getting learners to help you, write the notes as complete sentences.

Look at 2–5 and get learners to make sentences.

> 2 *I went to a new café called Copacabana yesterday. The coffee was really good and it wasn't very expensive.*
> 3 *I read a book by Stephen King. It was OK, but it was very long.*
> 4 *We went to a club called Los Banditos last night. It wasn't very good. The drinks were expensive and the music was really bad.*
> 5 *We went to a Chinese restaurant at the weekend. It was very cheap and the food was really good.*

b Play recording **2.25** to check.

PREPARATION

2 **a** *Writing.* Learners choose one of the topics.

   b Write a sentence. As they do this, go round and check.

   c Give time for them to prepare what they will say about the topic. Learners can write a few key words, but they shouldn't write complete sentences.

> **Alternative: Pairwork preparation**
>
> Working in pairs, learners choose a topic together and discuss what they will say about it.

TASK

3   👥👥👥 Learners tell each other about the topic they chose and ask the others if they agree.

> **Alternative: Mingling activity**
>
> Learners move freely round the class, talking about their topic to three or four other learners.

Round-up. A few learners tell the class something they heard from another learner.

Keyword *see, look at, watch*

Goal: to use *see*, *look at* and *watch* in collocations

Core language:

look(ed), see / saw, watch(ed)

1   Look at the pictures and the examples. Point out:
   – *watch = look at for a long time*
      (you could demonstrate this).
   – you look *at* something
      (we can't say ~~He looked the picture.~~).

   👤 / 👥👥 Learners complete the sentences.

> 1 *watch*   2 *saw / watched*   3 *watch*
> 4 *Look at*   5 *see*   6 *looked at*

2   *Speaking.* To introduce the activity, tell the class which things you did last weekend.

   Learners think about their own weekends, and tick the true sentences.

   👥👥 Learners tell their partner which things they did.

   Round-up. Ask a few learners if they did the same things as their partner.

7.4 Explore speaking

Goals: make requests
      reply to requests

Core language:

Requests: *Can I …?*
Replies: *No problem*; *Sure*; *Of course*; *Yes, you can*; *Sorry, you can't*
Other expressions: *I want to …*; *I'm thirsty, I'm hungry*

1 **a** Write on the board: *Can I …?* Read the situation and ask learners what questions they could ask. Introduce the verb *use*, and show how to say it: /juːz/.

> 1 *Can I use your computer?*   2 *Can I have a drink?*
> 3 *Can I use your bike?*   4 *Can I have something to eat?*
> 5 *Can I use your phone?*

> **Alternative: Presentation with books closed**
>
> Tell the class the situation: they are at a friend's flat, and they want a glass of water. Ask: *What can I say?* Use this to focus on *Can I …?*. Then open books and look at the questions.

   b Go through answers by listening to recording **2.26**.

2   *Giving reasons.* Read the sentences. Check that learners understand *I'm thirsty* (= I want to drink) and *I'm hungry* (= I want to eat). You could quickly ask learners round the class:
   Are you hungry? Are you thirsty?.

   👤 / 👥👥 Learners match the sentences and questions.

> b *Can I use your computer? I want to read my emails.*
> c *Can I use your phone? I want to call my sister.*
> d *Can I use your bike? I want to go to the shops.*
> e *Can I have something to eat? I'm hungry.*

3 a *Replies.* Play recording **2.27**. Pause after each conversation and ask which replies learners heard.

> 1 Yes, of course you can.
> 2 No, sorry, you can't.
> 3 Of course you can. No problem.
> 4 Yes, of course.
> 5 Yes, sure.

Point out that *of course* and *sure* mean the same – they are both ways of saying *Yes*.

b Focus on the question and answers. Point out that:
– *can* + *not* = *can't*.
– *can't* has a long sound: /kɑːnt/.

Practise saying /jʊ kæn/ and /jʊ kɑːnt/.

4 *Role play.* To demonstrate, take the part of A and ask a learner a question. Then choose a learner to be A and ask you a question.

👥 Put learners into A/B pairs. A asks two questions and B replies. Then they change roles and have a second conversation.

> **Conversation practice**
>
> You could do the conversation practice exercises on p118 at this point.

Across cultures: Housework

Goals: to give practice in reading short texts
to encourage learners to think about male and female roles and how they have changed

Core language:
do the housework, go shopping, buy food, cook meals, clean the flat, help

1 Introduce the topic by looking at the two photos. Ask what they show (A family in about 1950; a family now). Make sure learners understand *grandmother* and *grandfather*.

Reading for main idea. Learners read the texts quickly and find out which people the two photos show.

> 1 A   2 A   3 B   4 A

2 👤 / 👥 Learners read and decide if the sentences are true or false. They can use dictionaries to check new words. Ask learners to correct the false answers.

> 1 False – she stayed at home.
> 2 True.
> 3 False – he cooked barbecues.
> 4 True.
> 5 False – her husband works at home, she goes out to work.
> 6 False – he helps her.
> 7 False – her husband usually cooks the meals (so she sometimes cooks).

3 a 👥 Learners read the questions and compare answers.

b *Round-up.* Discuss the questions together. Find out from several different learners who does each job in their family, and whether they think this is 'typical'.

In mixed nationality classes, this will lead to a discussion of customs in different countries.

Look again

VOCABULARY

1 *Word pairs.* Learners find an expression that goes with *at work* (on holiday). Ask them why (you can be at work or on holiday).

👥 Learners find other pairs of expressions.

> boring – interesting   early – late
> breakfast – lunch   yesterday – last night
> cheap – expensive

Learners write sentences. Possible answers:

> 1 boring / interesting / cheap / expensive
> 2 early / late   3 at work / on holiday
> 4 yesterday / last night

2 a *Present and past verb forms.* Learners write the verb forms.

> get – got   have – had
> go – went   see – saw
> write – wrote   read – read
> meet – met

b Learners write sentences. Then a few learners read out their sentences for each item.

3 *in, on, at.* Learners fill in the gaps.

> 1 at   2 at; on   3 on; –   4 –   5 In

CAN YOU REMEMBER? Unit 6

4 a Learners suggest possible expressions to replace the highlighted words. Possible answers:

> 1 wake up / have breakfast / go to work / go to school / start work / start school ...
> 2 at home / in a café / in a restaurant / with friends ...
> 3 walk / cycle / go by car / go by tram / go by underground / go by taxi / go by train ...
> 4 read a book / read a magazine / watch a DVD / write emails / phone my friends ...

b *Writing.* To demonstrate, say two sentences about yourself and ask learners if they are true or false.

Learners write two true and two false sentences. Go round and check. Learners read out their sentences. The others guess which are true and false.

GRAMMAR

'be' past: was, were. Read through the tables.

5 Learners add *was* or *were* to the sentences.

> 1 Were   2 was   3 Was   4 were   5 was

Past simple. Read through the tables.

6 Learners add verbs to the sentences.

> 2 saw   3 stayed; listened   4 read; wrote   5 met; went

Self-assessment

To help focus learners on the self-assessment, you could read it through, giving a few more examples of the language they have learned in each section (or asking learners to tell you). Then they circle a number on each line.

Unit 7 Extra activities on the Teacher's DVD-ROM

Printable worksheets, activity instructions and answer keys are on your Teacher's DVD-ROM.

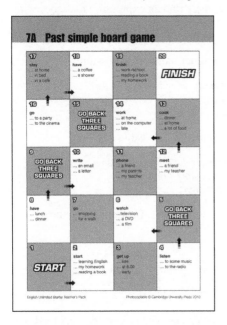

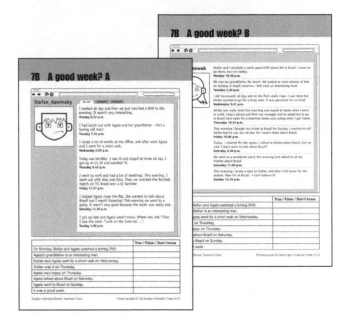

7A Past simple board game

Activity type: Speaking – Board game – Groups of four

Aim: To practise using past simple verbs

Language:
Past simple positive – Coursebook p55 – Grammar

Preparation: Make one copy of the worksheet for every four learners. Make sure you have one counter for each learner and one coin for every four learners.

Time: 20–25 minutes

7B A good week?

Activity type: Reading – Jigsaw reading – Pairs

Aim: To practise reading for gist and detail. To practise speaking about what somebody did in the past

Language: Past simple positive – Coursebook p55; *be* past – Coursebook p56–57 – Grammar

Preparation: Make one copy of the two worksheets for every two learners.

Time: 20–25 minutes

Unit 7 Self-study Pack

In the Workbook

Unit 7 of the *English Unlimited Starter Workbook* offers additional ways to practise the vocabulary and grammar taught in the Coursebook. There are also activities which build reading and writing skills, and a whole page of tasks to use with the DVD-ROM video, giving your learners the opportunity to hear and react to spoken English.

- **Vocabulary:** Place expressions; Adjectives
- **Grammar:** Past simple; *was, were; wasn't, weren't*; Questions with *was / were*
- **Time out:** Crossword
- **Explore writing:** *it, there*; *and, so, but*
- **DVD-ROM Extra:** Last weekend

On the DVD-ROM

Unit 7 of the *English Unlimited Starter Self-study Pack DVD-ROM* contains interactive games and activities for your learners to practise and improve their vocabulary, grammar and pronunciation, and also their speaking and listening. It also contains video material (with the possibility for learners to record themselves) to use with the *Workbook*.

- **Vocabulary and Grammar:** Extra practice of Coursebook language and Keyword
- **Classroom language:** Instructions (2)
- **Sounds and spelling:** /ɜː/, /ɜʳ/
- **Explore speaking:** Make and reply to requests
- **Video:** Last weekend

Places

Unit goal: talk about a place you visited

8.1

Goals: talk about a place you visited
say what you saw and did
say what you didn't see or do

Core language:

VOCABULARY	Past simple verbs: *saw, visited, went; had, watched, stayed, arrived, got up, bought*
GRAMMAR	Past simple – negative: *didn't (stay)*

We saw ...

READING

1 Check that learners understand 'Top five things to do' (show *top* with a gesture). For each one, ask learners to find the photo. Alternatively, let learners read and find the photos.

> 1 D   2 B   3 E   4 A   5 C

Present the word *visit* and give a few examples. Ask learners what places you can visit in your town.

> **Alternative: Lead-in with books closed**
>
> Write *Cairo* on the board (or show a picture of Cairo). Ask where it is and ask what learners know about it. Ask them to imagine they visit Cairo: What can they see and do there? Then open books and read the top five things to do.

2 *Reading for general idea.* Establish what a travel blog is (= a website where people write about places they visited).

Learners read the travel blog, then discuss together which of the five things they did.

> – They went shopping in the old market area. (2)
> – They visited the Citadel. (3)
> – They sat by the Nile. (4)

VOCABULARY Past simple verbs

3 *Reading for detail.* Learners cover the travel blog and add verbs in the gaps. Go through the answers together, or let learners check in the travel blog.

> 1 arrived   2 stayed   3 got up   4 went
> 5 bought   6 went   7 had   8 watched

Focus on the new verbs: *arrive – arrived* and *buy – bought*. Check that learners can say /əˈaɪvd/, /bɔːt/.

You could get learners to tell you (with the travel blog covered) the main things that Mike and Anna did in Cairo. Prompt them by giving sentence beginnings and asking questions, e.g.
– *First they ...*
– *What about the hotel? What was it like?*
– *What about Wednesday?*
Avoid using negative sentences at this point.

We didn't see ...

GRAMMAR Past simple negative

1 a *Presentation of past simple – negative.* Learners look at the travel blog again and find the three sentences. Write the negative forms on the board:
– *They didn't sleep ...*
– *He didn't buy ...*
– *They didn't see ...*

Show how we form the past simple negative:
did + not + main verb
He did not buy → He didn't buy

Point out that the main verb doesn't change into the past: so we say *He didn't buy* not *He didn't bought*.

b *Pronunciation.* Look at the table and play recording **2.28**. Practise saying the negative forms. Focus on the expressions /dɪdnt‿steɪ/, /dɪdnt‿baɪ/ and /dɪdnt‿siː/ and focus on how the /t/ runs into the next consonant.

c *Practice of past simple – negative.* Learners change the false sentences. Either do this with the whole class, or learners work in pairs.

> 1 False – they didn't see the Sphinx.
> 2 True.
> 3 False – they didn't visit Sakkara.
> 4 False – they didn't have kebabs for lunch.
> 5 False – they didn't stay for three days.
> 6 True.
> 7 False – they didn't buy a carpet.
> 8 True.
> 9 False – they liked Cairo.

WRITING

2 a To show what to do, write sentences on the board about a place you visited recently (this could be true, or you could make it up). Learners guess where you were.

👤 / 👥 Learners write sentences. As they do this, go round and check.

b *Round-up.* Learners read out their sentences. The rest of the class try to guess the place. Alternatively, learners could do this in pairs. Learners read their sentences and their partner guesses the place.

Classroom language: Instructions (3)

Goal: to understand simple classroom commands (positive and negative)

Core language:

Imperative forms: *Open ..., Write ..., Don't open ..., Don't write ...*

1 *Listening.* Explain that learners will hear a teacher in a classroom. Play recording **2.29** and establish what the teacher says.

> 1 Open your books.
> 2 Don't open your books.
> 3 Write a sentence.
> 4 Don't write – just listen.

Imperative forms. As you go through the answers, present imperative forms:
– positive: just use the verb (*Open ..., Write ...*).
– negative: use *don't* + verb (*Don't open ..., Don't write ...*).

You could give a few other examples, e.g. say to a learner *Open the door, please.* Then change your mind and say *No, don't open the door.*

2   *Practice of commands.* Demonstrate the meaning of *stand up* and *sit down.* Learners look at the pictures and decide what the teacher says. Play recording **2.30** to check.

> A Don't stand up.   B Sit down.   C Don't open the window.   D Don't eat food (in class).   E Don't talk.

Optional extension

Give a series of classroom instructions, using a mixture of positive and negative forms. Learners listen and do what you say, e.g.
– Stand up.
– Sit down.
– Don't stand up.
– Look at me.
– Don't look at me.
– Look left.
– Open your book.
– Don't open your book.
– Say 'hello' to the person next to you.
– Don't say 'hello'.
– Close your book.
– Don't close your book.

8.2

Goals: talk about a place you visited
talk about holiday activities
ask people what they did

Core language:

VOCABULARY   Expressions with *go* (+ *-ing*): *go swimming, go shopping, go walking, go skiing, go sightseeing, go camping*
Expressions with *go* (+ *to*): *go to restaurants, go to art galleries, go to museums, go to clubs or discos*
GRAMMAR   Past simple – questions: *Did you (go) ...?*

On holiday

VOCABULARY Expressions with *go*

1 a Look at the pictures one at a time and ask what they show. At this stage, simply use single words and singular forms of the nouns e.g. *skiing, shopping, a restaurant, an art gallery.*

> A skiing   B shopping   C an art gallery   D a restaurant
> E walking   F a museum   G swimming   H camping
> I sightseeing   J clubs or discos

As you identify each activity, you could ask one or two learners about it, using an expression with *go*:
– *Do you go skiing?*
– *Do you go shopping on holiday?*
Play recording **2.31** and practise saying the expressions.

b Look at the expressions in A and B, and establish that:
– the words in A are things you <u>do</u> (you swim, you walk, ...). With these, we use *go* + *-ing*.
– the words in B are <u>places</u>. With these, we use *go to.*

c *Speaking.* Tell the class what you often do on holiday, what you never do, etc.

👥 Learners go through the expressions and say which things they do and which they never do.

Round-up. A few learners tell you two things about their partner. Make sure they use the form *He / She (never) goes ... .*

LISTENING

2 a *Speaking.* Look at the photos and check that learners know where the places are. You could discuss what kind of place it is (e.g. a big city, very hot), but at this point don't go into what you can do there.

👥 / 👥 Learners look at each photo and say what they think you can do. Possible answers:

> – In Dubai, you can go swimming, go shopping, go skiing (in an indoor ski centre!), go to restaurants, go to clubs / discos.
> – In the Rocky Mountains, you can go swimming, go walking, go skiing (in the winter), go camping.
> – In Rome, you can go shopping, go sightseeing, go to restaurants, art galleries, museums, clubs or discos.
> – In Phra Nang, you can go swimming, go shopping, go to restaurants, clubs or discos.

b *Listening.* Play recording **2.32**, pausing after each speaker, and establish where it is and what activities they did.

> 1 Phra Nang: swimming, restaurants, club or disco
> 2 Dubai: shopping, swimming (in the hotel), restaurants
> 3 Rome: sightseeing, museums, art galleries, restaurants
> 4 Rocky Mountains: camping, walking

c Look at the sentences and ask which place they are about and what else each speaker said. Play the recording again to check.

> 1 Rocky Mountains (it was too cold)
> 2 Rome (they had lots of good food)
> 3 Phra Nang
> 4 Dubai (but he went shopping in his free time)
> 5 Phra Nang
> 6 Dubai

3   *Speaking.* Look on p97. To introduce the activity, choose a photo and say a few things you did, e.g. *We went sightseeing, went to art galleries. And we went swimming. Then in the evening we went to restaurants.* (Barcelona).

👥 In turn, learners choose a photo and say what they did. Their partner guesses the photo.

Round-up. Take each photo in turn and ask learners what they said about it.

Did you ... ?

GRAMMAR Past simple questions

1 a Introduce the topic by checking learners know where Singapore is. Ask what they think you can do there.

b *Listening for main idea.* Look at the photo of Masumi. Ask learners where they think she is from (maybe Japan, or the USA). Read through the sentences. Play recording **2.33**, then check the answers.

> 1 on a business trip   2 liked   3 a few days

c Learners complete the questions. Write them on the board and play recording **2.33** again to check.

> Did you have   Did you go   Did you buy

d *Past simple questions.* Look at the table. Show how we form past simple questions:
- we use *did* + verb.
- the main verb doesn't change into the past (so we say *Did you have ...?*, not ~~Did you had...?~~.

Play recording **2.30** and practise the questions. Focus on these points:
- *Did you* is said quite quickly and run together: /dɪdju/.
- the stress is on the main verb: *Did you háve ...?* .

> **Optional practice (books closed)**
>
> 👥 Learner A asks the questions. Learner B is Masumi and answers. Then they change roles.

2 *Practice in asking and answering questions.* Ask learners to imagine that you went to Singapore. Get them to ask you questions from the prompts and give suitable answers. The questions should be:

> 1 Did you stay in a hotel?   2 Did you go sightseeing?
> 3 Did you have good food?   4 Did you like Singapore?
> 5 Did you buy presents for your family?
> 6 Did you fly with (go with) Singapore Airlines?

👥 Put learners into A/B pairs. A asks questions.

A asks questions and B answers. Then they change roles.

SPEAKING

3 a Write a sentence on the board about a place you went to recently. Learners ask you questions.

Writing sentences. Learners write a sentence about a place they went to. Then collect the sentences and give one each to other learners.

b *Writing questions.* Learners read the sentence they received and write three questions. Go round and check.

c *Speaking.* Learners move round the class and find the person who wrote the sentence they received. They ask their questions. Then they move again to answer questions from other people.

> **Alternative: Pair work**
>
> If it is difficult for learners to move around the class, you could do this as pair work. Learners swap their sentence with the person next to them and write questions. Then they form pairs to ask and answer the questions.

Sounds and spelling: /ʃ/, /dʒ/ and /tʃ/

Goal: to pronounce the sounds /ʃ/, /dʒ/ and /tʃ/

Core language:
Words from Units 1–8 with the sounds /ʃ/, /dʒ/ and /tʃ/

1 Say the words or play recording **2.35**. Focus on the three sounds. Points to focus on:
- if learners have problems with /ʃ/, get them to say /s/, then move their tongue back and their teeth closer together.
- if learners have problems with /dʒ/, get them to say /d/ and /ʒ/ separately, then run them together (similarly with /t/ and /ʃ/ to make /tʃ/).

2 Learners put the words in the correct group. Go through the answers by listening to recording **2.36**.

/ʃ/	/dʒ/	/tʃ/
shower	vegetables	lunch
sugar	journey	China
Russia	jacket	much

3 a *Dictation.* Learners cover the words in **1** and **2**. Play recording **2.37**. Learners write the expressions.

b Learners read out the expressions. Check that they pronounce the /ʃ/, /dʒ/ and /tʃ/ sounds correctly. Check what learners have written (you could ask learners to write the expressions on the board).

8.3

Goals: talk about a place you visited
talk about months and weather
say when to visit a place
ask about a holiday or a business trip

Core language:
VOCABULARY   Months, seasons: *summer, winter*
Weather

Months

VOCABULARY Months, seasons

1 a *Months.* See if learners can say the months in the correct order. Play recording **2.38** to check and practise saying them.

> 1 January   2 February   3 March   4 April   5 May
> 6 June   7 July   8 August   9 September   10 October
> 11 November   12 December

Learners write the months in the calendar.

> **Note**
>
> The months may look similar in learners' own language but sound different. So focus especially on the pronunciation.

b *Summer, winter.* Discuss the questions. Use this to present *last* and *next* (show this with gestures) and *summer* and *winter*.

c *Birthdays.* Ask learners to say the month of their birthday round the class. Find out when most people have birthdays (you could do this by writing the months on the board as learners say them).

When to go

VOCABULARY Weather

1 a *Reading.* Look at the travel information and check that learners know where the four places are. Learners read and find adjectives.

wet	warm
dry	cool
sunny	cold
hot	

b *Reading for detail.* Learners read and find answers to the questions.

> 1 The best time is in February.
> 2 No (it's very hot).
> 3 It's hot and busy.
> 4 Yes (it's warm and dry) .
> 5 No (it's hot and very wet).

> 🔘 You could use photocopiable activity 8A on the Teacher's DVD-ROM at this point.

WRITING

2 🔘 / 🔘 *Writing.* Learners sit with people from the same country. Together, they write a 'When to go' text, using those in **1a** as a model. As they do this, go round and check and give help where necessary.

Round-up. Learners read out their texts.

Mixed nationality classes

Learners could tell the class about their country, using the information they have written. Other learners ask questions.

Single nationality classes

Learners read out their texts and see if other learners agree. Alternatively, you could build up a 'class' text together on the board.

Target activity: Talk about a place you visited

Goal: talk about a place you visited

Core language:

8.2 VOCABULARY	Expressions with *go*
8.2 GRAMMAR	Past simple – questions

TASK LISTENING

1 a Introduce the topic by asking if anyone in the class knows London. If so, what did they do there? Ask learners if they know what the photo shows (Big Ben, the London Eye).

Preparation for the listening. Learners match the questions and answers. Then discuss the answers together.

> 1 e 2 a 3 b 4 g 5 f 6 d 7 c

Focus on the question *What was it like? = Was it good, bad, interesting ...?*

b *Listening.* Play recording **2.39** to check.

Wh- questions. Read the questions in the table. Point out that we can ask two kinds of question:
– with *Did you* + verb.
– beginning with a question word (*Where, What, Who ...*).

In both kinds of question, we use *did* (so we say *Where did you go?* not ~~*Where you went?*~~).

Learners practice saying the questions.

c Learners cover the page and say what Alejandro did. You could do this round the class, getting one sentence from each learner in turn.

2 / 🔘 *Practice of questions.* Learners make questions for the answers. They could write the questions.

> 1 Where did you go?
> 2 When did you go?
> 3 What was the weather like?
> 4 Who did you go with?
> 5 Where did you stay?
> 6 What was it like?
> 7 What did you do (there)?

PREPARATION

3 Working alone, learners choose one of the topics and think about answers to questions 1–7 in **1a**. Learners should make brief notes, but not complete sentences.

TASK

4 a 🔘 Learners talk about the place they visited.

Alternative: Mingling activity

Learners move freely round the class, talking about their visit to three or four other learners.

b *Round-up.* A few learners tell the class something they heard from another learner.

> 🔘 You could use photocopiable activity 8B on the Teacher's DVD-ROM at this point.

Keyword *do*

Goal: use *do* and *did* to talk about activities

Core language:

do, did as a main verb

1 *Do, did.* Learners match the examples.

> 1 d 2 b 3 a 4 c

Point out that:
– we can use *do* as a main verb (just like *go, stay*, etc.).
– we say *I do, he / she does.*
– we often say *I do a lot* or *I don't do much* to say how we spend our time.

2 a Learners choose the sentences that are true for them.

🔘 They tell their partner their sentences, and ask questions to find out more.

Round-up. Ask a few learners if they do / did the same things as their partner, or not.

b 🔘 Learners ask and answer the questions.

8.4 Explore writing

Goal: Write about a sequence of events

Core language:
then, and, and then

1 Read the examples and ask how A and B are different. (A is two sentences. B is one sentence.)

Use this to show that:
– we use *and* or *and then* to join two sentences.
– *then* is usually at the beginning of a sentence.

2 **a** *Practice of writing sequences.* Learners decide the best order for the sentences.

b Look at the first example together and ask how to join the sentences. Write them on the board, e.g.

> – We arrived at the airport and had lunch. Then we got a taxi to the hotel.
> – We arrived at the airport and had lunch, and then we got a taxi to the hotel.

Learners join the other sentences. Possible answers:

> – I got up at 9.00 and went shopping. Then I cooked lunch.
> – I stayed at home in the morning. Then I met a friend and we went shopping.
> – We sat by the Nile and had coffee, and then we went back to the hotel.

3 **a** *Speaking.* Tell learners three things you did yesterday morning (or write them on the board), e.g.

I had breakfast. I went out. I read the newspaper.

Ask learners what order they think you did them in.

Learners think of three things they did and write them in the wrong order.

b Learners tell each other the three things they did. Their partner guesses what order they were in.

Across cultures: Hostels

Goals: to give practice in reading short texts
to give information about other parts of the world

Core language:
features of hostels; places in towns

1 Look at the pictures. Ask learners if they have ever stayed in a hostel, and if so, where and what it was like. Ask if they would like to stay in the hostels in the pictures.

Jigsaw reading. Put learners into A/B pairs. A looks on p93 and reads about the Three Black Catz Hostel. B looks on p96 and reads about the Lighthouse Hostel. They read the questions they will ask about the other hostel. As learners do this, go round and give any necessary help.

Speaking. Learners ask and answer questions about the hostels.

Round-up. Go through the questions about each hostel and ask learners what answers their partner gave. Ask if they would like to stay there, and why / why not.

Look again

VOCABULARY

1 **a** Learners find other groups of words and write them down. Then ask why they go together.

> – station, airport, bus station (places in towns)
> – May, August, October (months)
> – camping, swimming, walking (things you do on holiday / they all follow go ...)
> – warm, sunny, wet (weather)
> – museum, restaurant, art gallery (places in towns / places to visit)

b Learners complete the sentences. Possible answers:

> 1 week / month / year   2 camping / swimming / walking
> 3 station / airport / bus station / restaurant / museum / art gallery   4 May / August / October   5 warm / sunny / wet

2 Learners answer the questions and write the months.

> 1 April, June, September, November
> 2 February   3 January

3 *Past simple verbs.* Learners write the past forms.

> 1 saw   2 visited   3 watched   4 bought   5 went
> 6 got   7 stayed   8 arrived

SPELLING

4 Learners spell the words correctly.

> 1 shopping   2 bought   3 swimming   4 August
> 5 May   6 sightseeing

CAN YOU REMEMBER? Unit 7

5 Learners suggest possible replacements.

> 1 woke up / had breakfast / went to work / went to school / started work / started school / came home / met a friend ...
> 2 went to the cinema / went to a café / had a drink ...
> 3 at the cinema / out / ill / on holiday / at work ...
> 4 yesterday / this morning / at 6.30 / on Tuesday ...

6 A learner reads sentence A. The next learner reads B. The next learner reads C and adds a new expression. Continue in this way.

GRAMMAR

Read through the tables.

7 Learners correct the mistakes

> 1 Did you stay in a hotel yesterday?
> 2 I didn't visit the Pyramids.   3 Did she go shopping?
> 4 Did you stay at home?   5 They didn't buy anything.

8 Learners write the sentences.

> 2 We went to a restaurant last night.   3 I didn't see her at the party.   4 They bought a new DVD at the weekend.
> 5 Did you have a good time?   6 We didn't go swimming.

Self-assessment

To help focus learners on the self-assessment, you could read it through, giving a few more examples of the language they have learned in each section (or asking learners to tell you). Then they circle a number on each line.

Unit 8 Extra activities on the Teacher's DVD-ROM

Printable worksheets, activity instructions and answer keys are on your Teacher's DVD-ROM.

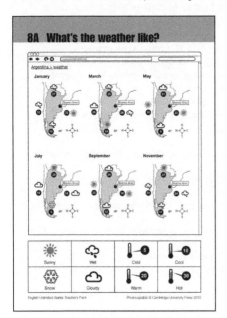

8A What's the weather like?

Activity type: Speaking – Picture matching – Pairs

Aim: To practise describing the weather

Language: Months – Coursebook p66;
Weather – Coursebook p66 – Vocabulary

Preparation: Make one copy of the worksheet for each learner.

Time: 15 minutes

8B Where did you go?

Activity type: Reading and Speaking – Information gap – Pairs / Groups of four

Aims: Asking and answering questions in the past

Language: Talk about a place you visited – Coursebook p67

Preparation: Make one copy of the first worksheet for every four learners. Cut along the dotted lines to make four cards. Make one copy of the second worksheet for every learner.

Time: 20–25 minutes

Unit 8 Self-study Pack

In the Workbook

Unit 8 of the *English Unlimited Starter Workbook* offers additional ways to practise the vocabulary and grammar taught in the Coursebook. There are also activities which build reading and writing skills, and a whole page of tasks to use with the DVD-ROM video, giving your learners the opportunity to hear and react to spoken English.

- **Vocabulary:** Expressions with *go*; Months; Weather, seasons
- **Grammar:** Past simple – positive and negative; Past simple – questions; *Wh-* questions
- **Explore reading:** Hotel reviews
- **DVD-ROM Extra:** *Where did you go?*

On the DVD-ROM

Unit 8 of the *English Unlimited Starter Self-study Pack DVD-ROM* contains interactive games and activities for your learners to practise and improve their vocabulary, grammar and pronunciation, and also their speaking and listening. It also contains video material (with the possibility for learners to record themselves) to use with the *Workbook*.

- **Vocabulary and Grammar:** Extra practice of Coursebook language and Keyword
- **Classroom language:** Instructions (3)
- **Sounds and spelling:** /ʃ/, /dʒ/ and /tʃ/
- **Explore writing:** A sequence of events
- **Video:** *Where did you go?*

9 Going out

Unit goal: invite someone to go out

9.1

Goals: invite someone to go out
 talk on the phone
 say what you're doing just now
 ask what people are doing

Core language:

VOCABULARY	Telephone expressions: *Are you busy?*; *I'm busy.*; *I'll call you later.*; *Can I call you later?*
GRAMMAR	Present progressive: *I'm / We're (just) going, having, cooking ...* *What are you doing?*; *Are you (having lunch)?*

I'm busy

VOCABULARY Telephone expressions

1 a Introduce the topic by looking at the two photos. Ask:
 – *Where are they?* (Tom is at home; Sue is at work)
 – *Are they busy?* (Sue is busy, but not Tom)

> **Optional lead-in (books closed)**
>
> Choose a learner and say: *You phone me. What can you say?* Use this to present:
> – *Hi. Hello.*
> – *It's (John). It's (John) here.*
> Tell the class *I'm busy. I can't talk to you. What can I say?* Use this to present:
> – *I'm busy.*
> – *Can I call you later?*

 Telephone expressions. Look at the conversation. Learners to put it in the correct order. You could write it on the board. Present:
 – *just now* = exactly now (show this with gestures)
 – *call* = phone
 – *later* = not now (give an example: *Now it's 2.00. I'll call you later* = maybe at 3.00 or 4.00)

b Play recording **2.40** to check.

 👥 Learners could quickly have a conversation like this in pairs.

2 a *Listening.* Read the expressions, then play recording **2.41**. Learners listen and underline the expressions they hear.

> | Are you busy? I'll call you later. Right.

 Establish why Sue is busy (She's in a meeting).

 Focus on the new expressions and get learners to practise saying them with the correct stress:
 Are you bu̇sy?
 I'll ċall you lȧter.

 Point out that *I'll call you = I will call you* (you could mention that this is a future form, but learners should just learn it as a fixed expression).

b 👥 Learners cover **2a** and complete the conversations. Then go through the answers.

> | 1 I'm; I'll; you   2 Are you; Can; you

3 *Role play.* To demonstrate the activity, choose a learner and have a phone conversation. Then have a second conversation as if you are calling a second time.

 👥 Learners have two phone conversations. Then they change roles and have two more conversations.

> **Conversation practice**
>
> You could do the conversation practice exercises on p119 at this point.

I'm ...

GRAMMAR Present progressive

1 a Introduce the topic by looking at the photos. Ask where the people are (at home; in the street; at home, in the kitchen).

 Listening. Play recording **2.42**. Pause after each speaker and establish which photo it is and what the person says.

> | 1 A I'm having breakfast.   2 C We're just cooking some food.   3 B I'm just going to a meeting.

b *Form of the present progressive.* Play recording **2.43**. Show the form:
 – *I'm* + verb + *-ing* → *I'm going*
 – *We're* + verb + *-ing* → *We're having*

 Point out that if the verb ends in *-e*, we drop the *-e* in the *-ing* form. Show this on the board:
 – *have* → *hav* → *having*

> **Language note**
>
> Verbs that end in a single vowel + consonant double the consonant before *-ing*:
> *sit* → *sitting*   *put* → *putting*
> This only applies to a few verbs at this level, so it is easier just to point out the spelling when it occurs.

2 a *Meaning of the present progressive.* Discuss the questions. Establish that:
 – *We have breakfast ...* = often, or every day.
 – *We're having breakfast.* = just now, at this moment.

b *Practice.* Learners write the verbs.

> | 1 We're having   2 We're cooking   3 I'm watching
> | 4 I'm driving   5 I'm working   6 I'm going

3 *Role play.* To demonstrate, choose a photo from **1** and have a phone conversation with one learner.

 👥 Learners choose photos and have conversations.

What are you doing?

LISTENING

1 a Look at the photo and the questions in the box. Ask what Aydin's answers might be.

b Play recording **2.44** to check.

> | *I'm at the airport.*
> | *No, I'm sitting in a café.*
> | *No, I'm having a cup of coffee.*

Ask what Aydin says about the plane and food.

> 1 The plane leaves in about half an hour.
> 2 They have food on the plane.

Look at the table and show how we form present progressive questions by changing the word order:

You are + -ing → Are you + -ing

SPEAKING

2 Look on p91.To show what to do, choose a picture and write a conversation on the board (or read it out):
   – *Where are you?*
   – *I'm at home.*
   – *What are you doing?*
   – *I'm reading the paper.*

Ask learners to find the picture (4).

👥 Working together, learners choose a picture and write a conversation. As they do this, go round and check.

Learners read out their dialogues. Other learners identify the pictures.

Classroom language: Talking about a picture

Goals: to understand questions about pictures
to talk about pictures using the present progressive

Core language:
Present progressive

1 a *Listening.* Play recording **2.45** and ask who it is about (Aydin). Then ask what the questions are and write them on the board.

> 1 What can you see? 2 Where is he?
> 3 What is he doing?

 b Ask what the answers are and play recording **2.45** again to check.

> 1 A man. 2 At the airport. 3 He's talking on the phone.

Point out that we use the present progressive to talk about pictures (= now, in the picture).

2 👤/👥 Learners read the sentences and find the pictures. Then go through the answers and learners point to the correct picture.

3 a *Present progressive.* Learners complete the forms of the present progressive. Then write them on the board.

wear	have
He's wearing	He's having
She's wearing	She's having
They're wearing	They're having

 b 👥 Learners find the pictures.

> 1 p16 2 p13; p22; p23; p28 3 p26 4 p27
> 5 p43; p44 6 p46; p50

 c 👥 Learners choose a picture from unit 7 and write a sentence about it. Go round to check and help with any unknown words.

Learners read out their sentences and other learners identify the picture.

 You could use photocopiable activity 9A on the Teacher's DVD-ROM at this point.

9.2

Goals: invite someone to go out
talk about arrangements
invite someone and reply

Core language:

VOCABULARY	Future time expressions: *today, tomorrow*; *this (Friday), next (Friday)*; *this (evening)*, *tomorrow (evening)* Present progressive verbs: *coming, going, staying, meeting, arriving, working*
GRAMMAR	Present progressive (future meaning): *I'm / We're staying, He's / She's staying, They're staying* *can, can't*

Time expressions

VOCABULARY Future time expressions

1 a Look at the diary page and establish which days are *today* and *tomorrow*.

 b Make sure learners understand the meaning of *this week* and *next week* (show this with gestures).

   Read the expressions in the box and establish what they mean.

> 1 this evening; this afternoon (today)
> 2 tomorrow morning (tomorrow)
> 3 this Saturday (this week) 4 next Tuesday (next week)

You could draw the diary pages on the board and indicate the day that each expression refers to:
   – we use *this* for the day or week (or month, year ...) we are in now. So, *this evening* means today, *this Tuesday* is this week, etc.
   – we can say *this Tuesday* or *on Tuesday*, *this evening* or *in the evening*, with the same meaning.
   – we say *tomorrow morning*, etc., not ~~tomorrow in the morning~~.

LISTENING

2 a *Listening for general idea.* Play recording **2.46**, pausing after each conversation. Ask what the people are talking about.

> 1 a meal 2 a meeting 3 a journey 4 a game of tennis
> 5 a walk

 b Play recording **2.46** again. Learners listen and write numbers in the correct places in the diary.

> 1 this evening 2 next Tuesday 3 tomorrow morning
> 4 this Saturday 5 this afternoon

If you drew the diary on the board, you could add notes in the correct places (e.g. *meeting 2.30*).

> **Note**
>
> The speakers use the present progressive to talk about future arrangements. Focus on the time expressions rather than the grammar at this stage. This is introduced in the next section.

This week

GRAMMAR Present progressive (future meaning)

1 a *Reading.* Look at the notice board and establish what it shows: these are Alan's notes, so that he remembers things. Present *write a note* and ask a few learners if they write notes like this, or if they use a diary.

Look at the notes and check that learners understand *hairdresser* (show the meaning with gestures).

👤 / 👥 Learners match the notes with the sentences.

Go through the answers. Look at each note in turn and ask which sentence it goes with.

> **1D 2A 3B 4E 5C**

b *Present progressive (future meaning).* Read the examples in the box and make it clear that we can use the present progressive:
– to talk about things happening now
– to talk about things we know are happening in the future (things we have arranged).

Look at the sentences in **1a**. Ask if they are about now or about the future (the future).

> **Note**
>
> If you can, compare these uses with learners' own language. This will help get a sense of how the tense is used in English.

2 a *Listening.* Play recording **2.47** and establish when Alan is free (Thursday afternoon).

b *Speaking.* Learners imagine they are Alan. They say what they are doing, including the days and the times. You could do this round the class, or learners could do it in pairs. Possible answers:

> B *I'm meeting Sophie for lunch at Pizza House.*
> C *I'm having a party on Saturday evening.*
> D *Carlos is coming to stay this weekend. He's arriving on Saturday at 6.30.*
> E *I'm going to the cinema on Friday at 7.30.*

> **Alternative: Role play**
>
> Learners act out a role play based on the listening. Learner A is Alan. Learner B is a friend who wants to find a good time to meet.

WRITING and SPEAKING

3 a *Present progressive – negative.* To present the negative, close books and write on the board: *I'm going out this evening.* Ask how you can add *not* to the sentence, and write on the board: *I'm not going out this evening.*

Writing. Look at sentences 1–5 one at a time. Ask a few learners whether the sentence is true for them and if not, to change it.

Learners re-write the sentences if necessary. As they do this, go round and check.

b 👥 Learners read out their sentences and find out which are the same.

Round-up. A few learners tell you things they and their partners are both doing.

4 a *Writing.* Tell the class something you are doing this week or next week and write it on the board, e.g.
– *I'm going to a wedding next Saturday.*

Learners write a sentence. Go round and check.

Mingling activity. Learners move freely round the class, telling other learners what they are doing. They try to find someone who is doing the same as they are.

> **Alternative**
>
> If it is difficult for learners to move around the class, they could form groups of four or five for the speaking stage, or talk to learners who are sitting nearby.

Invitations and replies

GRAMMAR can, can't

1 a *Invitations.* Look at the photo and see if learners can guess the question. Then play recording **2.48** to check and write the question on the board: *Would you like to come?* Point out we often say: *Would you like to ...?* when we *invite* someone (make the concept clear by giving a situation: *I'm having a party. I say, "Please come to my party"*).

b *Listening.* Play recording **2.48** again. Learners listen and answer the questions.

> **1** Saturday, 8.00   **2** At his flat
> **3** Sophie   **4** John. He's going out.

c *Replies.* Play recording **2.48** again. Learners listen and underline the expressions they hear.

> **1** Sorry, I can't.   **2** Yes, thanks, I'd love to.

d *can, can't.* Remind learners of *can* (= it's OK, it's possible) and *can't* (= it's not OK, not possible).

Practise saying the sentences with *can* and *can't*. Point out that:
– *can* is reduced to /kən/.
– *can't* has a longer sound: /kɑːnt/.

To practise, give a few other examples and ask two or three learners to respond to them each time, e.g.
– *I'm going to a café. Would you like to come?*
– *I'm going for a walk this afternoon. Would you like to come?*

SPEAKING

2 *Role play.* To prepare for the activity, suggest a few possible places in the town (e.g. a well-known department store, a café in the centre, a park).

👥 Learners choose a place and a time and invite their partner to go with them.

> **Conversation practice**
>
> You could do the conversation practice exercises on p119 at this point.

Sounds and spelling: The letter *u*

Goal: to recognise and pronounce the letter *u* with the sounds /ʌ/, /uː/ and /juː/

Core language:
Words from Units 1–9 with the letter *u*

1 /ʌ/, /uː/ and /juː/. Say the words or play recording **2.50**. Focus on the sounds and point out that:
   – /ʌ/ is similar to the 'a' sound in many languages (e.g. French, German, Spanish).
   – /uː/ is a long sound, and is pronounced with rounded lips.

2 Play recording **2.51**. Learners put the words in the correct group.

/ʌ/	/uː/	/juː/
bus	fruit	Tuesday
study	suit	student
number		usually

3 **a** *Dictation.* Play recording **2.52** or read the sentences. Learners listen to each expression and write it down.

   b Learners read out the expressions, checking that they are pronouncing the /ʌ/, /uː/ and /juː/ sounds correctly.

   Check what learners have written (you could ask learners to write the sentences on the board).

9.3

Goals: invite someone to go out
decide what to do and where to go
make suggestions

Core language:
VOCABULARY Going out: *football match, art gallery, theatre, rock concert*; *at + noun*
What's on (at ...)?
Suggestions: *Let's ...*; *How about ...?*; *We could ...*

What's on?

VOCABULARY Going out

1 **a** Look at the photos and ask where the people are. Learners make sentences with *They're at ... .*

> *A They're at the theatre.*
> *B They're at an art gallery.*
> *C They're at a rock concert.*
> *D They're at a football match.*

Point out that we say *at the theatre* (like *at the cinema*), but *at a concert*, *at a football match*, etc.

Optional extra

Ask questions (e.g. *What do you see at the theatre?*) and build up other related vocabulary on the board: *play, opera, actor; singer, musician; exhibition, painting, artist.*

   b Take each photo in turn, and ask a few learners whether they often, sometimes or never go there.

   c Ask learners when was the last time they went to one of the places in the photos. Ask them who or what they saw.

Alternative: Pair or group work

Learners discuss the questions together in pairs or groups. Then ask learners to tell you something interesting they found out from their partner (or from the group).

READING

2 *Reading for main idea.* Establish a 'What's on?' page is a page in a magazine or newspaper that tells you about films, concerts, restaurants, etc. You could ask learners how they find out about these things.

    Learners answer the questions. You could give them three minutes or stop when the first pair / group has answered all the questions.

   Go through the answers. Establish what each place is and present any new words.

> *1 Miami Police (at 8.45); Indian Summer (at 7.15)*
> *2 Yes – light meals 3 Yes (at the Olympic Stadium at 3.00) – €35 4 No – it opens at 6 p.m. 5 Romeo and Juliet (a play by Shakespeare) 6 Hollywood Super Bowling 7 At Club 17 – €15 8 An art gallery*

VOCABULARY Suggestions

3 **a** *Listening.* Play recording **2.53**.

> *They're going to the cinema (the Adelphi Cinema) and then they're going to Café Cuba.*

   b Ask learners if they remember what the people said.

   c Play recording **2.53** again to check.

> *1 We could go to a concert.*
> *2 How about a film?*
> *3 Let's go to Café Cuba.*

Focus on the expressions *It sounds good / nice* (= I think maybe it's good).

To practise, make a few suggestions (e.g. *Let's go to a concert. How about The Morgs?*) and ask learners to respond (e.g. *Yes, OK*; *Yes, that sounds good.*).

> 💿 You could use photocopiable activity 9B on the Teacher's DVD-ROM at this point.

Conversation practice

You could do the conversation practice exercises on p119 at this point.

Target activity: Invite someone to go out

Goal: invite someone to go out

Core language:
9.2 GRAMMAR	Present progressive (future meaning)
9.2 GRAMMAR	*can, can't*
9.3 VOCABULARY	Suggestions

PREPARATION

1 *Speaking.* To demonstrate, choose one learner. Suggest places to go out and get the learner to suggest places. Include some of the expressions in the speech bubbles.

   Learners look at the 'What's on?' page on p74 and make suggestions. Together, they choose two places.

TASK

2 a 👥 Together, learners write an email, inviting another pair to go with them to the place they chose. You could tell them which pair they are inviting (e.g. the pair next to them). As they do this, go round and check.

b Each pair passes their email to another pair.

3 a 👥 Learners read the email they received and write a reply. Go round and check.

b Learners pass their reply back to the original pair.

4 *Round-up.* Each pair tells you what they are doing, and if the other pair are coming with them.

Keyword *that*

Goals: use *that* to refer to things you can see
use *that* to respond to what someone has just said

Core language:

That's ...; That's nice, good, terrible, wonderful;
That's interesting; That's a good idea

1 Look at the pictures. Ask where the people are and what they are doing.

> *A They're looking at photos on a computer.*
> *B They're shopping. They want to go to a café.*
> *C They're in an office / at work. They're talking about holidays.*
> *D They're in a café. Someone is taking the man's coat.*

Ask which people are talking about things they can see (A and D), and which are replying to people (B and C). Use this to establish the two main uses of *that*.

Language note

We say *This is ...* for things which are near, or 'here' and *That's* for things which are further away (or 'over there'). Give a few examples to show this.
To talk about photos or pictures we can use either *this* or *that*.

2 *Practice of 'that' (for things you see).* To demonstrate, point to one item in the picture and say:
– *That's a (policeman).*

👥 Learners point to things in the picture and say what they are, using *That's ...* or *I think that's ...* .They write down the words for all the things they know.

Round-up. Found out how many words each pair knows. Point to the items in the picture and ask what they are. Write new items on the board.

a street	a policeman	a car
a tree	the sky	a ball
a bus stop	a police car	mountains
the sun	a boy	houses
a bus	a kiosk	buildings
a cat	a cloud	

3 a *Practice of 'that' (for replies).* Look at the first question together and ask learners to find a suitable answer (*Yes. That's a good idea.*).

👥 Learners match the questions and answers. Expected answers:

> *1 c   2 d   3 a   4 e   5 b*

b 👥 Learners cover answers a–e. They say sentences 1–5 and try to remember the answers.

Alternative

Put learners into A/B pairs. A closes his / her book. B reads out A's sentences in random order and A replies. Then they change roles.

4 *Speaking.* Put learners into A/B pairs. A looks on p91. B looks on p94. They look only at their own sentences.

If necessary, show what to do by asking one A learner to read out a sentence. Then ask one B learner to give a suitable reply using *That's ...* .

👥 Learners take it in turns to read out their sentences and reply.

9.4 Explore speaking

Goal: reply to questions

Core language:

Short answers: *Yes, they are; No, they aren't; Yes, I did; No, I didn't, etc.*

1 Play recording **2.54**. Pause after each conversation and ask questions **1** and **2**. Use this to establish that:
– in short answers, we repeat only the first verb (the auxiliary verb: *are, was, do, did*), not the main verb.
– in negative answers, we add *not* or *n't*.

> *1 are, was, do, did (the auxiliary verb)*
> *2 married, a good film, smoke, see her*

You could ask the questions round the class and get learners to answer. Make sure learners stress the verb in their answer:
– *Yes, I do.*
– *Yes, it was.*
– *Yes, they are.*

2 a 👤/👥 Learners think of suitable questions. E.g.:

> *1 Is that (Laura Matos)?*
> *2 Are you (at home)?*
> *3 Are you busy (tomorrow evening)?*
> *4 Would you like to (go to a restaurant)?*
> *5 How about (7 o'clock)?*

b *Listening.* Play recording **2.55** to check.

c *Noticing task.* Learners find the three kinds of answer.

Use this to emphasise that we don't always give a short answer to a question – we can answer in many different ways.

3   *Practice of replying to questions.* Ask the questions round the class, getting one or two learners to answer each time. Check the possible short answers.

> 1 Yes, I do. / No, I don't.   2 Yes, it is. / No, it's not.
> 3 Yes, I was. / No, I wasn't.   4 Yes, I am. / No, I'm not.
> 5 Yes, I am. / No, I'm not.

👥 Learners ask and answer the questions.

Language note

With *is / are* questions, there are two ways we can answer *No*:
– *No, it's not* or *No, it isn't*
– *No, they're not* or *No, they aren't*
Focus on this only if learners ask about it.

Across cultures: Family weekend

Goals: to give practice in reading short texts
   to give information about other parts of the world

Core language:

cook (a meal), go (shopping), sit (by the pool), drive (into the desert), eat (in restaurants), read (the paper), have (a picnic)

1   Books closed. Write on the board: *Saudi Arabia, Spain, Australia*. Learners imagine how families spend their weekend in each country. If you like, build up information on the board beside each country.

Open books. Learners read the texts and match them with the pictures. At this stage they should try to guess the meaning of unknown words.

> | A Riyadh   B Perth   C Madrid

Ask why they think each text is about the place they chose, e.g.
– *Riyadh: mosque, desert, weekend is Thursday and Friday.*
– *Perth: beach, swimming pool.*
– *Madrid: church, restaurant, drive into the country.*

2   *Vocabulary.* Learners read the texts again (using dictionaries if necessary) and note down the expressions.

> 1 go   2 sit   3 go   4 cook   5 drive   6 go
> 7 read   8 have

3   👤 / 👥 Learners write a few sentences about their country. As they do this, go round and check.

Round-up. Learners read out their sentences. See if other learners agree.

Mixed nationality classes

Learners from different countries tell the class about weekends in their country, based on what they have written. Other learners can ask further questions.

Look again

VOCABULARY

1   a   *Verb–noun collocations.* Do the exercise with the whole class, or learners do it in pairs.

> | go to a party   read the newspaper
> | have breakfast   meet a friend
> | cook some food   stay at home
> | talk to a customer

b   Learners write sentences. Possible answers:

> | I'm having breakfast.   I'm meeting a friend.
> | I'm reading the newspaper.   I'm talking to a customer.
> | I'm cooking some food.   I'm staying at home.

2   *Word order.* Learners write the words in the correct order.

> 1 Would you like to come?   2 Can I call you later?
> 3 What are you doing?   4 I can't go out this evening.

SPELLING

3   Learners correct the mistakes.

> 1 I'm having lunch.
> 2 He's meeting us tomorrow.
> 3 Two friends are coming for dinner.
> 4 We're just going to a football match.

CAN YOU REMEMBER? Unit 8

4   a   *Writing.* Put learners into A/B/C groups. They write sentences about their topic. If necessary, they could look quickly at Unit 8 as a reminder, but they shouldn't copy out information.

b   👥 Learners sit in groups of three: A, B and C. They tell each other what they remember.

Round-up. Ask learners what they remember and let them check the information in Unit 8.

GRAMMAR

Present progressive. Read through the examples and the table.

Alternative: Presentation with books closed

Write on the board:
– *They (stay) with friends.*   – *I (just get) up.*
Learners say the present progressive form. Then learners give forms with *he, she, you, we*.
Then learners make questions from the sentences. Write them on the board.

---

5   Learners write sentences with the present progressive.

> 1 is watching ('s watching)   2 am cooking ('m cooking)
> 3 are having ('re having)   4 Are; going   5 are; doing

can, can't. Read through the table. Learners say the sentences aloud.

6   Learners complete the sentences.

> 1 can't talk   2 can go   3 can stay   4 can't have
> 5 can meet / can't meet

Self-assessment

To help focus learners on the self-assessment, you could read it through, giving a few more examples of the language they have learned in each section (or asking learners to tell you). Then they circle a number on each line.

Unit 9 Extra activities on the Teacher's DVD-ROM

Printable worksheets, activity instructions and answer keys are on your Teacher's DVD-ROM.

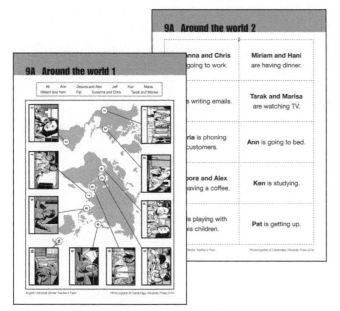

9A Around the world

Activity type: Speaking and Listening – Running dictation – Pairs / Whole group

Aim: To practise the present progressive

Language:
Present progressive – Coursebook p70 – Grammar

Preparation: Make one copy of the map for each pair of learners. Make one copy of the set of cards for the class. Cut along the dotted line into a set of 10 cards. Make sure the room is safe if learners are running.

Time: 15–20 minutes

9B Three phone calls

Activity type: Speaking – Role play – Groups of three

Aim: To practise speaking on the telephone and making arrangements

Language: Telephone expressions – Coursebook p70 – Vocabulary; Invitations and replies – Coursebook p73

Preparation:
Make one copy of the worksheet for each learner.

Time: 20–30 minutes

Unit 9 Self-study Pack

In the Workbook

Unit 9 of the *English Unlimited Starter Workbook* offers additional ways to practise the vocabulary and grammar taught in the Coursebook. There are also activities which build reading and writing skills, and a whole page of tasks to use with the DVD-ROM video, giving your learners the opportunity to hear and react to spoken English.

- **Vocabulary:** Telephone expressions; Future time expressions
- **Grammar:** Present progressive; Present progressive – questions
- **Time out:** Crossword
- **Explore writing:** *who, which*
- **DVD-ROM Extra:** *Are you busy?*

On the DVD-ROM

Unit 9 of the *English Unlimited Starter Self-study Pack DVD-ROM* contains interactive games and activities for your learners to practise and improve their vocabulary, grammar and pronunciation, and also their speaking and listening. It also contains video material (with the possibility for learners to record themselves) to use with the *Workbook*.

- **Vocabulary and Grammar:** Extra practice of Coursebook language and Keyword
- **Classroom language:** Talking about a picture
- **Sounds and spelling:** The letter *u*
- **Explore speaking:** Reply to questions
- **Video:** *Are you busy?*

10 People's lives

Unit goal: talk about your life

10.1

Goals: talk about your life
say when people were born and died
say when people did things
say what people did in their lives

Core language:

VOCABULARY Jobs: *writer, painter, musician, leader, singer*
Nationalities: *Italian, Egyptian, Indian,*
Russian, Chinese, Mexican, American
Years
Past simple verbs
I think, I don't know, I'm not sure;
possibly, probably, maybe

Famous people

VOCABULARY Nationalities, jobs

1 a Look at the words in the box and check that learners
know (or can guess) what they mean. Use the words
to ask questions, e.g. *Tell me the name of a writer in
your country. Who is your favourite painter?*

Learners look at the photos and say who the people
were. Then discuss this together.

b Play recording **2.56** to check.

> 1 She was a Mexican painter.
> 2 He was an Indian leader.
> 3 He was an Italian painter.
> 4 She was an Egyptian singer.
> 5 He was a Chinese leader.
> 6 He was an American musician.
> 7 He was a Russian writer.

Stronger classes

Learners say other things they know about the people, e.g.
Louis Armstrong: *He played jazz; he lived in New Orleans.*

VOCABULARY Years

2 a Play recording **2.57**. Pause after each one and ask who
it goes with.

> 1 Leo Tolstoy   2 Mao Zedong
> 3 Louis Armstrong   4 Frida Kahlo

Use the examples to show that:
– we say years in pairs of numbers: *19 – 48, 14 – 52.*
– we can say *1907* in two ways: *19 – oh – 7*
or *nineteen hundred and seven.*

b *Practice of years.* Play recording **2.58**. Learners say
the years. You could do this round the class, then
learners could practise them in pairs.

c Read the sentences and ask which person it is.

> 1 Frida Kahlo   2 Leonardo da Vinci
> 3 Mahatma Gandhi   4 Mao Zedong

Write *was born in* and *died in* on the board (the
meaning should be obvious).

---

d Learners test each other. In turn, they say a
sentence and find the person in **1a**.

You could use photocopiable activity 10A on the
Teacher's DVD-ROM at this point.

VOCABULARY Past simple verbs

3 a Learners match the sentences to the people in **1a**.

> 1 Louis Armstrong
> 2 Um Kulthum
> 3 Frida Kahlo
> 4 Leo Tolstoy
> 5 Mao Zedong
> 6 Leonardo da Vinci
> 7 Mahatma Gandhi

b Learners write the past verbs in the table.

paint – painted	go – went
live – lived	write – wrote
marry – married	become – became
study – studied	

Focus on:
– the spelling of *married, studied* (-*y* → -*ied*).
– the meaning of *became* (= before 1949 he wasn't
leader, then he was leader).

4 a Learners make sentences from the notes.

Discuss the answers together and write the verbs on
the board.

> 2 Che Guevara was born in Argentina in 1928.
> 3 Mozart died in Vienna.
> 4 Barack Obama became president of the USA in 2009.
> 5 Van Gogh painted Sunflowers.
> 6 Paul McCartney wrote Yesterday.

b Learners choose a well-known person and write
simple notes about him / her. Go round and check.

c Learners read out their notes. Other learners try
to make complete sentences about the famous person.

Who was Picasso?

LISTENING

1 Learners brainstorm things they know about
Picasso and write two lists: things they know and
things they think they know.

Discuss this together, getting ideas from different
pairs or groups. Build up a list on the board.

2 a *Listening.* Play recording **2.59**. Pause after each
answer to check what the people said. Ask the class:
Do you think they were right?

b *Reading.* Look on p94 and read the information
together. Ask which facts the people were right about.

> He was a Spanish painter.
> He lived in Spain (as a child) and France.

3 **a** Ask learners to complete the questions, and write them on the board.

> 1 What do you know about Picasso?
> 2 When was he born?
> 3 When did he die?
> 4 Where did he live?

b Play recording **2.60** and practise saying the questions. Focus on the stress pattern:
– When was he born?
– When did he die?

VOCABULARY *I think, I don't know ...*

4 *'Uncertainty' expressions.* Learners read the script on p127 and make a list of expressions.

Go through them together and write them on the board.

> I'm not sure; maybe; probably; possibly

SPEAKING

5 **a** Together, learners choose a famous person who is now dead, either from their own country or from another country. They try to answer the questions in **3a**.

b In turn, learners say what they think they know about their person. See if other learners agree or can give more information.

> **Homework option: Internet research**
>
> Learners check the answers to the questions on the Internet and report back in the next lesson.

Classroom language: Questions

Goal: ask what words mean

Core language:
What does ... mean?; How do you say ... in English?; What's this in English?

1 **a** *Listening.* Tell the class they will hear learners asking questions in class. Play recording **2.61**. Learners listen and write the questions correctly.

Discuss the questions together and write them on the board.

> 1 What does sofa mean?
> 2 How do you say también in English?
> 3 What's this in English?

b Ask what the answers are.

> 1 A long chair for three people
> 2 Also
> 3 Paper

You could quickly practise the questions by giving prompts, using English words and learners' own language: *Ask me about ... .*

2 **a** *Practice in asking questions.* Learners write three questions to ask. As they do this, go round and check.

b Learners ask their questions and try to answer their partner's questions.

Round-up. Learners ask you any questions they couldn't answer.

10.2

Goals: talk about your life
  talk about important events in your life
  tell someone's life story
  say when things happened

Core language:
VOCABULARY Life events: *grew up, went to school / university, got a job, met, went to (live in), moved to, got married, had a baby*
  Past time expressions: *in, for, until, from ... to*

My life

READING

1 **a** *Reading.* Learners read and answer the questions.

> 1 weren't 2 are

Ask learners if they could say the same about their own town (or the town where you are now).

b *Speaking.* Learners think about people in their family who moved to a different town or a different country. They could make brief notes.

Learners tell each other about their family.

> **Alternative**
>
> Talk about this with the whole class. Ask different learners to tell you something about people in their family.

LISTENING

2 **a** *Preparation for the exercise.* Read the sentences about Cheng and Donna. Check that learners understand *grew up in* (past of *grow up* = was there when he / she was a child) and *got married* (= married).

> **Language note**
>
> The verb *marry* and the expression *get married* mean the same.
> – They got married in 2010.
> – They married in 2010.

Learners put the events in order.

b Discuss the answers for Cheng, then play recording **2.26** to check. Then do the same for Donna.

Cheng	Donna
1 grew up in Hong Kong	1 was born in Canada
2 moved to London	2 grew up in a small town
3 went to school	3 went to live in Brazil
4 went to university	4 met my husband
5 studied business	5 moved to London
6 got a job	6 had a baby

c Discuss the questions. Let learners check answers in the script on p127, or play recording **2.26** again to check.

> 1 When he was 10.
> 2 business
> 3 Shanghai, China
> 4 Brazil
> 5 They both worked.
> 6 2005; a boy

VOCABULARY Life events

3 a Learners write the expressions in the lists.

> *Where you lived: was born, moved, went to live*
> *School, university: went to university, studied*
> *Work: worked*
> *People and family: got married, had a baby*

b Learners choose the expressions they could use about their life.
Go through the expressions. For each one, ask who chose it and ask them to make a sentence, e.g.
– *What about 'grew up'?*
– *I grew up in Istanbul.*

4 a *Speaking.* To show what to do, write an important year in your life on the board. Learners guess what you did.
Learners write about three important years.

b Learners take it in turns to read out their years and to guess what their partner did.
Round-up. Ask a few learners to tell you one thing their partner did and when.

> You could use photocopiable activity 10B on the Teacher's DVD-ROM at this point.

Life story

READING

1 a *Vocabulary.* Look at the photos and the title. Check that learners know *millionaire*. You could ask learners to guess how Erich Lejeune became a millionaire.
Read the sentences and check whether learners know (or can guess) what the words mean:
– *cleaner* = someone who cleans offices, hotels, etc.
– *grandmother* = the mother of your mother / father
– *salesperson* = someone who sells things
– *lost his job* = they didn't want him
– *poor* = they didn't have much money
– *left his job* = he didn't want the job

b *Jigsaw reading.* Put students into A/B pairs. A looks on p92. B looks on p94. Learners read their part of the story. As they do this, go round and help with any problems.

c A and B tell their part of the story to each other and ask about the main facts.
Round-up. Go through the story together, to establish what happened. B learners could tell you A's part of the story and A learners could tell you B's part.

GRAMMAR Past time expressions

2 Learners complete the sentences.

> *2 for   3 until   4 in   5 when*

Point out that:
– we use *for* to say how long (show this with gestures).
– we use *until* to say when something finished.

If necessary, give other examples, or draw a time line on the board:

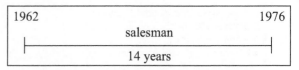

3 Learners complete the sentences. Possible answers:

> *1 ... when he was 7. / ... in 1951.*
> *2 ... when he was 18. / ... in 1962.*
> *3 ... until September 1976. / ... for a few months.*
> *4 ... until 1962. / ... until he was 18.*
> *5 ... when he was 7.*

4 *Speaking.* Learners re-tell the story round the class. Prompt them if necessary (e.g. ask: *Then what happened? What about his father? When was that?*).

> **Alternative: Pair work**
>
> Learners practise re-telling the story in pairs first, then go through it together.

Sounds and spelling: Revision

Goal: to review the pronunciation of difficult words
Core language:
Words from Units 1–10 with difficult pronunciation or spelling

1 Learners say the words. Then play recording **2.63** to compare. Practise words learners find difficult.

2 a *Dictation.* Play recording **2.64** or read the expressions. Learners listen to each expression and write it down.

b Learners read out the expressions. Check that they are pronouncing the words from **1** correctly.
Check what learners have written (you could ask learners to write the expressions on the board).

10.3

Goals: talk about your life
   talk about your past
   ask about someone's past

Core language:
GRAMMAR   Questions (in the past): *When ...?;*
            How long ...?

Questions

GRAMMAR Questions: *When ...? How long ...?*

1 a Look at the photo and discuss the question.

> *She got no money.*

b You could talk (or ask) about Galápagos and what it's like. Establish that there are lot of unusual animals there, so it's an important place to study animals. Focus on the photo of Anne and discuss the question.

> *She studied animals.*

2 a *'When? How long?'* Learners complete the questions.

b Play recording **2.65** to check.

> When did you leave school?
> How long did you stay in Galápagos?

Practise saying the questions. Focus on the stress pattern: *did you* is unstressed and spoken more quickly:
– When did you leave school?
– How long did you stay in Galápagos?

c 👤/👥 Learners complete the questions.

> 1 When
> 2 How long
> 3 How long
> 4 When

d *Question forms*. Look at the examples and discuss the questions. Use this to establish that:
– questions with *was / were* change the word order:
  I was → When were you ...?
– questions with main verbs add *did*:
  I stayed → How long did you stay?

LISTENING

3 *Listening for main idea*. Read through the questions, then play recording **2.66**. Learners listen and answer the questions.

> 1 I first travelled to Quito in Ecuador (to learn basic Spanish).
> 2 I studied iguanas.
> 3 I went back to Manchester.
> 4 I worked in a café.
> 5 I studied Biology.

If necessary, play the recording again, pausing to focus on the answers.

SPEAKING

4 *Role play*. Put learners into A/B pairs. You could give time to prepare: A learners think what questions they will ask; B learners think how they will answer the questions.

👥 Learners ask and answer questions.

Optional extra

B learners move to a new pair and have the conversation again.

Target activity: Find out about someone's life

Goal: talk about your life

Core language:
10.1 VOCABULARY Life events
10.2 GRAMMAR Past time expressions

TASK WRITING

1 a Learners write three sentences about their life. You could prepare by eliciting verbs and writing them on the board (e.g. *was born, grew up, moved to*).

Learners exchange sentences with the person next to them.

---

b *Writing questions*. Learners look at the sentences and write questions to find out more information. You could prepare for this by writing question words on the board (e.g. *When? How long? What? Who? How? Why?*).

TASK

2 a 👥 Learners take it in turn to ask their questions.

b Learners tell the class about their partner, including the sentences and the answers to their questions. They check with their partner if the information was correct. Other learners could also ask further questions.

Keyword *how*

Goals: ask questions with *how*
ask questions about age, distance, price and length of time

Core language:
How ...?; How old ...?; How much ...?; How far ...?

Optional lead-in

Books closed. Write *How ...?* on the board and learners think of possible questions. You could also give situations to prompt questions, e.g. *You want to go to the airport. What can you ask?*
Open books. Do **1a**.

---

1 a 👤/👥 Learners match the questions and the answers.

b Discuss the answers together and play recording **2.67** to check. Show the meaning of *How far?* (= *Is it near, or is it far?* Show this with gestures).

> 1E 2C 3B 4A 5D

2 a *Writing*. Learners write items for each of the four categories, as in the example.

b *Preparation for the activity*. Look at the four categories and ask learners what questions they could ask about each item. Possible questions:

> 1 When did you go there? How long did you stay? How was the weather?
> 2 Where did you buy it? How much was it?
> 3 How is he? How old is he?
> 4 Where is it? How far is it (from here)? How can I get there?

Alternative

Write four items of your own on the board, as in the example. Get learners to ask you questions about them (prompt them by saying *Ask me when. Ask me how. ...*).

---

c *Speaking*. 👥 Learners ask and answer questions.

Round-up. Ask a few learners what they found out from their partner.

10.4 Explore writing

Goal: write when things happened

Core language:

when, after

1 a Learners read the texts. Ask which word goes in each gap.

> 1 When 2 After

Use this to show how we use *when* and *after*:
– *When she was a child, she lived in a village ...*
  = these things were at the same time
– *After they got married, they lived together ...*
  = first they got married, then they lived together.

(You could show the two different meanings with gestures.)

b Read the examples. Ask learners to say the sentences in the texts in a different order.

> *She lived in a small village <u>when</u> she was a child.*
> *They lived together in Mexico City <u>after</u> they got married.*

2 a 👤 *Writing.* Learners join the sentences.

b 👥 Learners compare their sentences and see if they had different answers.

Discuss the answers together and get learners to suggest different ideas. Possible answers:

> *I got a job in a bank after I left university.*
> *When I went to Tokyo, I didn't know any Japanese.*
> *After I left school, I moved to Spain.*
> *When I lived in Berlin, I spoke German all the time.*
> *I wrote my first novel when I was 16.*
> *After I finished university, I worked in the USA for a year.*

3 a *Writing.* Learners write two true sentences. As they do this, go round and check.

b *Round-up.* Learners read out their sentences. Other learners listen and ask further questions.

Across cultures: Birthdays

Goals: to give practice in reading short texts
to give learners information about birthday customs in different parts of the world

Core language:

invite, present, special, adult, important

1 a *Prediction.* Look at the pictures. Ask learners what they think they show and what people do in each country. Use the pictures to introduce vocabulary, e.g. *dance, flag, birthday cake, candles, envelope, noodles*.

b *Reading.* Learners read the texts on p92. Then discuss together whether they were right and what the pictures actually show.

> *China: people invite their family and eat noodles.*
> *Germany: people invite friends and family for a meal.*
> *Britain: people make a birthday cake with candles.*
> *Denmark: people put a flag outside their house.*
> *Argentina: on their 15th birthday, girls dance the waltz.*
> *Vietnam: children get a red envelope with 'lucky money'.*

2 *Reading for detail.* Discuss the questions together. If necessary, learners read the texts again to find the answers.

> *China: Noodles are long, so the child will have a long life.*
> *Argentina: Her father.*
> *Denmark: By the child's bed (in the night).*
> *Germany: The person who has the birthday.*
> *Britain: One candle for each year.*
> *Vietnam: The first day of New Year.*

3 a Present the word *custom* (= things people usually do).
👤/👥 Learners make a list of birthday customs in their country. Go round and give help where necessary.

b 👥/👥 Learners sit together and compare their lists.

Round-up. Ask different pairs / groups what they wrote and what was the same or different.

> **Mixed nationality classes**
>
> Learners from the same country make lists together. Then they use this to tell the rest of the class about birthday customs in their country.

Look again

VOCABULARY

1 a *Verb-noun collocations.* Do the exercise with the whole class, or learners do it in pairs.

> *paint a picture*
> *study biology*
> *go to university*
> *write a novel*
> *play jazz*
> *become president*
> *lose your job*

b Learners write sentences.

> *1 She painted a picture.*
> *2 I studied biology.*
> *3 He went to university.*
> *4 She wrote a novel.*
> *5 They played jazz.*
> *6 She became president.*
> *7 I lost my job.*

2 a *Years.* Learners say the years round the class. Alternatively, they do this in pairs.

> *1914 – nineteen fourteen*
> *2010 – two thousand and ten (twenty ten)*
> *1492 – fourteen ninety-two*
> *1930 – nineteen thirty*
> *1900 – nineteen hundred*
> *2001 – two thousand and one*
> *1848 – eighteen forty-eight*
> *1789 – seventeen eighty-nine*

b Learners choose three people in their family and write the years they were born.

👥 Learners tell each other about the people they chose. Alternatively, do this with the whole class together.

3 a *Past simple verbs.* Ask learners to give the past simple forms. Write them on the board.

> 1 met
> 2 studied
> 3 went
> 4 moved
> 5 grew up
> 6 had
> 7 got
> 8 wrote

b Learners write three sentences. As they do this, go round and check.

Learners read out their sentences. Other learners listen and ask further questions.

CAN YOU REMEMBER? Unit 9

4 a 👤/👥 Learners think of ways to continue the questions and sentences. Possible answers:

> 1 ... like to come?
> 2 ... call you later? / ... call you this evening?
> 3 ... busy? / ... at work?
> 4 ... going out. / ... working. / ... busy. / ... not here.

b Learners suggest expressions to replace the ones highlighted. Either do this with the whole class, or let learners discuss it in pairs and then go through the answers together. Possible answers:

> 1 a party / a restaurant / the theatre
> 2 in a meeting / having breakfast / going to work
> 4 meet you for lunch / come to the meeting / go out

5 A learner reads the first speech bubble. The next learner reads the second speech bubble and adds a new expression. Continue round the class, with each learner repeating what the others have said and adding a new day and a new activity.

> **Alternative: Group work**
>
> Learners sit in groups of four or five. They play the game round their group, going round twice.
> *Round-up.* Ask one person from each group to remember all the things their group said.

GRAMMAR

'be' past – questions. Read through the table.

> **Alternative: Presentation with books closed**
>
> On the board, write the sentences from the table (the left-hand column). Beside them, write the question words from the right-hand column: *When ..., Where ..., How long ... .* Ask learners to complete the questions.

Past simple – questions. Read through the table.

> **Alternative: Presentation with books closed**
>
> Write the sentences from the table on the board (the left-hand column). Beside them, write the question words from the right-hand column: *When ..., How ..., How long ... .* Ask learners to complete the questions.

6 Learners write the questions in the correct order.

> 1 When were you in Japan?
> 2 Where did you meet your husband?
> 3 Did you stay at home?
> 4 When was your daughter born?
> 5 How long did you live in Argentina?

Past time expressions. Read through the tables, and ask learners to say the sentences aloud.

> **Alternative: Presentation with books closed**
>
> Write the questions from the table on the board with gaps instead of the words in orange.
> Ask learners to add the missing words.

7 Learners complete the sentences.

> 1 for; in
> 2 from; to
> 3 when
> 4 until / in

Self-assessment

To help focus learners on the self-assessment, you could read it through, giving a few more examples of the language they have learned in each section (or asking learners to tell you). Then they circle a number on each line.

Unit 10 Extra activities on the Teacher's DVD-ROM

Printable worksheets, activity instructions and answer keys are on your Teacher's DVD-ROM.

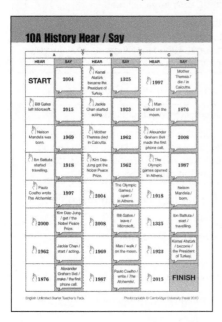

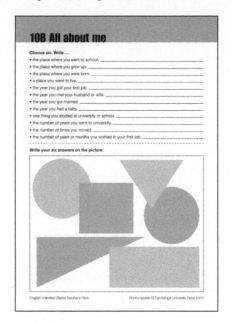

10A History Hear / Say

Activity type: Speaking and Listening – Hear / Say – Groups of three

Aim: To practise years and the past simple

Language: Years – Coursebook p78 – Vocabulary

Preparation: Make one copy of the worksheet for every three learners. Cut along the dotted lines into three separate cards.

Time: 15–20 minutes

10B All about me

Activity type:
Speaking – Personalised guessing game – Pairs

Aim:
To practise asking and answering questions about life events

Language: Life events – Coursebook p80 – Vocabulary

Preparation:
Make one copy of the worksheet for each learner.

Time: 20–25 minutes

Unit 10 Self-study Pack

In the Workbook

Unit 10 of the *English Unlimited Starter Workbook* offers additional ways to practise the vocabulary and grammar taught in the Coursebook. There are also activities which build reading and writing skills, and a whole page of tasks to use with the DVD-ROM video, giving your learners the opportunity to hear and react to spoken English.

- **Vocabulary:** Nationalites, jobs; Past simple verbs; Years; Life events
- **Grammar:** Past time expressions; Questions
- **Time out:** Odd one out
- **Explore reading:** Job ads
- **DVD-ROM Extra:** Duggal's life

On the DVD-ROM

Unit 10 of the *English Unlimited Starter Self-study Pack DVD-ROM* contains interactive games and activities for your learners to practise and improve their vocabulary, grammar and pronunciation, and also their speaking and listening. It also contains video material (with the possibility for learners to record themselves) to use with the *Workbook*.

- **Vocabulary and Grammar:** Extra practice of Coursebook language and Keyword
- **Classroom language:** Questions
- **Sounds and spelling:** Revision
- **Explore writing:** Write when things happened
- **Video:** Duggal's life

Writing Essentials worksheets

Writing Essentials Worksheets are designed as a series of targeted activities to encourage learners to 'notice' aspects of literacy, such as letter formation and spelling patterns. The materials use all four skills to develop strategies to improve learners' reading and writing; they also encourage learner autonomy.

The worksheets provide supplementary reading and writing activities for adult learners with a specific focus on literacy, spelling and handwriting. They enable learners to complete authentic, practical tasks, and in the process work with the meaning of texts, rather than acquiring a range of isolated skills.

The worksheets are based on these principles:
- learners should only work with words they understand
- they should be encouraged to look for patterns
- they should learn words in context, embedded in a text
- they should start from the words **they** want to write.

Who are the worksheets for?

The skills practised in *Writing Essentials* are an integral part of English-language learning for anyone but especially those who are unfamiliar with Roman script.

The activities can be used for individuals, pairs, groups, or for whole classes.

How do the worksheets fit into the course?

The worksheets can be used alongside the Coursebook. The *Can be used* heading at the beginning of the teacher's notes indicates where the activity could be included. This takes account of the vocabulary and structures covered up to that point in the Coursebook. The worksheets can also be used at any subsequent point in the course or independently, as stand-alone materials.

The worksheets can be used as part of a group or paired activity, when all the learners are at a similar level, or can be used for individuals or pairs, to give extra practice. They can be used at the beginning or end of a lesson, or given as homework. An estimate of the time each activity will take is given in the teacher's notes.

What skills will the learners develop?

Handwriting

The development of legible, cursive script is a fundamental part of Writing Essentials. Learners are taught to join letters together from the very beginning. To be effective, handwriting training should be taught systematically, with attention to the detail of letter formation. Attention is given to the shape, joining and placing of letters relative to the line. When learners are confidently doing this correctly, they are encouraged to develop their own distinctive, fluent style. Learners of all levels can benefit with work on handwriting. Learners in high-level classes may have relatively advanced oral skills, and good grammatical and syntactic skills, but still need to work on their handwriting.

Spelling

English spelling is challenging for all learners, but particularly for those who are not familiar with a language which does not have a clear sound-symbol correspondence. Writing Essentials provides a wide variety of strategies for enabling adult learners to improve their spelling, whilst giving learners phonic strategies for the 80% of words that are phonically regular. These include:

- **Whole word recognition**

  Many of the worksheets enable the learners to work with high-frequency and everyday words, building up a core sight vocabulary.

- **Spelling patterns**

  Many of the worksheets are designed to help learners identify and predict spelling patterns, useful for both reading and writing.

- **Phonic strategies**

  Several of the worksheets are designed to help learners to work with common phonic patterns, working on sound discrimination and production.

- **Punctuation**

  Several worksheets give learners practice in using punctuation and word spacing, focusing on communication and meaning.

We hope that you and your learners find these materials useful and enjoyable.

Cathy Brabben
Rachel Thake

Writing Essentials worksheets

Printable worksheets and activity instructions are on your Teacher's DVD-ROM.

1 Handwriting – writing patterns

Aim: To improve learners' handwriting; to encourage pen control as preparation for handwriting in an unfamiliar script

Can be used: at any point in the course

Activity: Individual work

Focus: Handwriting

Materials: One copy of Worksheets 1.1 and 1.2 per learner

Estimated time: 15 minutes

2 Handwriting – capital letters

Aim: To improve learners' handwriting; to show the starting point for each letter and the order in which each 'part' of the letter is formed

Can be used: at any point in the course

Activity: Individual work

Focus: Handwriting

Materials: One copy of Worksheets 2.1 and 2.2 per learner; copies of Worksheet 7.1 (*Handwriting guidelines*), optional

Estimated time: 15 minutes

3 Handwriting – lower-case letters

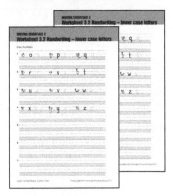

Aim: To improve learners' handwriting; to show the correct formation and the point to join lower-case letters

Can be used: at any point in the course

Activity: Individual work

Focus: Handwriting

Materials: One copy of Worksheets 3.1 and 3.2 per learner; copies of Worksheet 7.1 (*Handwriting guidelines*), optional

Estimated time: 15 minutes

4 Handwriting – capital and lower-case letters

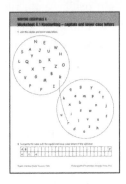

Aim: To check that learners are able to match capital and lower-case letters accurately, and know the name and sound of letters, whether they are capitals or lower case

Can be used: at any point in the course

Activity: Individual work

Focus: Letter recognition

Materials: One copy of Worksheet 4.1 per learner; copies of Worksheets 2.1, 2.2, 3.1 and 3.2, optional

Estimated time: 15 minutes

5 Handwriting – letter families

Aim: To focus learners' attention on the position of the letter, relative to the line; to look at the shape of the letters, introducing letters that start with the same basic structure

Can be used: at any point in the course

Activity: Individual work

Focus: Handwriting

Materials: One copy of Worksheets 5.1 and 5.2 per learner

Estimated time: 15 minutes

6 Handwriting – joining letters

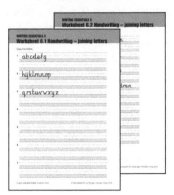

Aim: To encourage learners to join their letters correctly; to enable them to write more fluently

Can be used: at any point in the course

Activity: Individual work

Focus: Handwriting

Materials: One copy of Worksheets 6.1 and 6.2 per learner; copies of Worksheets 1.1 and 1.2 optional

Estimated time: 15 minutes

7 Handwriting guidelines

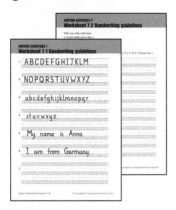

Aim: To help learners regulate the size and positioning of letters

Can be used: at any point in the course

Activity: Individual work

Focus: Letter formation

Materials: One copy of Worksheets 7.1 and 7.2 per learner

Estimated time: 15–20 minutes

8 Look, Say, Cover, Write, Check

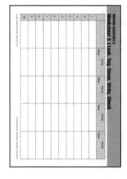

Aim: To encourage learner independence and help learners to develop habits for learning the spellings of new words

Can be used: at any point in the course

Activity: Individual work

Focus: Strategy for learning spelling

Materials: One copy of Worksheet 8.1 per learner

Estimated time: 15–20 minutes

9 Word spacing

Aim: To make the boundaries between words clear and establish the recognition and practice of word spacing

Can be used: from Unit 1 onwards

Activity: Individual or pair work

Focus: Word spacing

Materials: One copy of Worksheets 9.1 and 9.2 per learner; scissors for class; glue sticks

Estimated time: 20 minutes

10 I am

Aim: To familiarise learners with common, high-frequency words; to write, using a parallel-text model

Can be used: from Unit 2 onwards

Activity: Individual work

Materials: One copy of Worksheet 10.1 per learner; highlighters, optional

Focus: Reading and writing high-frequency words

Estimated time: 30 minutes

11 Listening to sounds (consonants)

Aim: To develop the ability to recognise individual (consonant) sounds and their position within words.

Can be used: from Unit 3 onwards.

Activity: Pair work

Focus: Sound recognition

Materials: One copy of Worksheets 11.1 and 11.2 per pair; one copy of Worksheet 11.3 per learner; scissors for the class

Estimated time: 30–40 minutes

12 Which vowel: *a e i o* or *u*?

Aim: To help learners differentiate between short vowel sounds to aid spelling and pronunciation

Can be used: from Unit 4 onwards

Activity: Pair work

Focus: Short vowel sounds

Materials: One copy of Worksheet 12.1 per learner; one copy of Worksheet 12.2 per learner, with vowels section cut off (to be handed out separately); scissors for class

Estimated time: 30–40 minutes

13 Shopping dominoes

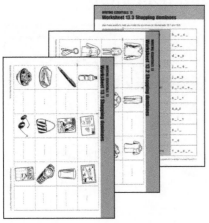

Aim: To reinforce recognition and spelling of shopping words; to develop skills of sequencing and turn taking

Can be used: from Unit 5 onwards

Activity: Pair work

Focus: Spelling

Materials: One copy of Worksheet 13.1 per learner; one copy of Worksheets 13.2 and 13.3 per pair, photocopied on card or thick paper; scissors for class

Estimated time: 20–30 minutes

14 Word chunks

Aim: To help learners recognise syllables and build up words by assembling separate syllables.

Can be used: from Unit 6 onwards.

Activity: Individual or pair work

Focus: Word syllables and chunks

Materials: One copy of Worksheet 14.1 per pair (or per learner if done individually); scissors for class; dictionaries, optional

Estimated time: 20 minutes

15 Word shapes

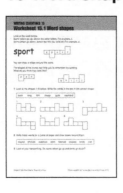

Aim: To encourage learners to be aware of the different letter shapes in English

Can be used: from Unit 7 onwards

Activity: Individual or pair work

Focus: Shapes of words

Materials: One copy of Worksheet 15.1 per learner; sheets of plain paper; sheets of squared paper, optional

Estimated time: 30–45 minutes

16 Days and months Bingo

Aim: To improve the recognition and spelling of familiar words

Can be used: from Unit 3 onwards

Activity: Group or class work

Focus: Spelling and recognition of familiar words

Materials: One copy of Worksheets 16.1 and 16.2 per group of five, cut up into cards

Estimated time: 20–30 minutes

17 Email addresses

Aim: To enable learners to exchange email addresses

Can be used: from Unit 9 onwards

Activity: Pair work

Focus: Reviewing and practicing the alphabet; dictating and writing

Materials: One copy of Worksheet 17.1 per pair, cut into A and B sections; one copy of Worksheet 17.2 per pair cut into 'cards'; one copy of Worksheet 17.3 per pair, and one copy cut up so that there is one address per learner

Estimated time: 30–40 minutes

18 Buddhi and Ikuko

Aim: To extract information from a short text and complete a form

Can be used: from Unit 10 onwards

Activity: Pair work

Focus: Reading and extracting information to present in a different form

Materials: One copy of Worksheets 18.1 or 18.2 per pair, cut into sections; one copy of Worksheet 18.3 per learner

Estimated time: 30–40 minutes

EXPLORING
SHIPWRECKS

EXPLORING
SHIPWRECKS

KEITH MORRIS · PETER ROWLANDS

WINDWARD

Executive Managers Kelly Flynn
Susan Egerton-Jones
Designer Ruth Levy
Editor Barbara Segal
Production Peter Phillips
Barbara Hind

This edition published 1987 by WINDWARD
an imprint owned by W.H. Smith & Son Limited
Registered No 237811 England Trading as WHS Distributors
St John's House, East Street, Leicester LE1 6NE

Devised and researched by Keith H. Morris
Written by Peter Rowlands
Edited and designed by the Artists House Division
of Mitchell Beazley International Ltd.
Artists House
14–15 Manette Street
London W1V 5LB

"An Artists House Book"
© Mitchell Beazley Publishers 1988
Text © Keith Morris and Peter Rowlands 1988

ISBN 0 7112 0503 5

Typeset by Hourds Typographica, Stafford
Reproduction by La Cromolito s.n.c., Milan
Printed in Portugal by Printer Portuguesa Grafica Lda

The joint authors of **Exploring Shipwrecks** would like to
express their personal thanks to the following for their
generous advice and contributions:
Geoff Barker, Michael Mensun Bound, Collins and Chambers
Ltd, Alec Double, Patricia Hipwood, Jack Jackson,
Terry Kruger, Bill Lewis, Amanda Ludlow, Tony Marshall,
Clare Morris, Layla and Lee Morris, Lorraine O'Malley,
Oxford University Shipwreck Trust, Jane Rowlands,
Peter Sieniewicz, Reg Vallintine, Virgin Islands Tourist
Board, Joanna Yellowlees.

CONTENTS

INTRODUCTION

by Reg Vallintine

Few words stimulate the imagination as much as "shipwreck". Down the ages echo the desperate cries of seamen and passengers, trapped in a threatened ship amid wild and breaking seas. Those who have seen the death of a ship are held irresistibly by the sight and the memories never leave them.

For divers today, however, the mention of a wreck brings visions of swimming along companionways inhabited by fish, delving into cabins and over bridges where once humans trod, and above all it brings thoughts of treasure.

For the marine archaeologist, wrecks are "time capsules" in which a moment of time can be preserved in a way that can never happen above the surface. The contents of a seaman's pocket on the *Mary Rose* lie preserved in the silt of the Solent illuminating a lifestyle centuries old; and a tiny fragile oil jug links us directly to the Etruscans and a civilization which existed long before Rome.

For the marine biologist, wrecks are natural laboratories, providing homes for millions of tiny animals and plants which in turn attract thousands of others that graze and prey on them. The sight of the *James Egan Layne* lying on a sand bottom off Plymouth, covered with a carpet of plumose anemones and dead-men's fingers, is never forgotten.

Finally, for the underwater photographer, wrecks provide a dramatic challenge to his techniques and equipment in capturing both the mystery and excitement that he feels, while at the same time recording it all in photographs and on film.

The Eternal Quest

For many centuries, wrecks have provided a profitable source of income to divers searching for cargo or guns, and salvors have sometimes become rich beyond their wildest dreams. Before the birth of Christ, divers in the Levant were employed in the business of bringing up valuables from wrecks. They were paid a percentage of the value which increased with the depth of the wreck.

Since that time, ingenious inventors have produced designs and "machines" to allow man to stay under-

(Right) Personal effects from The Mary Rose that give an insight into life in Tudor times.
(Top, far right) An Etruscan pot saved from one of the oldest shipwrecks in the world.
(Below, far right) Marine plants such as large plumose anemones favour wrecks lying in temperate waters.

water. In 1531 a small portable diving bell, invented by a local man called Lorena, was used to try to raise the Emperor Caligula's pleasure galleys that had lain at the bottom of Lake Nemi in Italy for a thousand years. The bell covered the top half of a man's body and his hands could be used under the rim. By 1658 an improved version of the diving bell was being used down to a depth of 35 metres (110 feet) to recover cannon off Gothenburg, and in early, futile attempts to salvage the Swedish warship *Wasa*, a ship that eventually was raised successfully in 1961. A larger bell that could accommodate several divers was used in 1665 on the famous Tobermory treasure galleon in Scotland recovering several cannons. One of the most successful treasure hunters to use a bell was William Phipps, who, in 1685, brought up treasure worth several millions from a Spanish galleon sunk off Cuba.

The 18th century astronomer, Edmund Halley, recognized and studied the problem of foul air in diving bells; and he came up with a design in which the air could be repurified from barrels sent down from the surface, and by which divers could also work away from the bell for short periods by breathing air through tubes.

The father of diving was John Lethbridge of Newton Abbot in Devon who designed his own apparatus in 1715. He built a tube in which he could lie protected from the water pressure, and look through a small glass window, his hands hanging out of the bottom through two specially insulated holes. He had to be pulled up at intervals so that his assistant could renew the air. Lethbridge could not go deeper than 20 metres (60 feet) because of the water pressure on his arms, but his "machine" worked well and his dream of recovering treasure came true as he travelled the world for the Dutch East India Company.

By 1750 the first, primitive diving helmets were being used. These were usually made of brass with the diver wearing a leather dress. The main problem was water pressure – an atmosphere every 10 metres (30 feet) – which made it difficult to breathe unless the air was fed to the diver at the same pressure.

Two other Englishmen, John and William Braithwaite, designed a special helmet to work on the sunken *Earl of Abergavenny* and they successfully recovered £75,000 in dollar coins from a depth of 20 metres (60 feet). The best helmet, however, was developed by John Deane of Whitstable in Kent. Its use became standard for the next 150 years, and originally it had two large round windows and was fixed to a watertight dress, but Deane improved it further during his 40 years of diving when he worked the wrecks of both the *Mary Rose* and the *Royal George* in the Solent. He was so fascinated by

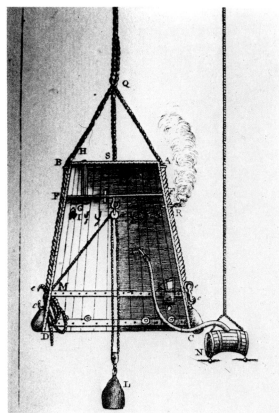

(Far left) One of the first divers' helmets was this strange bell-shaped arrangement of leather and metal.
(Left) Edmund Halley's bell was supplied with air pumped down from a fire engine. The basic principle behind these diving bells still operates today, even in the commercial diving world.

his discoveries that he made careful sketches of the artifacts recovered, thus making a pioneering contribution to the science of underwater archaeology.

The use of "free" diving apparatus, whereby the diver is independent of air tubes to the surface, dates from the middle of the 19th century. William James in England, and Charles Condert in America both came up with designs which featured compressed air held in a metal reservoir fixed round the diver's waist. A variation on this design came from France and was called the "Aerophore", and in this case a small metal cannister was carried on the diver's back containing air at a pressure of 40 atmospheres. Rouquayrol and Denayrouze, the inventors, also introduced a "demand valve", or "regulator" whereby the pressure of the air could be adjusted to that of the surrounding water by the diver. The equipment proved successful, and Jules Verne equipped Captain Nemo and his crew with an "improved version" in *20,000 Leagues Under the Sea*.

Gradually cylinders were developed that could hold higher pressures of air and by 1900 another Frenchman, Louis Bouton, had a compressed air breathing set with two cylinders holding air at nearly 200 atmospheres pressure.

Much of the development of the present day aqualung or SCUBA (Self-contained underwater breathing apparatus) has taken place in France. Yves Le Prieur evolved an apparatus in which the air cylinders were attached to the diver's back and air fed to a full face mask instead of goggles, and he was a founder of the first diving club in Paris in 1935 using the new equipment. His apparatus was not perfect of course; much of the air was wasted, and the pressure still had to be adjusted manually. In 1939, Georges Commeinhes produced the first fully automatic aqualung with a demand valve mounted between the diver's shoulder blades, and Jacques Cousteau, with engineer Emile Gagnan, produced the final version of it which is used by millions of amateur divers today.

Diving clubs, schools and organizations proliferated in the years after the war and amateur divers became the "eyes under the sea" reporting to scientists, biologists and archaeologists. Inevitably, many of these land-bound experts learnt to dive themselves, and their arrival underwater spawned several important diving techniques as well as major scientific discoveries.

Photography

Back in 1856, a William Thompson had taken the World's first underwater photographs off the

(Far right) Diving suits developed from diving bells and were advertised in the Illustrated London News *on November 24th 1855. (Above) A contemporary illustration etched on a silver cup shows John Lethbridge, his diving boat, crew and barrel.*

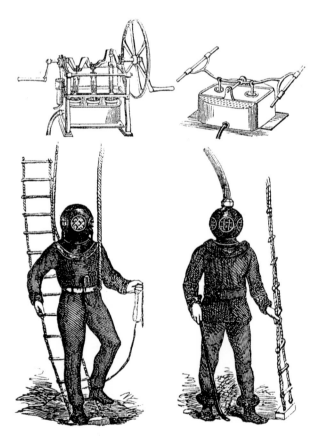

Weymouth coast in Britain. His leaking camera recorded a dim image of sand and seaweed. Then in 1893 the Frenchman, Louis Bouton, used a wet plate camera sealed in a copper housing. It weighed 400lbs underwater and, using a diving helmet, Bouton produced the first underwater flash photographs.

By the 1950s diving biologists, using cameras, had discovered many kinds of nudibranchs or sea slugs unknown when the only means of discovering them had been the net or the line. Underwater photography became not only an important scientific and strategic operation, but a popular pastime, and now fully amphibious and very sophisticated cameras are available, and photographs and films have introduced the underwater world to millions.

History Under the Seas

Underwater archaeology is now a recognized science. The pioneer in this field was George Bass of the University of Pennsylvania, who was the first to excavate ancient wrecks in the Mediterranean to the high standards of land archaeology. The work on the *Mary Rose* achieved worldwide publicity, but that extraordinary underwater excavation was only possible because of the contribution of hundreds of amateur divers who helped the archaeologists with the excavation and survey.

The Dream comes true

The aqualung has given a new lease of life and new hopes of great fortunes to the modern treasure hunter. Mel Fisher, for instance, spent 16 years of patient research and searching in the Florida Keys. Quite recently he discovered the wreck of the Spanish galleon *Atocha*, and he found the cargo too: gold and emeralds worth four hundred million dollars.

The wrecks covered in this book range in time from the Etruscan cargo ship of 600 BC to the *Umbria* and other casualties of World War 2. Locations range from the Mediterranean to the Pacific and from the Great Lakes to Bermuda – seven of the greatest shipwrecks explored by amateur divers. Some, such as the Etruscan wreck, have given us new knowledge of the past. Others, such as the *Umbria* and the *Rhone*, are unique because they are so perfectly preserved and are inhabited by rich sea life. Some have tragic histories, the *Royal Oak* and the Japanese wrecks of Truk Lagoon. Their stories are fascinating enough, but the photographs bring these relics of human endeavour and disaster back to life.

(Far left) *This old print shows hard hat divers retrieving the cargo from a recently sunken ship and ignoring the bodies of those who drowned.*
(Left) *The marine world boasts hundreds of types of nudibranchs. Most of them are brightly coloured.*

WRECK SITES

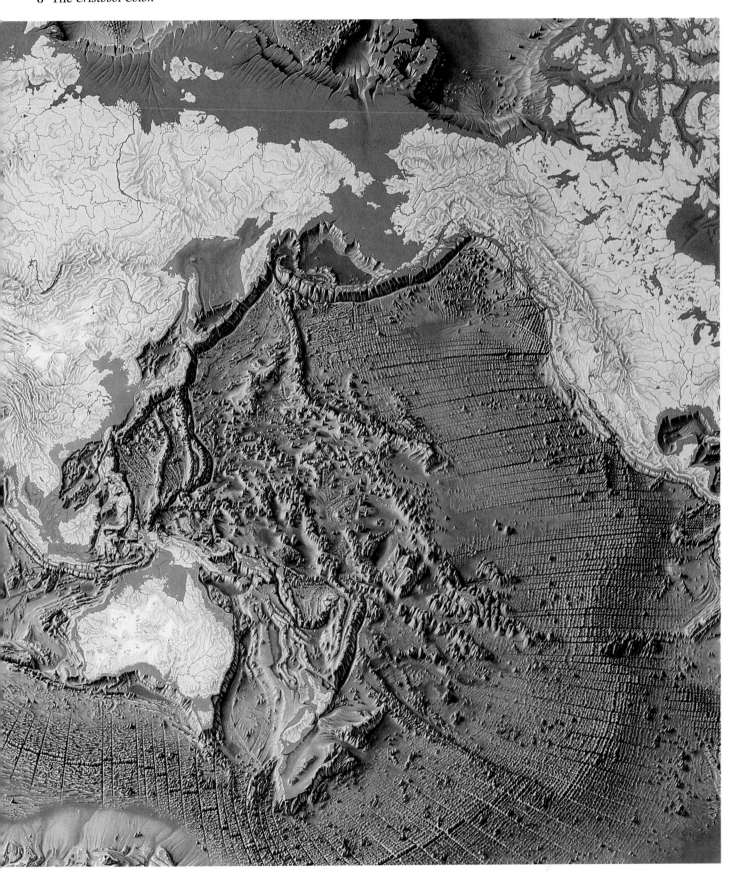

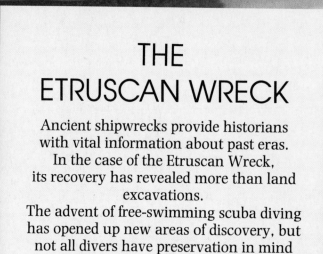

THE ETRUSCAN WRECK

Ancient shipwrecks provide historians
with vital information about past eras.
In the case of the Etruscan Wreck,
its recovery has revealed more than land
excavations.
The advent of free-swimming scuba diving
has opened up new areas of discovery, but
not all divers have preservation in mind
and rapid recovery is needed to safeguard
the ancient and valuable remains.

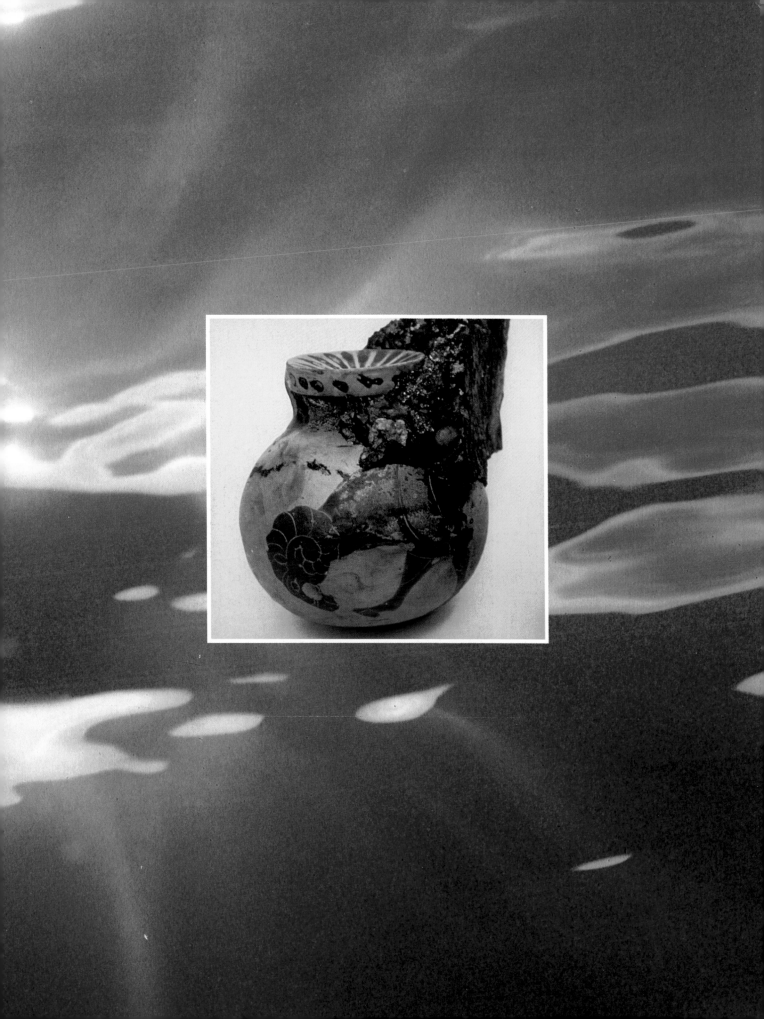

The first task of a wreckhunter, through often long and arduous research, is to pinpoint the location of a wreck and then to collect enough evidence to identify it. Hours, days, weeks and often months can be spent ploughing through old manuscripts which give copious, but possibly confusing details of ancient cargoes and of the ships which carried them.

For most divers, the object of their work lies on or under the seabed, undisturbed and undiscovered for centuries. Such locations can have two effects on the wreck. Either the relentless movements of the sea gradually reduces it to a heap of fragmented remains or the marine covering that colonizes it can actually preserve the ship, saving it in a submarine time capsule. In most cases, historic wrecks are first discovered through painstaking research on dry land. Divers only enter the water after the research team has established the most likely site. The more fortunate teams make significant discoveries within the first few dives. For those less fortunate, diving continuously for days and weeks may not produce anything of significance. Such lack of results could lead to the cancellation of a project, an event that could damage the morale and future capability of the team.

Vital clues

Modern technology has provided marine wreck researchers with the means to stay underwater for long periods of time (such periods being limited more by human endurance than equipment). This is achieved by using a breathing apparatus, the aqualung. Since its invention in 1948 it has enabled millions of humans to sample and become, however briefly, part of the underwater world. The interest and activities of so many amateurs has, in many cases, reversed the way discoveries are made. Instead of researching and then diving, they dive first and then, when they surface with man-made artefacts, set about identifying them. However, such advantage in mobility and exploration can, and often does, have negative repercussions.

Such problems have beset a wreck

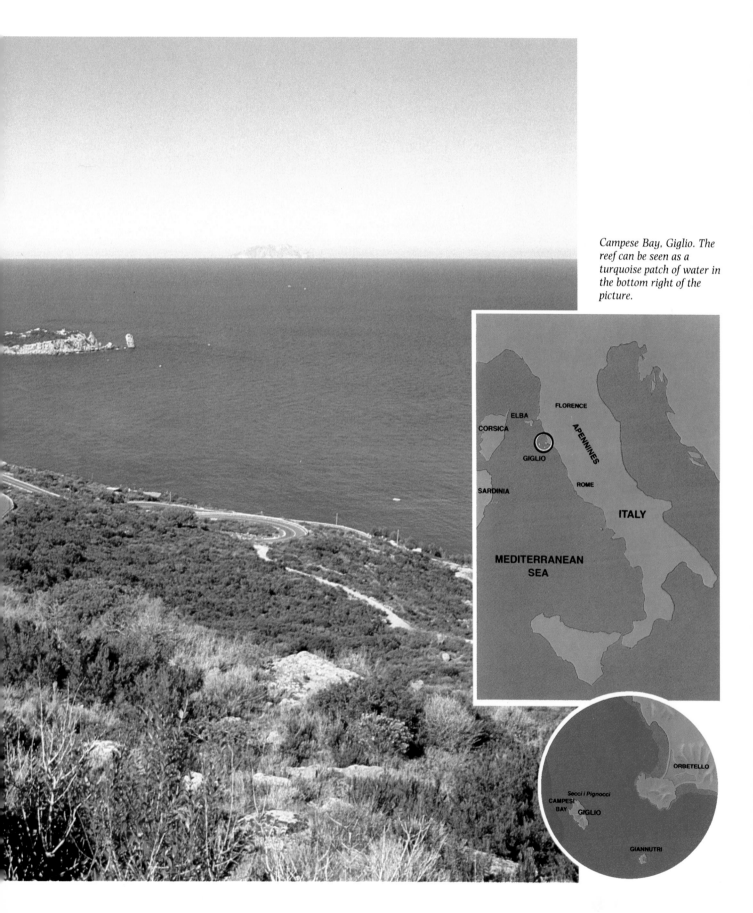

Campese Bay, Giglio. The reef can be seen as a turquoise patch of water in the bottom right of the picture.

which was discovered by chance over 25 years ago and is only now recognized as the oldest shipwreck in the world. (It is likely that an even older wreck has since been discovered.) This particular wrecksite has been robbed of some of its most precious and historically vital clues by amateur divers, driven by tales of underwater booty and treasure chests. To an individual diver a single small vase is simply a trophy destined to become a conversation piece on a mantlepiece: to the serious marine researcher it may well provide the vital link in the long chain of clues needed to identify the site.

Today, the site of this ancient wreck, off Giglio island, is a protected reserve. Controlled scientific excavations are taking place around it to unearth new knowledge about an era of which so little is known, the Etruscan era.

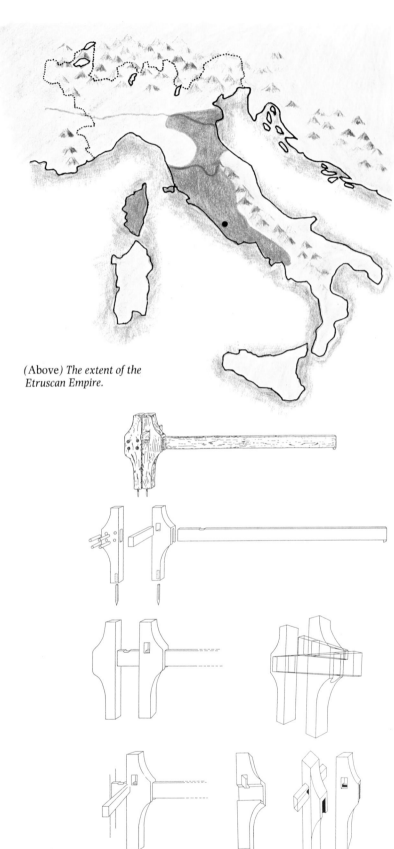

(Above) *The extent of the Etruscan Empire.*

(Above) *An Etruscan earing from between 400 and 250 BC.*

(Above) *Callipers found under concretion in 1985.*

Etruscan times

Despite claims that theirs was the earliest culture to write, the Etruscans have left little written evidence to give us an insight into their era. What we now know has been collated from archaeological finds.

The Etruscans lived in the area between the Tiber and Arno in northern Italy. Their land was very fertile and supported rich crops that created their trading surplus. With the sea to the west and the Apennines inland, they were protected and able to flourish. Their efforts brought a great deal of wealth to the area and enabled them to purchase quality goods from the established civilizations of Egypt and Greece. Members of a strong and informed society provided Rome and her empire with the first three generations of kings. The Etruscans could therefore claim to be the founders of the Roman empire and it is certain they were the purveyors of taste and style now associated with the Romans. Evidence uncovered in recent decades shows that the Etruscans enjoyed a high quality of life, with sports and artistic entertainment playing an important part.

The work on Giglio is of such importance that from now on anybody wishing to study the Etruscans would be well advised to study the remains of the excavation. Such work being a tribute to the determination of Mensun Bound and the tireless efforts of a widely differing group of people — academics and divers, professionals and amateurs — who for four years from 1982 to 1986 undertook a major and difficult project which has certainly advanced historical learning.

The importance of such work led to the formation of the Oxford University Maritime Archaeology Research Group, MARE, to continue the study and excavation of wrecks from antiquity.

(Above) *A panel of an alabaster cinerary urn showing horseman, musicians and a sacrificial sheep.*
(Left) *Sarcophagus of seianti Thanunia Tlesnasa.*

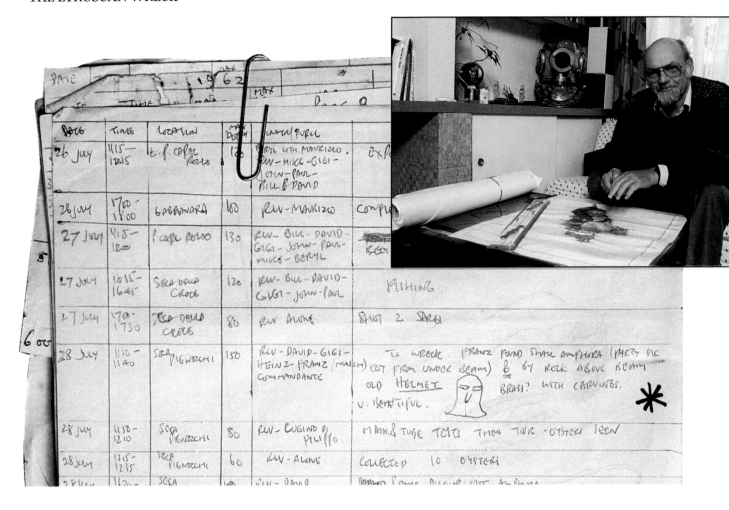

The discovery

Encouraged by the boom in air travel and financed by a cash-rich society, the diving world in the early 1960s experienced a pioneering explosion, the effects of which were felt both above and below the waterline. Without realising the consequences, if any, of his actions, intent only on making a living from his hobby, Reg Vallintine, a member of the diving fraternity, left his native London to set up one of the first diving schools abroad. He hoped that the warm climate and clear waters of the Mediterranean island of Giglio, just off the west coast of Italy would attract divers to his school as a holiday venue.

Fortunately for wreck researchers, Reg logged his dives meticulously, even though he made repeated dives each day to sites with which he was totally familiar. On 2 August 1961 he logged yet another dive taking a group down into the deeper waters off Campese Bay. His party consisted of photographers and spearfishermen, all looking for their

(Above) *Reg Vallintine at home in London with his log book from his days as a dive guide in Giglio.*

(Left) *The first item raised from the wreck. On the dive during which the wreck was found in 1961, Reg Vallintine had with him another diver called Beryl Boomshooft who slipped this into her pouch. They afterwards decided it was an Etruscan doorknob! Beryl kindly gave this vase to the excavating team, and now it is back with all the other materials in Florence.*

(Near left) *Of all the items that Reg Vallintine raised in 1961, and which he hoped would be the core of a new museum collection, only two copper ingots survived. They were refound by the team in an old storage room.*
(Left) *Draughtsman, Mike Wright, drawing one of the ingots. Rich metal deposits first attracted other nations of the Mediterranean to Etruria.*
(Centre) *Reg Vallintine and Mensun Bound.*
(Below) *This Etruscan handle was spotted by Mensun Bound in a private collection in England.*

own forms of underwater booty. High on both of their lists would be Grouper — large fish with menacing looks but harmless to man. These fish grow up to 2 metres (6 feet) and were plentiful in the Mediterranean before the advent of snorkelling and then scuba diving spearfishermen.

On this particular dive around a submarine island known as *Secci i Pignocchi*, Reg and his diving party came across a large grouper which seemed to be guarding the entrance to a cave. It was in this area 40 – 50 metres (150 feet) down, that the group found interesting remains and shapes in the sandy seabed.

As word of the wreck spread, the site fast became a client-drawing attraction for Reg. However, despite his need to earn a living, he became increasingly concerned by the amount of individual "souvenir collecting" each time he took divers to the site. He tried to interest the local authorities in starting a small museum but, although the support was there, it was not as widespread as he had hoped. Archaeologists on the island were also indifferent. After a few years Reg left the island and returned to London to continue his career in diving, eventually to become the Chairman of the British Sub Aqua Club.

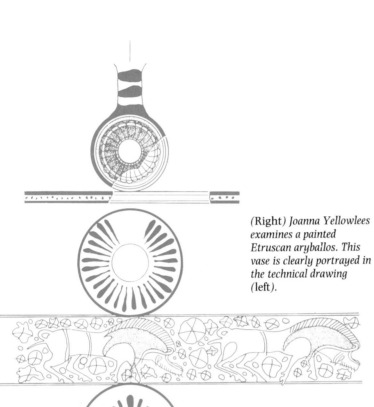

(Right) Joanna Yellowlees examines a painted Etruscan aryballos. This vase is clearly portrayed in the technical drawing (left).

Divers no longer visited the site and, for a time, its existence was almost forgotten. New historic shipwrecks, such as the *Mary Rose* in the English Channel were in the headlines. To marine archaeologists this was an ideal opportunity to examine closely aspects of Tudor England, an era when maritime skills were the foundation of the country's widespread power. Investment potential encouraged by Royal patronage, together with the evocative and romantic history of the wreck, created worldwide interest in the *Mary Rose*. It was inevitable that Reg Vallintine would sooner, or later meet an Oxford don, Michael Mensun Bound.

Mensun's consuming interest in marine archaeology drove him to locate and arrange a meeting with Alexander McKee, the first person to find the *Mary Rose*. Mensun wanted to talk about preserving wrecks in general and, in particular, to learn whether the experience gained on the *Mary Rose* might help him in his project to preserve wrecks off the Falklands Islands.

During his first visit to McKee's house, Mensun Bound noticed a piece of rough pottery in the shape of a handle. Alexander had found the artefact while diving with Reg Vallintine in 1963. Mensun was fascinated, and his knowledge of such artefacts led him to believe that this piece dated back to Etruscan times. McKee put Mensun in touch with Reg and the first of many meetings was set up to discuss the Mediterranean site of Giglio and its potential. Mensun was convinced that this wreck held information which would fill in the considerable gaps in our knowledge of the era prior to Roman dominance, over 2,500 years ago.

One of the major problems was that over the years visiting divers had removed many items from the site. Now scattered across the world, it would be necessary to trace these to identify and date the wreck. The existence of these artefacts and their authentication would raise the credibility of fundraising schemes to finance a formal excavation of the site, and would also, convince the Italian authorities.

The research

Undaunted by the enormity of the task, Mensun and his companion Joanna Yellowlees set about locating some of the removed pieces. Their only pieces of evidence were Reg's notes and three old photographs of some of the finds and their new owners before they left the site for good.

Of particular interest was a vase whose existence would establish the wreck's date to within the 20 years between 610 BC and 590 BC. Initially, the whereabouts of this all important vase eluded them, but, after detailed studies of Reg's notes, the owner was tracked to Monte Carlo. Having changed her name twice in the inter-vening years she was hard to find. When she was located, the study of the vital vase revealed that it was made of yellow clay and painted with a chequered band. Other decorations confirmed a date of close to 600 BC for the wreck. It was the vital evidence they needed to attract the finance necessary for serious underwater exploration to get underway.

(Left) This little amphora from the Greek Island of Samos was found in an apartment off Harley Street in London. (Below) The first item uncovered when the wreck site was refound was the top of a large iron concretion with an Etruscan amphora handle – later stolen – on it.

Rediscovery

To the newly formed team the few remains which they had located on land, together with Reg's photographs, suggested that they had found the oldest shipwreck in the world. However, their own interest and enthusiasm was not shared by any potential financiers. For some time they had difficulty find-ing outside help. Then, through the co-operation of Professor John Boardman, a classical archaeologist, Mensun and his team secured the backing of Oxford University. It was the support they so badly needed if the project was to have a chance of success.

Eventually, the "Giglio Project" was formed under the wing of the University and the World Ship Trust, an organiza-tion set up by Prince Philip some years previously to preserve ships all over the world. Reg was offered the post of Chief Diver which he excitedly accepted as it would lead him back to the area he had enjoyed so many years ago.

For Reg it was to be a nerve-racking time as he dived again and again in the once familiar area without finding the site. It is surprising how the mind plays tricks with the imagination especially

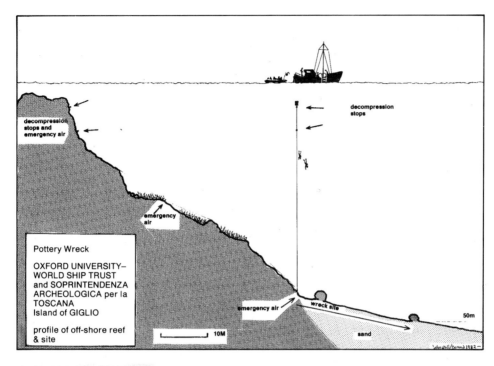

Pottery Wreck

OXFORD UNIVERSITY–
WORLD SHIP TRUST
and SOPRINTENDENZA
ARCHEOLOGICA per la
TOSCANA
Island of GIGLIO

profile of off-shore reef
& site

*(Opposite) Divers
decompressing under the
boats. A waterdredge sits
in a sling waiting to be
lowered.*
*(Centre) The excavation
team's boats in position
over the site.*
*(Left) Section of the reef
showing how the site was
excavated.*

when you are being relied upon to relocate a site you last visited underwater over 20 years ago. He only had a few days with the team and, in true pioneering fashion, it was not until one of the last days that the site was found again. They were unable to establish good bearings and spent a fraught few days after Reg's departure trying to find the wreck again! Eventually they did, using a metal detector which revealed a large iron concretion on which an Etruscan amphora handle adhered. A short

distance away, Mensun found a small vase used for carrying oil or perfume. Having rediscovered the wreck, sensibly, they now buoyed it.

However, it was to be these buoys that would not only help the archaeological team but would also pinpoint the site for the groups of souvenir hunters who would soon gather in the area.

Diving on the Etruscan wreck

In the warm shallow waters of the Mediterranean, divers do not have to wear restricting wetsuits as the temperatures are so high that a tee-shirt is enough protection from the cold. Go deeper, as the divers on this site had to, and you will experience a strange underwater phenomenon known as a thermocline where the much colder water from the depths meets the sun-warmed shallower water. This meeting of the waters is clearly visible. The colder water is much clearer and has a shimmering quality not dissimilar to mirages seen on hot days on land.

For the diver, the impressive visual appearance of a thermocline is spoilt by the sudden drop in water temperature which it represents. The drop can be as much as 10 degrees so if you are to stay

for any length of time below the thermocline full wetsuits are essential. As if the colder water was not enough to contend with, the greater part of the wrecksite lies in 50 metres (150 feet) of water where the effects of breathing air at such pressure cause temporary narcosis. At this depth, "the narcs", as it is known, can cause a sense of panic and fear which can induce a diver to endanger or even attack his diving companions, or a heady euphoria encouraging him to go deeper and even remove his mouthpiece. However, with acclimatized divers under proper supervision, this should never happen. Jacques Cousteau is credited with calling this effect "Raptures of the deep".

A diver's time at such a depth is strictly limited. In order to avoid decompression, you would only be able to spend around seven minutes at such a depth before having to make for the surface. Longer bottom time results in long periods of decompression (hanging midwater in the shallows waiting for the absorbed gases to dissipate from the bloodstream without forming minute circulation- stopping bubbles).

Descending slowly down into the deep blue Mediterranean water through the thermocline and past 20 metres (60 feet), your time underwater becomes as

23

much a recording exercise as a dive. You have to time your dive accurately to make sure you don't stay too long and, at the same time, you have to keep a check on your air supply so that, if you do intend to decompress, you will have enough air to allow this.

In shallow water, it is normal diving practice to make for the surface when your cylinder is down to 50 atmospheres (most tanks start with at least 200 atmospheres when full) but with such a deep dive where decompression is planned, this figure would normally be increased to 60 to 80 atmospheres for sensible safety. It is for this reason that divers working on such a project have to be sufficiently experienced that these considerations and calculations become second nature. They can then go about the main purpose of carrying out the tasks set by the organizers to survey the site.

Still further down, as you dive, the colours and light levels fade; your weight increases as your wetsuit compresses under the water pressure and all sound distorts, muted by the density of the water. You are left with a feeling of intense aloneness, which is both exciting and disturbing. The sensation of diving to depths greater than 30 metres (100 feet) is one of the sport's major, and sometimes fatal, attractions. For some, underwater photography in the bright shallow waters is totally absorbing, but for others the sole purpose of

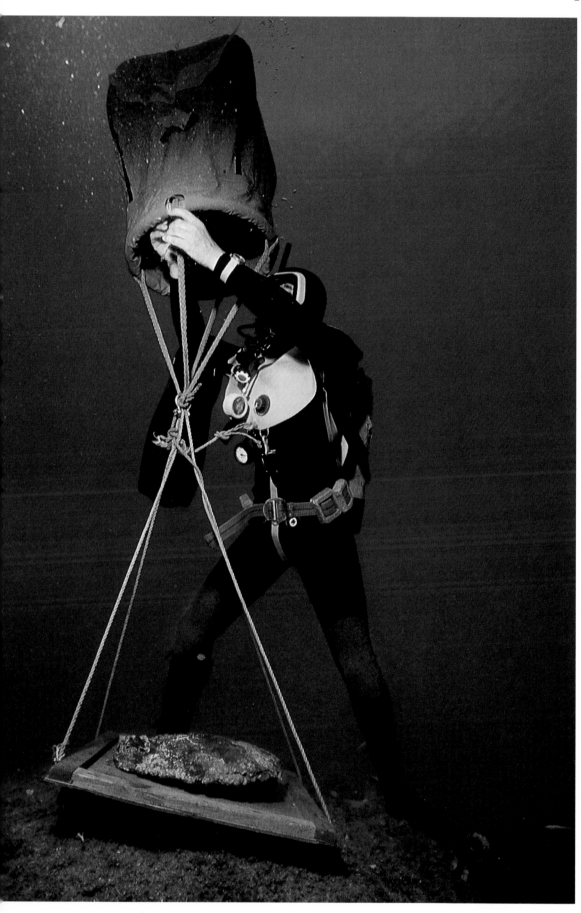

(Far left) *Mensun Bound and Reg Vallintine inspect the ancient remains.*
(Centre) *After working underwater, a diver holds onto the latest find as he decompresses on the reef face.*
(Left) *A lifting bag and tray were used to take heavy objects to the surface.*

diving is to go as deep as possible. The physical limitations of such practices are complicated and personal co-ordination and mental skills become severely reduced. Even for the sport diver, these limitations are relevant but for the marine archaeologist they present a number of problems which restrict the progress that can be made on any one dive.

If the team on the Giglio Project were to make significant progress in such a limited amount of time, they would need many more divers to help them in their work. The academic world of Oxford, and members of the British Sub Aqua Club, responded with a regular supply of visiting divers on site, attracted not by the money, for they had to pay their own way, but by the thought of diving on and helping to unearth the oldest deep ocean vessel known to man at that time.

Such obvious activity attracted the unwanted bounty hunters and early work on the site, and the project itself, was nearly terminated in early 1983 when, under cover of darkness, unofficial divers took down a portable airlift and sucked up large quantities of evidence from the site. An airlift is the most economic and efficient way of uncovering large volumes of sand and small objects from an area. Unfortunately, the airlift cannot distinguish between small rocks and delicate Etruscan vases. It will never be known just how much damage was caused both underwater, and to the research in general, as hundreds of vital pieces — including two intact painted Greek vases — disappeared up the airlift's wide suction tube.

In the days following the raid, archaeologists set about sifting through

the debris and pieced together fragments to give more evidence of the ship's history. The early problems of underwater piracy were eventually terminated with the help of local police and the use of simple radios so the work could be continued under strict control. Undeterred by the events, the serious diving commenced in the summer of 1983 and by the end of the summer of '84, the team had uncovered many important pieces that were then safely lodged with the Museum of Archaeology in Florence.

In order to record such a site and gain the maximum potential, the area must be referenced so that working divers know exactly where they are in relation to the site as a whole. There are several ways of doing this including the most commonly used permanent grid of iron squares, but as this site covered such a large area, it was decided to depart from traditional surveying methods and divide it into smaller areas dictated by the underwater terrain, each with an identifying name — Victor, Whisky, X-ray, Zulu and so on. These areas were then further subdivided for accurate positioning. On top of the need for accuracy, speed was essential to prevent looters removing precious pieces. In this case, a decision had to be taken to contravene traditional archaeological guidelines: to lift as much material as possible, as quickly as possible, and to make sure that artefacts were preserved in safety for study on the surface.

This practice does not meet with widespread approval within the archaeological world, but it has to be remembered that most archaeologists are used to land sites, generally easier to police. Unless a vessel is kept over an

(Far left) One night, looters broke a big wine-mixing crater. The seabed was later sifted and re-sifted. Fragments – such as the one inserted into the tracing below – were collected in plastic containers, and then pieced together jig-saw fashion in "treatment traps" by the team's conservator. The design slowly emerged of little pot-bellied figures dancing over a row of birds and animals.
(Left) To establish the exact location when pieces were found, a grid system was used for reference. The known size of the grid squares gave scale to the artefacts when they were photographed.

underwater site day in, day out, it is difficult to prevent determined looters. Such policing is expensive and not always effective either.

Despite the surface complications, the underwater team began to make several finds which established the identity of the wreck and its original purpose, as well as providing new insight into everyday life over 2,500 years ago. The site, in common with so many ancient wrecks, is difficult to imagine. What the original vessel looked like lying on the seabed with its valuable cargo spilt onto the sand must be kept for the story books, although reconstructions have been done to show her just after sinking. The reality is an unremarkable area of seabed

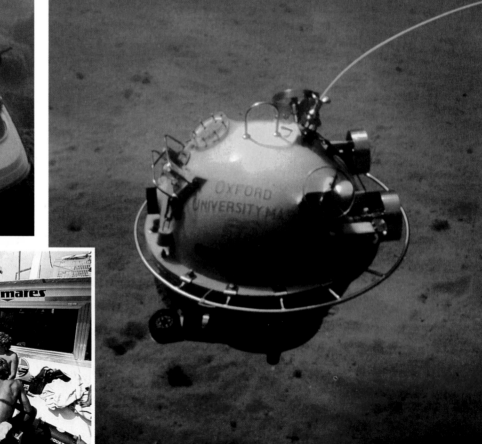

(Left) *Conservator at work in the expedition's "pot" shed sorting fragments brought up from the wreck site.*
(Opposite, top) *The boats at anchor over the site.*
(Opposite, centre left) *End-of-summer flash storms were always a fear. Caught without warning in one such storm, the excavation team's dory was overwhelmed by the sea and sank in seconds.*
(Opposite, bottom left) *On board the expedition's research vessel at Campese Bay in 1986. The recompression chamber at one side is kept there in case a diver suffers a bend.*
(Opposite, bottom right) *The ROV (remote operated vehicle) swimming along underwater.*

(Left) *Some of the team gather outside the derelict building that was home for five years. The sign reads: "Private property – admission prohibited – Beware Dangerous Building".*

(Above) *Divers gather for a break beside the excavation truck – the workhorse that made it all possible.*

where marine growth combines with large rocks and thick layers of sand dotted with fragments and artefacts.

Speedy excavation by an airlift would mean the possible loss of some pieces as it would inevitably break some items. Careful use of machinery was needed to quicken the removal of sand and light covering debris, but at that depth, a water dredge was more controllable. This simple device passes pressured water from the surface which creates a much gentler and more controllable suction on the seabed. The results of this controlled dredging provided a host of small artefacts such as arrow heads, fishing weights and lump-metal money, all of which combined to give the team a more detailed view of Etruscan life.

The treasures

It is often the case that although some finds are dazzlingly glamorous and large, it is the small pieces which give us a true insight into the everyday lives of the ordinary people of the era under scrutiny. A good example was the discovery of olive pips in some of the Etruscan amphora. They confirmed that the vessel was shipping olives and olive oil. But posed the question whether from or to Italy. Olive trees were not recorded in northern Italy until at least a century after this shipwreck was thought to have occurred, but could these pips indicate a much earlier olive industry in Italy? Olive oil was an important commodity used for lighting, cooking and cosmetics.

In the "Victor" area, large quantities of spilled pitch pine were found. This covered the site where it had flowed out

(Above) *An Etruscan amphora full of olive pips; a mound of pips is in the foreground.*
A Greek lamp retrieved from the wreck. The charring on its lip indicates that it would have been used on the ship.

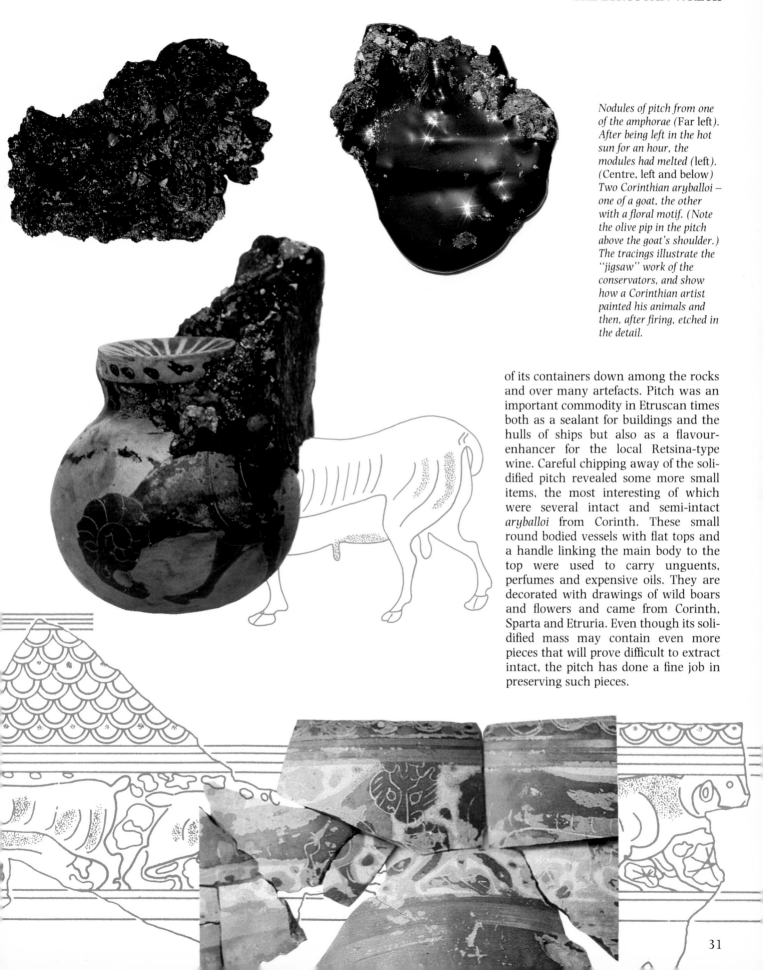

Nodules of pitch from one of the amphorae (Far left). After being left in the hot sun for an hour, the modules had melted (left). (Centre, left and below) Two Corinthian aryballoi – one of a goat, the other with a floral motif. (Note the olive pip in the pitch above the goat's shoulder.) The tracings illustrate the "jigsaw" work of the conservators, and show how a Corinthian artist painted his animals and then, after firing, etched in the detail.

of its containers down among the rocks and over many artefacts. Pitch was an important commodity in Etruscan times both as a sealant for buildings and the hulls of ships but also as a flavour-enhancer for the local Retsina-type wine. Careful chipping away of the solidified pitch revealed some more small items, the most interesting of which were several intact and semi-intact *aryballoi* from Corinth. These small round bodied vessels with flat tops and a handle linking the main body to the top were used to carry unguents, perfumes and expensive oils. They are decorated with drawings of wild boars and flowers and came from Corinth, Sparta and Etruria. Even though its solidified mass may contain even more pieces that will prove difficult to extract intact, the pitch has done a fine job in preserving such pieces.

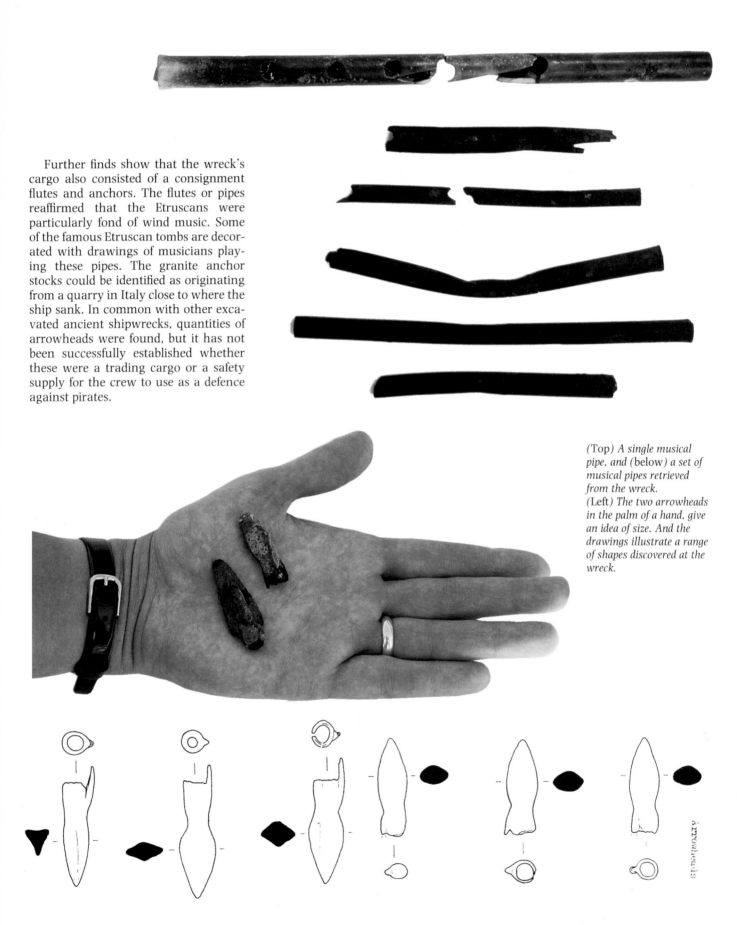

Further finds show that the wreck's cargo also consisted of a consignment flutes and anchors. The flutes or pipes reaffirmed that the Etruscans were particularly fond of wind music. Some of the famous Etruscan tombs are decorated with drawings of musicians playing these pipes. The granite anchor stocks could be identified as originating from a quarry in Italy close to where the ship sank. In common with other excavated ancient shipwrecks, quantities of arrowheads were found, but it has not been successfully established whether these were a trading cargo or a safety supply for the crew to use as a defence against pirates.

(Top) *A single musical pipe, and (below) a set of musical pipes retrieved from the wreck.*
(Left) *The two arrowheads in the palm of a hand, give an idea of size. And the drawings illustrate a range of shapes discovered at the wreck.*

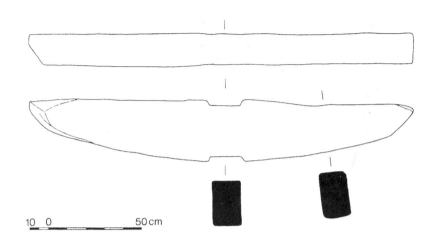

10 0   50 cm

(Left) Some years ago looters were caught raising stone anchor stocks from the site. One still survives in the basement of the local coastguard building. Here we see the team with the stock in the basement.

(Above) A section profile of the stone anchor stock illustrated left.

(Below) Another anchor stock excavated by the team, was first transported into shallow water in a sling under one of the boats, lowered to the seabed, and then simply walked out of the water by a gang of divers.

The most spectacular find to date was a bronze helmet engraved with drawings of boar and snake heads. This was one of the "finds" taken during the years of Reg's diving school by a German diver. Its existence had been logged by Reg but its whereabouts were difficult to trace since the diver had long since returned home. With their usual tenacity, Mensun Bound and Joanna Yellowlees traced the diver who was now in poor health. He had realised the importance of the helmet and kept it in a bank vault. Anxious that it should remain in his care, he did, however, allow Mensun and Joanna to inspect the helmet and take photographs and drawings of it, worn on the head of a model.

Close inspection revealed that his helmet had been shaped from a single piece of bronze, using skills long since forgotten. Even in Etruscan days it would have been considered a valuable item since it was so well made and exquisitely engraved. Despite persistent pleas, the helmet remains in a German bank vault destined only for its owner's eyes, rather than in the public safety of a museum. It is hoped that one day, this piece will be returned to Italy to form the centre piece of the museum exhibit of the wreck.

(Right) This helmet shaped from a single piece of bronze remains the most spectacular find. Its exquisitely engraved detail (facing and below) was clearly evident after cleaning.

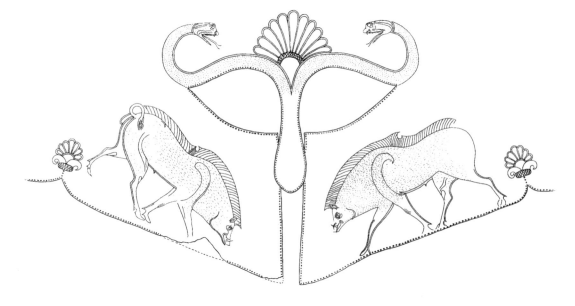

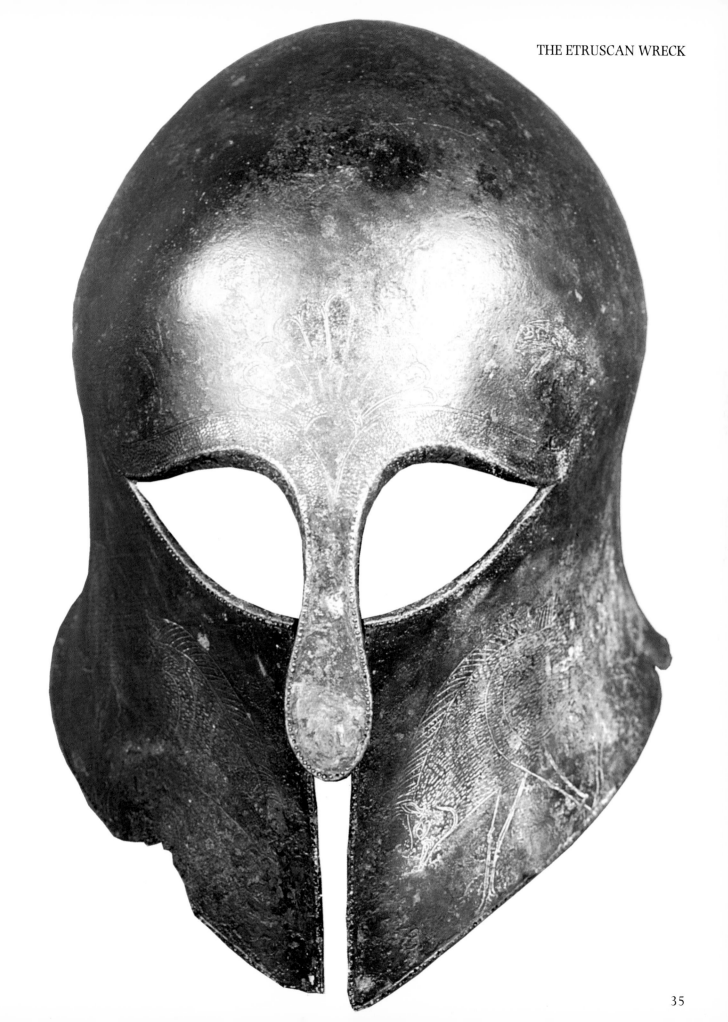

During the summer of 1984, the diving team uncovered a large section of the keel of the ship. Initial studies showed this was either made of pine or oak and, though not of particularly complex construction, it gave the first insight into how the Etruscans joined wood to make it waterproof. In 1985, the keel section was raised in the full glare of cameras and press, and brought ashore in a specially constructed box. Detailed study on land showed that the vessel was of "sewn" construction – the main components having being bonded together with cord.

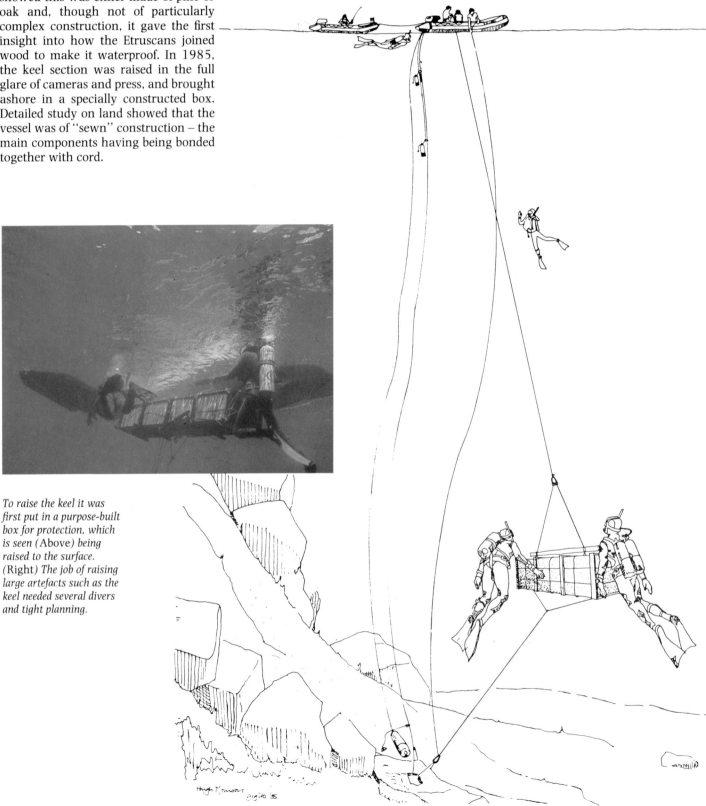

To raise the keel it was first put in a purpose-built box for protection, which is seen (Above) being raised to the surface. (Right) The job of raising large artefacts such as the keel needed several divers and tight planning.

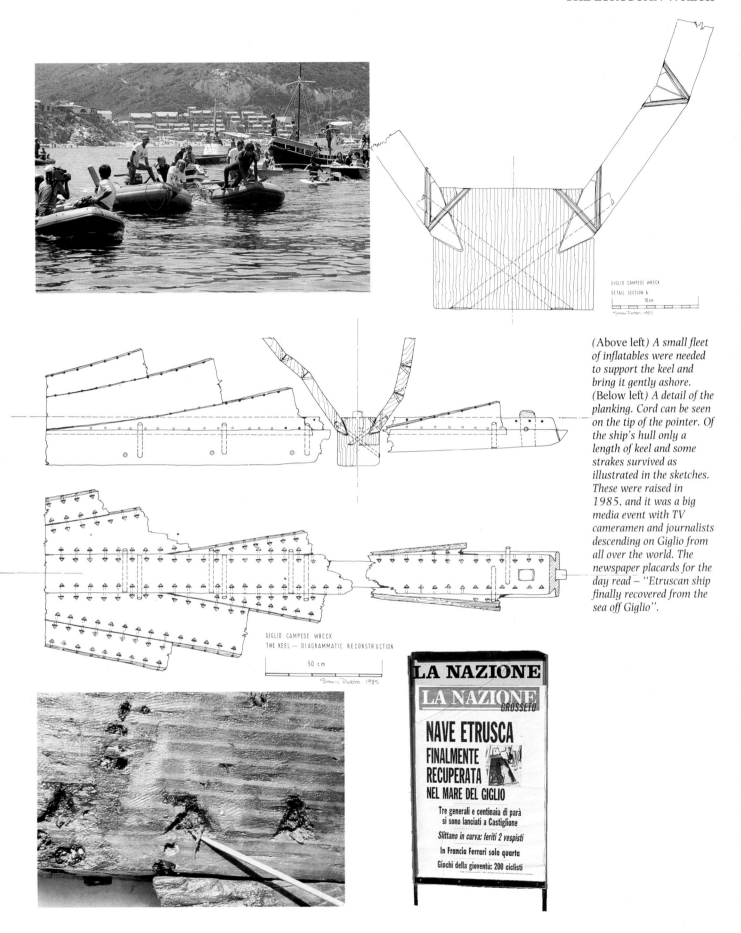

GIGLIO CAMPESE WRECK
DETAIL SECTION A
10 cm
Simon Dobbs 1985

GIGLIO CAMPESE WRECK
THE KEEL — DIAGRAMMATIC RECONSTRUCTION
50 cm
Simon Dobbs 1985

(Above left) A small fleet of inflatables were needed to support the keel and bring it gently ashore. (Below left) A detail of the planking. Cord can be seen on the tip of the pointer. Of the ship's hull only a length of keel and some strakes survived as illustrated in the sketches. These were raised in 1985, and it was a big media event with TV cameramen and journalists descending on Giglio from all over the world. The newspaper placards for the day read – "Etruscan ship finally recovered from the sea off Giglio".

LA NAZIONE
LA NAZIONE GROSSETO
NAVE ETRUSCA
FINALMENTE
RECUPERATA
NEL MARE DEL GIGLIO
Tre generali e centinaia di parà si sono lanciati a Castiglione
Slittano in curva: feriti 2 vespisti
In Francia Ferrari solo quarta
Giochi della gioventù: 200 ciclisti

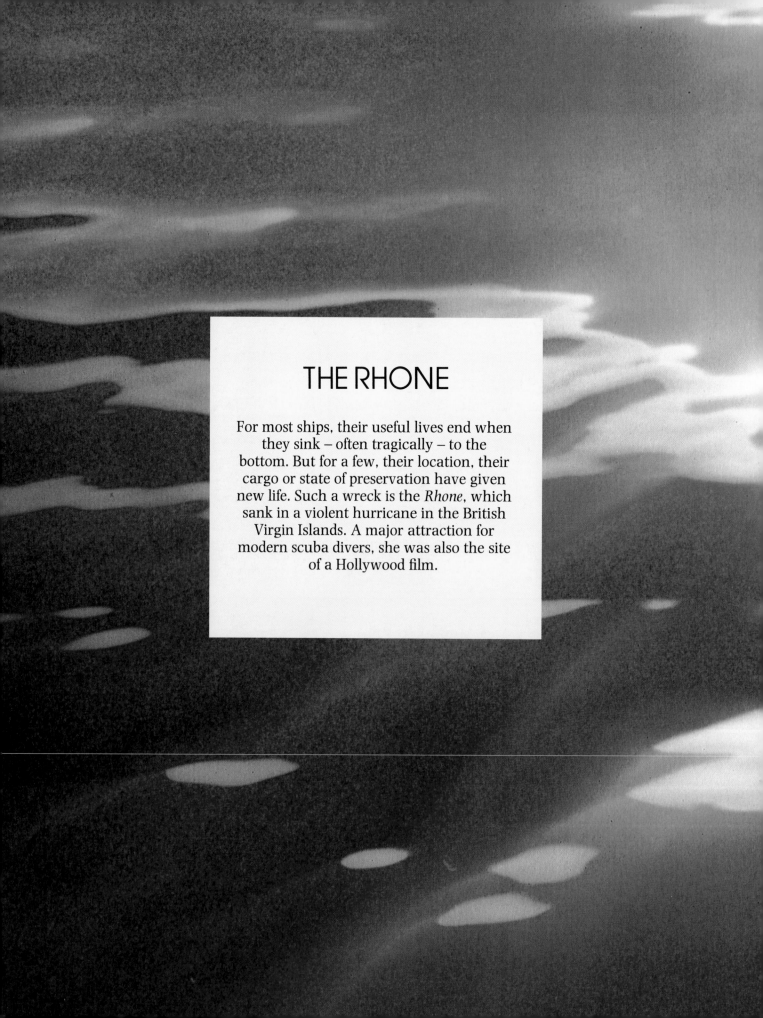

THE RHONE

For most ships, their useful lives end when they sink – often tragically – to the bottom. But for a few, their location, their cargo or state of preservation have given new life. Such a wreck is the *Rhone*, which sank in a violent hurricane in the British Virgin Islands. A major attraction for modern scuba divers, she was also the site of a Hollywood film.

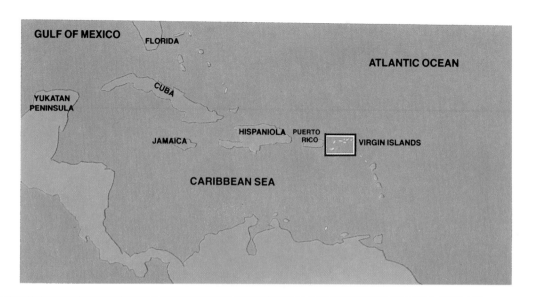

THE ROYAL MAIL STEAM

Built by the Millwall Iron Works, England. Launched February 1865.

Length: 310 feet. Breadth: 40 feet. Displacement: 2738 tons. Accommoda

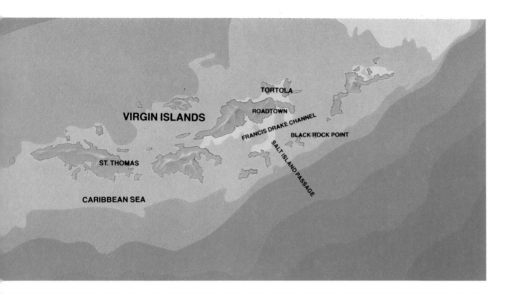

R RHONE

d off Salt Island. October 1867.

253 first. 30 second. 30 third.

© ROGER BURNETT 1981.

Designed & Published by Roger Burnett, P.O. Box 496, East End, British Virgin Islands.

The useful life of a ship ends dramatically when it sinks. It becomes just one more statistic in maritime journals. The memory of the human tragedy fades too. But, underwater, the marine world starts almost instantly to colonize the latest arrival.

There are, however, some instances where the nature of a ship's sinking has brought her more fame than she ever had in her floating career. Such a ship was the Royal Mail Steamship, *Rhone*, whose two year life ended in one of the worst storms ever experienced in the Caribbean. It was a tragic event for the inhabitants of the British Virgin Islands, and indeed it shocked all the Caribbean island communities. However, before the name of the *Rhone* was forgotten, the invention of the aqualung stimulated a sudden resurgence of interest in this particular wrecksite.

Divers, seeing the wreck for the first time, enthused about her location and quality as a wreck dive. The word spread throughout the diving world that the *Rhone* was one of the world's best wrecks. As scuba diving increased in popularity, time has since revealed larger and better wrecks, but the *Rhone* still has a special reputation which has made her more famous now than ever in her working life.

RMS Rhone

RMS *Rhone* was commissioned by the Royal Mail Steam Packet Company and launched in February 1865 to serve as a mail-carrying passenger ship in Caribbean waters. Built by the Millwall Iron

Works of London, she was much admired for her fine lines, two masts, an abundance of sails as well as her coal-fired steam-driven engine. On board, there were 253 first class, 30 second class and 30 third class cabins together with cargo holds for mail. At 310 feet long and 40 feet wide, she weighed 2,738 registered tons and was capable of 18 knots to speed her from Southampton to South America (with a stopover at St Thomas in the Caribbean US Virgin Islands to take on more coal).

St Thomas was a fast expanding sea port catering for the pioneering packet companies who traded between England and America. In the mid 1800s, however, a scourge of yellow fever swept St Thomas causing visiting ships to transfer to the smaller port of Roadtown, capital of the British Virgin Islands. This smaller harbour had not experienced such rapid expansion but provided sheltered anchorages and easy access to the main shipping channels.

The hurricane

RMS *Rhone* set sail from Southampton on 2 October 1867 and arrived in the British Virgin Islands with a full complement of passengers and loaded with mail. She anchored outside Great Harbour, Peter Island, just across the main channel from Roadtown to offload passengers and take on cargo, fuel and

The usually calm, warm waters of the Caribbean can become a sea of boiling turbulence when hurricane-force winds blow. Such winds are fortunately rare but, when they do occur, the results are often tragic.
(Inset) The nearer to land the more turbulent will be the waters. Here, Black Rock Point looks safe on a calm day but, on the night RMS Rhone sank, it would have been a mountain of foaming spray and raging waves.

new passengers for the return trip to England. She was under the command of Captain Wooley who had anchored her alongside RMS *Conway*, her sister ship, under Captain Hammock. Neither captain expected a hurricane as the season was over. They assumed that a sudden fall in barometric pressure was the signal of a wind arriving from the north. As such a wind would make them dangerously exposed, they decided to head for the shelter of Roadtown Harbour, protected by hills to the north. As a further safety measure, non-swimming passengers were transferred from the *Conway* to be strapped to bunks on the "safer" RMS *Rhone*.

At 11 am, and before they could move, the barometer again fell steeply and a strong wind blew up from the northwest. For an hour, the speed of the wind increased by the minute until it reached hurricane proportions and forced both ships to face the storm with engines running at full power. Any mechanical problems now would have allowed the wind to drive them onto the rocks of Peter Island. After an anxious hour, the wind died down sufficiently for both ships to head for the safety of Roadtown. The *Conway* managed to complete the journey despite losing her funnel and some of her rigging but the *Rhone* snagged her 3,000 lb (1,360 kg) anchor and was forced to abandon it with 300 feet (91 m) of chain. Wooley decided now that the only chance of survival was to head for open water through Salt Island Passage in the hope that they could weather out the renewing hurricane in deeper water away from land.

With the engines steamed up to provide maximum pressure and revolutions, the *Rhone* again battled against the hurricane — which had now altered course completely and was blowing from the southeast. Salt Island Passage was a mass of boiling, foam-covered water, visibility was severely reduced and then, just as open water seemed a possibility, the *Rhone* was hit by an even stronger blast of wind which forced her onto Black Rock Point, the westernmost tip of Salt Island. Her superheated boilers exploded as they were flooded by the cool Caribbean waters. The *Rhone* broke in two and sank instantly in 25 metres (82 feet) of water.

Twenty-three crew members, some of whom were not rescued from the water until the following day, and one passenger, an Italian, survived. It is believed that, of the 173 who died, most were killed by the exploding boilers and the rest were dashed onto the rocks of Salt Island or faced the sharks known to frequent the normally crystal clear and calm waters. The bodies that were washed ashore were buried in shallow graves, covered in the same razor-sharp coral against which the *Rhone's* iron hull had crumpled on impact.

The ferocity of the hurricane caused havoc to the surrounding islands where over 500 lives were lost and as many as 75 vessels foundered on the rocks or sank at sea. The tragedy had another effect — although not so immediately dramatic — the island lost its reputation as a safe stopover anchorage.

Throughout the Caribbean Islands, the hurricane had brought widespread devastation. Only 18 houses remained on the mainland of Tortola while in Kingston, Jamaica, only four of the original 80 houses still stood.

As the days passed and the hurricane blew itself out, the water calmed down and revealed the *Rhone* with her stern in shallow water just 50 metres (164 feet) from a sandy bay. The *Rhone* remained undisturbed after early bounty hunters, using primitive diving apparatus, managed to salvage some china and crystal together with £60,000 of bullion. The storm, the salvage and the *Rhone* survived in local folklore while the British Virgin Islands returned to comparative tranquility.

"The Deep"

It was not until the invention of sophisticated breathing apparatus, over 100 years later, that the *Rhone* was rediscovered, entombed in waters that are nearly always warm and crystal clear. The abundance of sheltered bays made the Virgin Islands a perfect area for sailors and sports divers. Their proximity to the American mainland has resulted in a highly profitable tourist trade. This has escalated ever since

planes could land at the large airport at St Thomas and the smaller one at the northern tip of Tortola.

Divers from all over the world now gather expectantly to sample the beauty of the Caribbean underwater world and, more especially, to dive on the *Rhone*.

Her fame was further enhanced in 1976 when the glittering world of Hollywood film-making descended to use her tranquil setting as a background to the underwater action in *The Deep* — a multi-million dollar motion picture starring Robert Shaw, Jacqueline Bisset and Nick Nolte.

The normally quiet Roadtown was suddenly transformed by the arrival of a large film crew and attendant reporters lured to the site of the most ambitious

underwater film ever made. It was based on Peter Benchley's book *The Deep*, the sequel to his popular first book, *Jaws*. That book had become one of the largest box office successes when it was converted to film by a young and up-and-coming director, Steven Spielberg. *The Deep* was an extremely ambitious project even by Hollywood standards.

Underwater cameramen were consulted for their specialist knowledge and the top job — the shooting of the underwater footage — was eventually given to Al Giddings from the West Coast of America. His first problem was that no camera existed that could film underwater to the scale and quality demanded. So, in the true tradition of

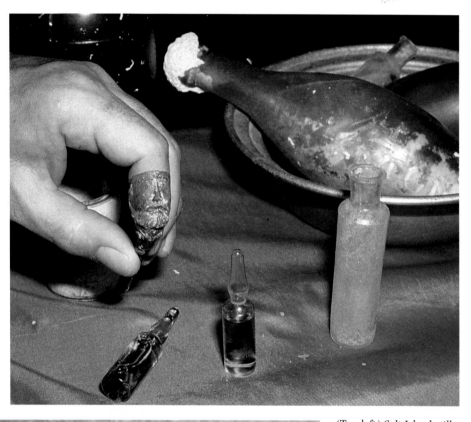

(Top left) Salt Island still bears the graves of those who perished when the Rhone sank. They are covered in the same razor-sharp corals which ripped open her hull and sent her to the seabed.
(Above) Even after countless visiting divers and over a century underwater, artefacts are still being uncovered. The rate at which they are unearthed is increased after violent storms when, even at depth, the powerful water movements on the surface dislodge parts of the wreck to reveal more small items. This delicate clay pipe has survived as well as the more robust glassware.
(Left) The Rhone was laiden with a general cargo of wines together with china and cutlery for the crew and passengers, but coral growth has covered most items forever.

45

(Far right) The Rhone now lies on her starboard side with her mast firmly on the seabed.
(Right) The saltwater has corroded the Rhone's hull and allows easy access to her insides.
(Below) The explosion of the boilers has left a huge open section into which a diver can swim in complete confidence. The light streams in to illuminate your way.

ingenious film-making, he built three underwater housings for land motion picture cameras. This took just 90 days. The housings not only worked but proved reliable for the entire length of filming.

As an indication of Gidding's drive and flair, he not only produced the housings in shining Ferarri Red but managed to make them with a style and simplicity of operation which reassured even the most cynical Hollywood mogul. Made from cast aluminium to match the contours of the cameras, these housings included external controls which activated all the main functions of the camera. On land they weighed over 30 kg (66lbs) but, underwater, they were neutrally buoyant.

The housings became known as the "Petermars" after the two Peters — Peter Gruber, the producer and Peter

Bisset swimming along the side of the *Rhone* and catching sight of something glittering just inside the wreck. She can't quite reach the tempting item and, as she stretches her arm inside the small opening she is suddenly and forcibly yanked by the arm and smashed against the wreck. The shock makes the audience jump with a mixture of fright and pain as they watch her with her arm still held and then jerked twice more with a terrific force by this mysterious creature inside the wreck. Finally freeing herself, she hurtles to the surface while Nick Nolte tries to restrain her, not knowing what has just occurred. This results in her kicking his valve out of his mouth and further escalating the panic.

What the audience does not know is that the scene is real. The incident happened during another dive and just happened to be filmed by the camera. The director liked the reality of the footage so much that he edited it into the opening action.

The logistics of filming underwater are more complicated than those on land. Communication underwater is virtually impossible except by writing tedious notes on waterproof slates. As a result, detailed briefings were needed on the surface to make sure that when action was signalled the correct movements took place. In addition, time underwater was limited, due to the depth at which they were filming. The crucial scenes were filmed at 25 metres (82 feet) where a diver can stay for only 30 minutes. Staying longer meant time must be spent during the ascents for decompression.

Even so, the filming involved many hours spent decompressing underwater each day. That meant hanging on to a length of weighted rope in mid-water to ensure the correct depth for decompression was kept. The longer you stay down at depth, the longer you have to decompress so the principal cameramen and their assistants were brought fresh air tanks from the surface to keep them underwater as long as possible. Any failure to supply the continuous air tanks would have brought on a massive embolism that would have resulted in slow and painful death. The nearest recompression chamber, where medical

Yates, the director. Both highly acclaimed men in their fields, neither had ever ventured a foot underwater and were more than a little concerned about trying to control the film from the surface. In the end, overcoming their reservations, they learned to dive and then to extend their production skills to the underwater location.

Apprehension about diving was not restricted to those behind the camera. Jacqueline Bisset was known to be afraid of water — even in a swimming pool. Some delicate training was needed, to coax her out of her inbuilt fear. With good and sensitive tuition, she gradually relaxed and felt more and more at home with the valve and equipment necessary to allow her to breathe normally for the first time at 25 metres (82 feet) under the Caribbean Sea.

Three expert underwater camera-men were hired, as was a large crew of assistants to help arrange lighting, lay lighting cables and act as safety cover. Not only was the filming of *The Deep* to be a severe test for the camera equipment but it was also an endurance test for the underwater film crew. They notched up hundreds of underwater hours in the drive to ensure every detail was taken care of.

The film maker had chosen the *Rhone* from a long list of possible wrecks. Relatively undisturbed previously, now, in 1976, she was about to experience an unheralded period of intense activity: 1,465 dives took place within 35 days.

With Jacqueline Bisset much more confident in her diving skills and with Robert Shaw and Nick Nolte already keen divers, the filming could begin. The opening scene sees Jacqueline

help might remedy a disaster, was too far away to reach in time.

The actors' time underwater was therefore carefully planned to make most use of the limited time available. They would wait until everything was set before beginning their dives. But, even with this organization and pre-planning, they had to decompress when a particular scene had to be reshot.

After the excitement of filming, the boredom of decompression led to many practical jokes being played on the more experienced divers. Air valves were turned off to see if they would panic, but all the jokers saw was a cool hand reaching back to slowly turn the air on again. Diving safety checks are second nature to such experienced camera-men.

To pass his decompression time more productively, Chuck Nicklin, the third cameraman, perfected the technique of reading a book underwater. The trick was not to let the book dry out for it is then that the paper tears. A carefully handled book lasted long enough underwater for Chuck to finish it.

The job of organizing the diving equipment and safety was given to George Marler who, together with his wife, Luana, had been diving on the *Rhone* for many years. They run the Aquatic Dive Centre on the mainland and have introduced hundreds of divers to the wreck. They have preserved many fascinating artefacts and made several new discoveries including the anchor lost during the hurricane. George's brief from the film makers was to ensure that enough air tanks were filled and ready for use, as well as help with the lighting underwater. He enjoyed 35 lucrative, busy days. Then the Hollywood sideshow left to complete filming in Bermuda. The *Rhone* was left once more as a tourist attraction for visiting divers and an ideal prop for underwater photographers.

Exploring the Rhone

The boat trip across Francis Drake Channel to Black Rock Point, Salt Island, takes just 20 minutes and provides time for a full briefing on the wreck. Your dive boat is anchored carefully over the wreck and the diving platform at the rear lowered to give easy

(Top right) *The prominent bows still remain intact although covered in coral growth. Designed and built to slice through the water at 15 knots this section now lies on a hard rock seabed. Guided dives on the* Rhone *begin here and work back to the stern in shallower water.*
(Right) *The combination of clear water and large open sections make the* Rhone *a safe dive. Inside, the cargo has become "concreted" together into a heap of unrecognizable shapes covered in silt. The more interesting artefacts are to be found on the outside where the water action has discouraged too much growth and so keeps them recognizable.*

access into the warm, clear water. The remains of the *Rhone* cover a large area and lie in depths from 25 metres (82 feet) almost up to the surface. For safe diving it is best to go to the deepest section first and then work your way back into shallow water. Fortunately, this route provides the best opportunity to see the *Rhone* in her entirety. The blue Caribbean waters soon clear even after the rare but sometimes most

violent storms so you catch your first glimpse of the wreck as soon as you hit the water.

The bow section is virtually intact, with the proud bowsprit heeled over and pointing to deeper water. The sleek lines of the hull are still clearly visible lying on her starboard side on a solid rock seabed. The sunlit surface, 25 metres (82 feet) above, provides plenty of general light but a diving torch is a

useful accessory that reveals the true colours of the wreck and the marine growth that has made the structure even more attractive. The water at this depth absorbs most of the colours and leaves only blacks, blues and greys. Your dive light will restore these to vivid reds, greens and purples.

It is the bow section that gives the *Rhone* its special attraction. The traditional bowsprit conjures up images

THE RHONE

The most unusual remains
of the Rhone are the
supports for the timber
deck. The deck has rotted
away leaving these iron
columns standing upright.
In the foreground, a small
signalling cannon
protrudes from the
wreckage.

(Above) A small signalling cannon lies wedged under the wreck. Being iron, it has little commercial value and so has remained in situ since the ship sank.

(Far right) The barrel of the signalling cannon has been colonized by marine encrustacean.

(Right) The nooks and crannies on any wreck are ideal homes for a variety of marine life. Large Moray eels lurk in the wreckage. They appear ferocious but will only attack and bite if severely provoked.

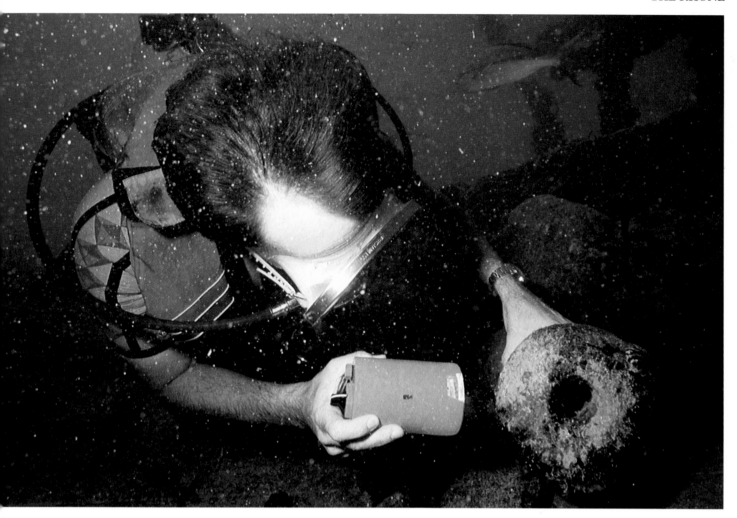

of the "tall ships" era when ships were elegant as well as practical and designed for speed and appreciation rather than pure function. This section also gives the diver a definite sense of scale as it is intact save for a few small areas reshaped during the sinking.

The keel faces deeper water and is less interesting than the deck area in between the bowsprit and aft of the foremast. Here, the anchors would have been strapped to the deck with the heavy links of chain leading down to the chain locker below. Rigging would have reached up to the foremast to support auxiliary sails — still considered by the designers of the era necessary to supplement the engines, or to take over in the event of mechanical failure.

Swimming now towards the stern, the first major landmark is the forward mast which now lies as if glued to the seabed. Two-thirds of the way up the mast the crow's nest is clearly visible

and from the very top of the mast you can look back, see the whole of the forward section and appreciate the overall size of the wreck.

The luxury of clear water is often taken for granted by those who have never experienced the claustrophobic darkness of temperate waters after rough weather, but to see whole sections of a wreck in clear water is an experience most divers aim for. Fortunately, the visibility on the *Rhone* rarely disappoints.

To your right as you swim up, the centre section opens up and allows easy access to the inside of the hull. The internal decking has rotted away and fallen to the seabed leaving the site looking like a large warehouse. From the side of the wreck, the davits which once supported lifeboats now reach out in the open water. Behind the davits is an area of columns reminiscent of a classical Greek ruin. They are in fact supporting girders for decking which

has long since rotted away. They rise in serried ranks, superbly decorated by marine growth.

Just below these columns there is a small signalling cannon firmly wedged under large metal plates. These plates are ideal homes for long moray eels that lie with heads protruding slightly and toothy mouths slowly opening and closing filtering water through their gills. The *Rhone* is a catacomb of such lairs, and care should be taken not to be too curious with your hands unless you are absolutely sure that no dangerous animals are at home. Just after the "Greek columns" and 50 metres (164 feet) from the bowsprit, the scene changes dramatically. Here are the boilers that exploded with such force. Fortunately for divers, the explosion opened up an area that allows entry into the main section — a large opening at least 10 metres (33 feet) wide, gradually narrowing as it tapers towards the bows.

Inside, the scene is rather like a scrapheap as areas have either rotted or been blown away. The heaps of mangled metal covered in fine silt are not particularly interesting, but, as you swim slightly further into the *Rhone*, you can begin to pick out light coming from the forward mast area. These shafts of light gradually increase until you come to gaps where you can swim out of the wreck and back towards the bows. The openings are not large but are safe. They were created by doors rotting away from their metal bulkheads. You have to be careful that your air tank does not hit the steelwork and this calls for experienced control over your buoyancy.

Swimming in and out of the *Rhone* is an exhilarating experience. Most wrecks are either so distorted that they are hazardous or are so confined that they are unwelcoming. The *Rhone* feels safe and does not pose problems.

From here, the wreck changes totally. There are no formal structures as you make your way from one piece of wreckage to another. The largest item is one of the boilers and a little to the right, in slightly deeper water, there are the condenser tubes. Further small areas of wreckage lead you into shallower water where the debris changes direction abruptly and leads to your left. The shapes again become more familiar as another boiler appears. The aft mast lies to the left in a similar condition to the foremast but detached from its base. From now on, the waters, being shallower, are much brighter.

The engine lies just aft of the gearbox housing and from here into the shallows your eye is drawn to the massive propshaft that transferred the power of the 600 horsepower engine down to the propeller. The shaft is supported at intervals by steel blocks, easily recognized as they stand above the general level of the seabed. Portholes mark areas that were probably first class cabins but which now lie flattened in 10 metres (33 feet) of water.

(Centre) *Looking out from inside the* Rhone *the blue water contrasts with the black of the wreck. Divers must take care not to snag their cylinders when swimming out through the holes.*

(Top left, inset) *The stern section is in much shallower water with the huge prop still clearly visible.*

(Bottom left, inset) *The main drive shaft runs from the engine, through the gearbox housing and on to the propeller.*

(Left) *The gearbox housing is only just recognizable, as the faster coral growth in the shallower water camouflages the original shape.*

(Bottom left) *One of the blades of the* Rhone's *massive single propeller was broken as it crashed to the seabed while still turning at full speed.*

Evidence of the lifestyle enjoyed by the passengers now lies encrusted in solid coral. Necks of champagne bottles protrude from the solid marine growth, which will, in time, cover much of the wreckage in shallower water. All over the *Rhone* there is a luxurious covering of colourful marine growth which varies from hard corals to soft filter feeding sponges.

Unfortunately for the careless or unprotected diver, there are large areas of staghorn coral — a hard coral that inflicts a painful sting if touched with an unprotected hand. This coral is covered with minute hairs, just like nettles on land, and contains a painful poison. A thin pair of gloves will reduce the risk but, in such warm waters, short wetsuits are usually worn leaving knees and elbows exposed. Many is the time when a muffled cry signals that a diving companion has experienced a brush with staghorn coral.

Despite such minor obstacles for human visitors, the *Rhone* is an ideal habitat for marine life. The protection of the larger sections accomodates shoals of bluestriped grunts and yellow tailed snappers. In the surrounding areas nutrient-rich sand provides pasture for goatfish, probing avidly under the surface of the sand with their special front feelers.

For those divers who want to attract fish, there is one sure method — food in a plastic bag. You only have to make a move towards your wetsuit pocket to pull out a food bag and you will be

(Far left) *The comical Trumpet fish tries to blend in with the coral for camouflage but is obvious to the diver's eye.*

(Centre) *So many divers have visited the Rhone that the fish are not shy. In fact, they are so friendly that when a bag of food is produced, the feeding diver can virtually disappear in a swarm of pecking fish. They will not go away until they are sure there is no more food.*

(Below) *The various coral growths are both attractive and potentially dangerous. This fire coral inflicts a nasty sting when touched with a bare hand.*

instantly surrounded by a shoal of fish so thick that you will not be able to see open water. The ball of frenzied activity will completely surround you. The fish dart all over you and they will peck at anything. It may be fun for a moment but, after a while, it can become quite claustrophobic. Thrashing your arms to scare them away makes no difference. The only way to escape is to push your way through the ball and gradually the fish will subside as they realize the food has run out.

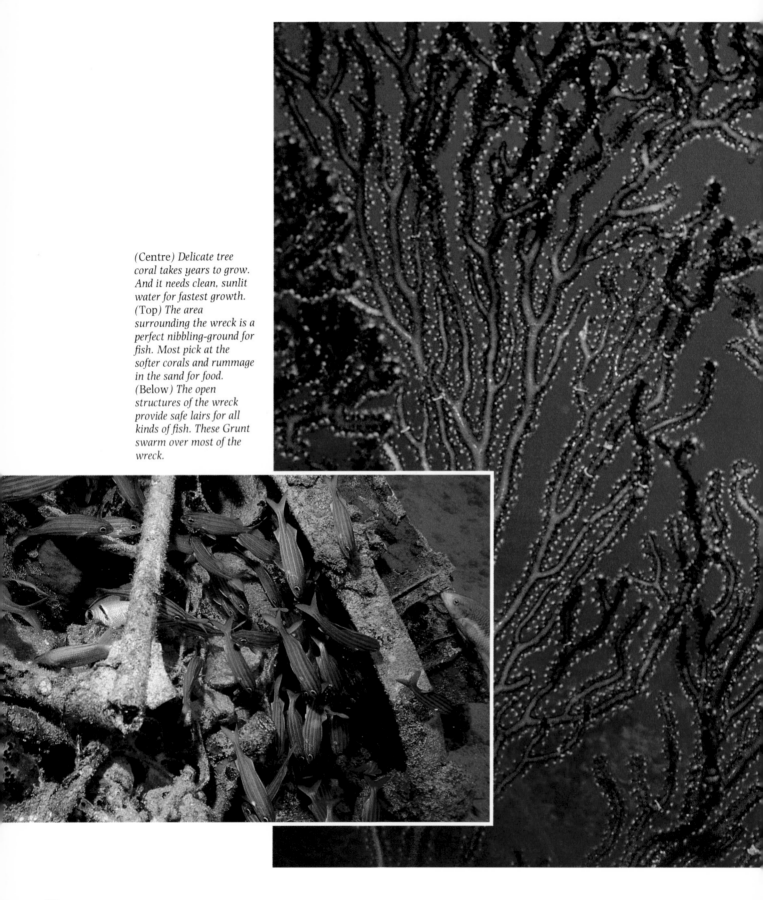

(Centre) Delicate tree coral takes years to grow. And it needs clean, sunlit water for fastest growth. (Top) The area surrounding the wreck is a perfect nibbling-ground for fish. Most pick at the softer corals and rummage in the sand for food. (Below) The open structures of the wreck provide safe lairs for all kinds of fish. These Grunt swarm over most of the wreck.

(Top) *These Yellow Stripes prefer the shelter between the wreck and the seabed.*
(Above) *Funnel-like sponges like the calmer waters inside the wreck.*
(Centre) *The vibrant life over a coral reef is one of the thrills of diving – fish, soft corals and sponges.*
(Top right) *These Big-eyes seek the safety of the wreck.*
(Below right) *The sandy seabed can come up with exciting surprises. This large Eagle Ray will swim off slowly if disturbed.*

Despite this self-inflicted hazard, the marine life on the *Rhone* is a fascinating revelation of successful colonization. Its conservation is ensured by law, for the site of the *Rhone* is a nature reserve. Several underwater plaques, placed in strategic locations, make sure that it remains undisturbed by the thousands of divers who visit her every year. As long as such laws are observed, the *Rhone* will continue to attract divers from all over the world to the tropical paradise of the British Virgin Islands.

THE GREAT LAKES

The fresh water of the Great Lakes in
North America preserves huge timber
wrecks which represent an era of shipping
that declined as fast as air cargo and road
transport developed.
The action of gale-force winds across a
large expanse of fresh water results in
wave formations that no shipbuilder could
overcome, but it has given the diving
world an exciting legacy.

To most people, inland water is a calm stretch of cold water, usually surrounded by hills and small enough to be able to see the other bank on all but the wildest of days. The Great Lakes, on the border between Canada and the United States of America, cover an area larger than the combined total of England, Wales and Scotland. The longest stretch of uninterrupted water in the area is over 450 km (280 miles) long. With statistics such as these, the Great Lakes move up the importance ladder.

(Above) The Strathern – *a fine example of early Great Lakes shipping – was the last of the barques. (Right) Early settlers coped with severe conditions.*

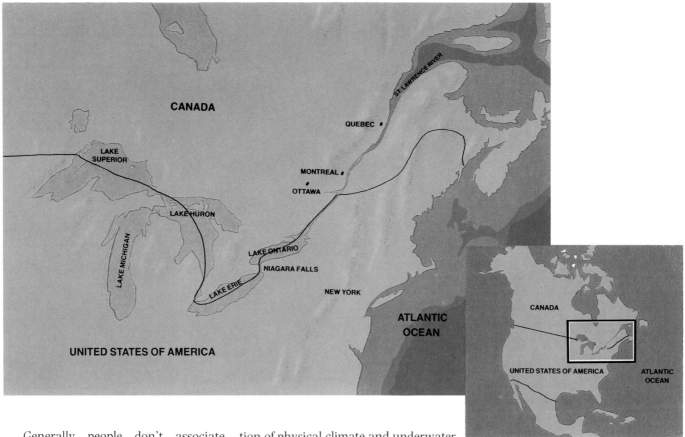

Generally people don't associate shipwrecks with what they instinctively feel are placid expanses of water. Mention freshwater to most divers and you will be greeted with an unexcited response. This almost sterile environment is regarded as one that is only to be tolerated during the winter months when the surrounding seas are too rough to dive but training programmes must continue.

Such attitudes, although understandable and commonplace, are misguided. Not only are freshwater shipwrecks as numerous as those in the open sea, but they are usually better preserved, enabling divers to study their structures and cargoes more easily. The mainstay of this surprising statistic are the five Great Lakes where many such wrecks are to be found. Despite the relatively small area of water and small percentage of shipping involved, these land-locked waterways have contributed to hundreds of shipwrecks. What is staggering is that shipping first came to the Great Lakes just a little over two hundred years ago.

Here in the Great Lakes a combination of physical climate and underwater conditions have given divers an array of interesting sites. These waters are extremely cold and ice cover is a common occurrence. Although physically uncomfortable for divers, this is an advantage: cold, fresh water restricts marine growth and so acts as a preservative. Since wrecks are kept in prime condition, diving on them is much more productive as you can easily recognize sections of the wrecks. Instead of shunning freshwater wrecks, divers should be more enthusiastic about diving on some of the cleanest wrecks in the world.

The Great Lakes

As explorers fought their way all over the globe to make new discoveries and colonize territories, the vastness of our planet became evident. Pleasant and temperate climates were the first to support visitors, and it was not until these had been fully explored, that man ventured into the colder northern climates. Here survival was never guaranteed and the terrain became extremely difficult and hazardous.

The first maritime explorers sailed across the Atlantic Ocean and stumbled on what is now the St Lawrence River. They had no idea at this time that it would lead them to the vast expanses of inland water which would eventually support the gradual colonization and exploration of these then empty and inhospitable lands.

In these days prior to the advent of ice-breaking ships, the St Lawrence was iced over for much of the year as the temperatures dropped from summer highs of 20°C (68°F) down to −10°C (14°F). These may not seem to be too excessive but it should be borne in mind that the average annual temperature is just 5°C (41°F) and the summer highs are short lived. The result is a very damp climate with high rain and snowfall figures. We are, it must be remembered, in an area about 45° above the equator but although this is on the same level as London, the Lakes are in the centre of a huge land mass which does not benefit from the warm waters of the Gulf Stream.

Traders moving up the St Lawrence founded the early settlements of Quebec, Montreal and Ottawa, the capital of Canada. Later, all of these three cities derived their early growth from shipping carrying cargoes from east to west. The traders realised that the huge inland waterways would allow the movement of cargoes over long distances, impossible overland. At first these early traders experienced difficulty in approaching the lakes: the nearer one got to a lake, so it became more and more hazardous. For example, the area close to the Niagara Falls. Here the 50 metre (164 feet) drop had to be bypassed with a man-made canal. Today there are now internationally maintained canals linking all of the five lakes — Ontario, Erie, Huron, Michigan and Superior.

The Shipwrecks

It is the huge size and inhospitable climate of the Great Lakes which have led them to play host to an inordinate number of shipwrecks. No significant naval warfare has ever taken place on their surfaces yet well over 500 ships have sunk in the short time since shipping first appeared in these waterways. Local climate and prevailing winds combined with the effects of the different physical properties of freshwater are responsible for sometimes impossible conditions.

Just as on the open waters of the oceans, the surface water conditions are dictated by the wind. The larger the area of open water, the greater the effect the wind will have. But these facts

*Canada's contrasts:
(Above) Quebec and Laporte Bridges in Quebec span the St Lawrence River.
(Middle) The Desjardins' business complex in 20th century Montreal.
(Bottom) Ships are specially designed to cope with the ice.*

(Left) Montreal, combines
modern and old style
buildings. Her financial
base has stemmed from
Great Lakes trading.
(Below) The Canadian
mountain ranges present
picturesque but
inhospitable landscapes.
Snow lies most of the year.

and conditions are no different to those experienced in open oceans so why do the Great Lakes pose such a threat? The problem lies in the difference between fresh and saltwater. Saltwater is much denser and so is more supportive and slower to react. As an indication of this increased support, laden ships going from fresh to saltwater will rise around 15 cm (6 inches). Freshwater is whipped up more quickly by the wind and has much smaller distances between wave peaks.

It is this difference that causes Great Lakes shipping so many problems. Whereas a seagoing vessel could plough down into a wave trough and rise up with the peak, fresh water, being less supportive means that the short distances between peaks can lead to a ship going into a trough and never pulling out of it. Wave heights of 13 metres (43 feet) are not uncommon.

In the case of Lake Huron, the winds generate from the northern area of Sault Sainte Marie and pick up speed as they blow down towards the warmer land masses to the south. They travel over the uninterrupted surface of Lake Huron and can raise the water level 3 metres (10 feet) higher at one end.

These hazardous conditions are a threat to both large and small ships. One of the largest vessels to sink was a 580-foot ship which went down into a steep trough and just kept going down.

The Great Storm of 1913 is a measure of the power of local conditions. In just one night, the winds blew so severely and whipped up the surface so fiercely that 57 ships, some up to 500 feet long, went down complete with cargoes and this was just on Lake Huron. The cargoes were, in the main, iron ore being shipped from the mineral rich mountainous areas out through the St Lawrence and into the trade routes of the high seas.

Under the Great Lakes

In saltwater, timbers and metals can be quite quickly reduced to powder as marine growth and chemical corrosion etch their surfaces but, in freshwater, there is very little life and the composition does not provide the destructive chemicals so evident in saltwater. Here, structures which have been underwater for nearly two centuries attract very little marine growth. Even in shallow water where there is the maximum of ambient light, the only major growth is a thin layer of weed. The result is clean wrecks, held in a deep-freeze state, awaiting the exploration of divers.

One of the most productive areas for a wreck diver is Georgian Bay to the east of Lake Huron. This is a large extension of the Lake separated by Bruce peninsula at the end of which is Tobermory. A recently published account of the diveable wrecks in the Georgian Bay area listed at least 55 known wrecks. The most prolific area is just off Tobermory where over 20 wrecks lie in close proximity to each other.

The most famous are not only of interest to divers, they are also tourist attractions which can be viewed from the safety of a glass-bottomed boat. The popularity of the wrecks had led to the formation of a 116 square kilometre (45 square mile) protection zone known as the Fathom Five Provincial Park. It extends from Dunks Bay, to the east of Tobermory, to Bears Rump Island in the North East, across to the west to include Cove Island and back to the mainland at Cape Hurd. The aim of the park is to emphasize the historic and natural resources of the marine environment and to promote greater public awareness.

The Sweepstakes

Probably the most exciting wreck in the area is the *Sweepstakes*. Lying in such shallow water that she can be seen from the surface, she plays host to a constant procession of approved observation

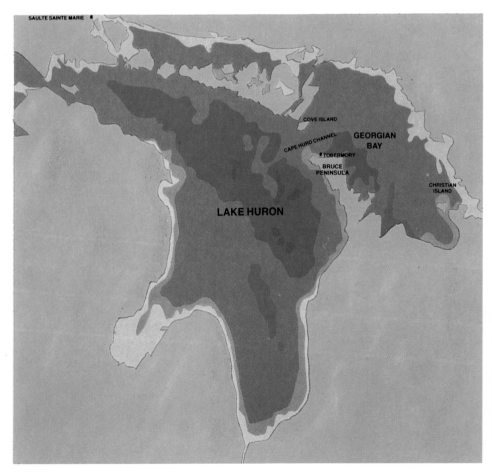

boats. Built in 1867, the *Sweepstakes* was launched from Wellington Square, Ontario. At 120 feet long, she was an unusual ship by most ocean-going standards in that she had a "drop keel". This design was and still is very common on dinghies and small yachts where storage and access to shallow waters are prime requirements. The use of this drop keel schooner design on larger vessels was that it gave them greater manoeuvrability in shallow water harbours that constant dredging kept operational.

Carrying a cargo of coal, the *Sweepstakes* sank in 1896 probably having suffered damage passing through Cape Hurd Channel in just 8 metres (26 feet) of water. The real facts are still unknown. The *Sweepstakes* is intact but for the stern section. This area was not damaged during the sinking but subsequently has been crushed, separated and moved by ice which covers the area for as much as four months of the year.

For about one month of this period, the ice forms packs rather than flows and is subject to a downward movement. Being up to 2 metres (6 feet) thick, this mass causes more damage each year.

Despite the damage, the *Sweepstakes* is a perfect example of a Great Lakes schooner and her construction can be clearly investigated. Lying just 40 metres (130 feet) from the head of Big Tub, she has continued to deteriorate underwater and is not really a safe wreck to go inside but for those who do, the structure could be weakened by a rush of bubbles causing timbers to fall to the lakebed. There has even been some underwater repairwork undertaken to make the wreck safer for divers.

Most of the surrounding land is privately owned, so access to the *Sweepstakes* is by boat from Tobermory. More energetic divers have to swim from the Government docks in Big Tub, Tobermory, to the wreck site.

(Above) *The inland water of the Great Lakes can provide calm, safe sailing.* (Left) *The open landscape, however, offers little resistance to strong winds that can turn a tranquil scene into a dangerous and rough expanse of water in a very short space of time.*

(Far right) *The 120-ft* Sweepstakes *lies in just 8 metres (26 ft) with her prominent anchor winch and gearing still intact.* (Below right) *The solid timbers still remain but they are being gradually eroded by ice which covers the wreck for as much as four months every year.* (Right) *Divers can swim inside the wreck to view her clean timbers, but gradual deterioration has made it risky. To safeguard themselves, divers have started to repair the wreck so that they can explore inside in greater safety.*

Being in such shallow water, the ambient light levels are good but the water can be very cold. A surface temperature of 60°F/15°C can drop by as much as 10° by the time you descend 8 metres (25 feet) so all divers wear full wetsuits, hood, boots and gloves. For the professional and wealthier divers, dry suits make cold water more tolerable.

The sun's rays do penetrate down to the *Sweepstakes* where they provide attractive shafts of light, rather than any significant warmth. The clarity of the water rarely exceeds 10 metres (33 feet) but a lack of planktonic life helps keep the colour cast much bluer than normal. Where there is a heavy deposit of plankton and marine organisms, the colour cast of the water is usually heavy green. This becomes darker and darker, the deeper you dive.

Reflecting the difficulties she was in prior to her sinking, the *Sweepstakes* is in a poor state, with decking rotted away and crucial structural supports in danger of folding. Although this makes her internal areas more accessible there is constant risk of shifting timber. The light levels are high: the sun's rays stream down through the holes in the decking and there is plenty of room for a diver to swim without feeling claustrophobic.

The ribs of the ship and her general timber construction details are clearly visible both internally and externally. At the bows, the solid keelstrip still stands proudly vertical, but the attached smaller timbers show signs of marine wear and tear. Also, at the bows of the *Sweepstakes* is the large anchor winch with its two capstans and central gearing. The railings running the length of the vessel are still intact, but towards the stern they break up, as does the ship itself, crushed by successive years of grinding ice.

Open hatches allow the safety-conscious diver to view the inner areas from a distance and perhaps they are sensible as well as safe for the coal cargo leaves wetsuits in a dirty state.

The last ten years have seen a rapid deterioration of this wreck. Eventually, the *Sweepstakes* will crumble as a result of ice weathering.

The wreck of the City of Grand Rapids

To add to the attraction of the area around Tobermory, there are another 20 wrecks in shallow water. One of these, the *City of Grand Rapids* is situated close to the *Sweepstakes*. Although this 122-foot long steamer lies in just 3 metres (10 feet) it is not as accessible as the *Sweepstakes*. Over the years, silt has partly buried her and when she sank she filled with debris.

Built in 1879, the *City of Grand Rapids* was a wooden steamer designed to carry passengers and cargo. On 29 October 1907, she was lying at anchor in Little Tub when a small fire broke out on board. Fanned by the wind, the flames soon went out of control and the crew fled. The tug, *Clucas*, was hired to tow her out into open water but the heat from the flames was so intense that they had to cut loose and watch the *City of Grand Rapids* drift towards the head of the Big Tub. Here she went aground, continuing to burn until the flames were extinguished when they reached the waterline.

Underwater, the structure which was not burned is now covered in silt. The larger engine section with its huge boiler remains intact. The rudder and propeller were lifted in 1968 and are on display in the local Peninsula & St Edmunds Township Museum.

(Far left) Close to the Sweepstakes *lies the* City of Grand Rapids. *Sunk by fire, her remaining structure is covered in silt but the engine and boiler section is still evident. (Above) The once solid timbers have slowly rotted leaving the retaining bolts exposed. Being in shallow water, the* City of Grand Rapids *can be visited by divers and snorkellers. (Left) Just below the surface, the remains of the wreck have suffered from wave action and silt.*

(Top right) *Being in deeper water, the* Arabia *has remained impressively intact. Even the chains from bowsprit to the deck are still in place.*
(Above) *Her huge hull lies upright in deep water and provides an interesting dive for experienced divers. But, the combination of cold water and depth has proved fatal to some novices.*
(Below right) *One of the main prizes on any wreck is the anchor, and the* Arabia's *is prominent on her deck.*
(Right) *As well as her anchor, the* Arabia *still displays her main wheel which has served as a "prop" for many underwater photographers.*

The Arabia

Just outside Tobermory's harbour, the wreck of the *Arabia* lies just off Echo Island in 33 metres (107 feet). Carrying a cargo of 20,000 bushels of corn, she sprang a leak during a fierce gale on Lake Huron on the night of 4 October 1884. Early next morning the Captain ordered the exhausted crew to abandon ship. From the lifeboats, they watched as the 131-foot *Arabia* sank beneath the waves.

It was to be her cargo of corn which would give divers an indication of her whereabouts. Searching the area, they asked local fishermen about the best fishing areas since fish are known to favour wrecks. The fishermen not only told them of a good area but volunteered that the fish they caught there nearly always had black corn in their stomachs. A more concentrated search revealed the wreck of the *Arabia.*

Lying in deep water, the *Arabia* is reached by passing through two thermoclines. Depending on the time of year, these thermoclines move up and down but the temperatures at depth do not vary much. It is a consistent 2°C (36°F) when you dive below 25 metres (82 feet). This mind and body-numbing temperature could account for the high number of diving fatalities which have occurred here over the years.

Once again, the only advantage for divers of such low temperatures is the preservation of the wreck in good condition. The intact bows still have chains lined out from the main winches and the bowsprit provides a powerful photographic subject when silhouetted against the light which just reaches down from the surface. A classic anchor lies strapped to the deck and probably most interesting of all, the ship's wheel still stands in position. Here divers pose in traditional and now somewhat hackneyed way as if they were the captain going down with his ship.

The *Arabia*'s location will keep her intact for some time to come and her reputation will grow as an excellent deeper dive. The most worrying aspect is that she seems to attract novice divers who frequently underestimate the adverse conditions which must be endured to view this example of Great Lakes shipping in its heyday.

Mapledawn

At the head of Georgian Bay in 10 metres (33 feet) lies one of the Great Lakes most popular wreck dives.

The *Mapledawn* was launched in 1890, a 350 foot steel-hulled steamer displacing 3100 tons. In 1924 she went aground during a snowstorm and despite her size, became a total loss. Sections of the wreck were removed in salvage work undertaken during World War 2.

Nevertheless, she is still an excellent dive just 100 metres (328 feet) from the shore. At low tides her bows break the surface, so locating her is easy and she provides safe holds to tie a boat up to. As you drop into the cool waters you cannot fail to be impressed by the twin boilers which are at least 5 metres (16 feet) in diameter. The lack of growth and shallow water will afford you a clear view of this large wreck with its huge decking and plates, some of which are buckled from the salvaging. About 15 metres (49 feet) away from the stern, lies the propeller, the tips of its huge blades broken off by the impact of going aground on the west side of Christian Island.

As with most large wrecks, the engine and boilers remain solid, providing perfect compositions for underwater photographers to capture on film.

(Left) Despite being partly salvaged during World War 2, the Mapledawn is still an impressive sight and, being in shallow water, the light levels are good and the water is slightly warmer.

(Top, far left) The huge twin boilers are the most prominent part of the Mapledawn. They are each over 5 metres (16 feet) in diameter and will remain intact long after the rest of the ship has flattened.

(Top left) Twisted metal surrounds the intact boilers with their huge retaining bolts.

(Above) The steel hull has been ripped apart during salvage but still retains its shape. Holes in line show where solid rivets would have held one plate against another.

(Top right) Slightly deeper than the boilers is the large single propeller which suffered major damage when the ship sank. The tips of the blades are broken off.

(Centre) *The* Michigan *lies in such shallow water that snorkellers can dive down to view the winch gearing.*
(Top, far left) *The rudder of the* Thomas Cranage *lies on a rocky lake bottom.*
(Below, far left). *The propeller of the* Seattle *is about 2 metres (8 feet) across.*
(Below) *The anchor of the* Marquette *lies on sand with her impressive hull upright behind.*
(Left) *The anchor chain of the* W.L. Wetmore *will remain in its untidy heap for centuries.*

The future of the Great Lakes wrecks as sites for divers, tourists and marine life is being preserved by the formation of marine reserve parks. This will help to provide a selection of dives for the keen wreck diver. As waterborne lake transport declined in the 20th Century, the possibility of new wrecks has decreased. However, since there are so many existing wrecks, it is difficult to imagine divers ever running out of wreckdives on the Great Lakes.

THE UMBRIA

If one wreck has stimulated an interest in
the underwater more than any other, it
must be the *Umbria*. First explored by
Hans Hass and made famous in his books
about diving in the Red Sea, the *Umbria*
forms one of the finest centres for scientific
study – she supports a wide and colourful
variety of marine life – and photographic
enjoyment.

Originally owned by The Hamburg South American Lines (a major line in Hamburg where she was built by Reihersts), the *Umbria* started her service in 1912 as the *Bahia Blanca*. In 1935 her name was changed to the *Umbria* (sometimes spelt *Umbrea*) after she had been sold to the Italian Company Lloyd Triestino Di Navigazione and was registered in Genoa.

At 491 feet long and 59 feet wide, the *Umbria* was a twin screw cargo ship that, for most of her life, was connected with South America as a destination and as a country of ownership. Her maritime life was the uneventful transportation of cargoes from one port to another and, like thousands of other vessels, she fulfilled a basic function, earning a living for her owners.

The events of 1940 brought an abrupt halt to her humdrum life. On 12 June 1940, the news that Italy had entered World War 2 and allied herself to Germany reverberated all over the world, particularly in places where Italians lived and traded. The *Umbria*, at this time, was in the British-controlled Port Sudan, half way down the west coast of the Red Sea, and she was carrying a cargo of cement and munitions en route to Rangoon via Eritrea.

She lay at anchor off Wingate Reef. British reaction to Italy's alliance was swift: all Italian assets in Port Sudan were taken over. They included the *Umbria*, just about to set sail. The British Authorities trustingly, or

stupidly, assumed that her crew would obey orders from their new owners, and certainly the *Umbria* needed a sizeable crew to keep her operational. But the Italian crew, once the gravity of the situation had sunk in, decided otherwise.

They opened the ship's seacocks and very effectively, denied the British the double prize of the *Umbria* and her cargo. The *Umbria* was slow to sink, so, in order to prevent any attempt to save her, the Italians declared that timed fuses had been placed in the holds that contained large quantities of munitions. The British had no choice but to let her sink.

Location

The *Umbria* sank in an area of busy shipping movements in and out of Port Sudan – the most important harbour on the whole length of the Sudanese Red Sea coastline. It was not the sort of place where any obstacle was likely to be ignored, but strangely enough it was her cargo of munitions which saved her from salvage. Any plan to remove the new obstacle was blocked for fear that the salvors could trigger the increasingly unstable cargo. Had she been blown up, the detonation would have resulted in the generation of a huge tidal wave. The concave shape of Wingate Reef would have reflected this back on to Port Sudan, and the conse-

(Above) Ships of all nationalities have used Port Sudan to take on cargo and supplies.
(Left) The glowing sunsets reflected in the waters of the Red Sea inspired early settlers to give it its name.

quences of such a wave on such a strategic port could have meant the difference between victory and defeat.

Early underwater explorers

So, despite the inconvenience of her new location to the harbour and shipping authorities, the *Umbria* remained where she sank on one of the most prolific coral reef areas in the world. After the War, these reefs provided a superb environment for the famous adventurers, Jacques Cousteau and Hans Hass to carry out some of the first underwater scientific research on the rates of growth of corals and marine life. Previous expeditions had taken them to possible locations all over the world but, finally, it was the reefs around Port Sudan on which these pioneers chose to spend so many productive years diving and carrying out their underwater scientific experiments.

Cousteau built the very first under-water habitat. Inside it scientists could stay underwater for days, both observing marine life and conducting research into diving medicine. Later on, other research groups came from England to continue Cousteau's work. They set up research platforms on the tops of the reefs as well that provided non-stop access by divers to the shallow coral waters where the diversity and quantity of marine creatures was so attractive.

For Hans Hass, however, it was the *Umbria* herself which first captured his imagination. He was the first civilian to dive on her after the War and his book *Under The Red Sea*, first published in 1952, found a large and enthusiastic public. In his book, he describes how he managed to dive on the *Umbria* initially without official permission in late 1949. The wreck was protected to safeguard the volatile cargo but, of course, her location was hardly a secret, for she lies with her starboard davits breaking the surface in just over 20 metres (60 feet) of water at the stern.

(Centre) One of the first underwater habitats was set up by Jacques Cousteau to establish rates of coral growth as well as man's ability to survive long periods underwater. The structure has attracted a luxurious growth of Table corals.
(Inset top, left) The Cousteau habitat is shallow enough for snorkellers to dive down and inspect in more detail.
(Inset below, left) Close to Cousteau's habitat is the "garage" where divers stored their underwater vehicles.

When Hass first visited the *Umbria*, there was no such thing as an aqualung breathing apparatus: he had to dive using an oxygen rebreather set which limited his time and depth to 10 metres (30 feet). Below this depth the partial pressure of the normally life-sustaining gas would become dangerously toxic. Such a limitation did not deter him, as most that is fascinating about *Umbria* is in such shallow water that any experienced snorkeller can easily explore this huge artificial reef. In fact this was how Hass first investigated the *Umbria* as he did not wish to waste his precious oxygen supply until he was sure that a particular dive was worth using the breathing set.

Even from a snorkeller's restricted viewpoint, Hass appreciated immediately the wealth of the *Umbria* as a natural science resource. The tropical sun and the clear shallow waters provide a nutrient-rich environment and, over a surprisingly few number of years, a brand new structure for the developing marine life to colonize. By 1949, the *Umbria* was transformed into a garden of multi-coloured corals through and around which almost solid

(Top) *The combination of sunlit waters, a sheltered location and low pollution provides ideal conditions for fast and profuse coral growth. The deeper you go, the less the light and the slower the coral growth.*
(Bottom, far left) *The shelter of the Umbria's large structure is ideal for swirling shoals of Glass fish. They part as a diver approaches and then quickly reform.*
(Bottom left) *Portholes, once watertight windows, are now just playthings for the fish to swim through. The brass porthole surrounds remain intact mainly because visiting divers could not carry them back on an aeroplane!*

shoals of a huge variety of fish sauntered in search of food and shelter. "Teeming" is an often over used word, but it was accurately used here by Hass to describe the marine life he saw.

The rapidly developing life on the *Umbria* has been left unchecked and, indeed, since she sank it has been positively encouraged. There is a total ban on fishing around the wreck and on unapproved visitors of any sort. Such a ban

Corals are quick to form on any new structure, given the right conditions. Soft coral grows rapidly while hard coral takes longer.

THE UMBRIA

has provided today's visiting diver with a unique opportunity to experience nature's progress when she is set free of man's restrictions.

For Hass, it must have been an incredible experience as he floated, hovering over the *Umbria*, the very first diver to see her and her newly acquired marine life. Of his second dive he says, "I now considered her almost in the light of a personal possession that I had won in a competition".

Umbria's topside career may not have been particularly eventful but she now provides a foundation of such fecundity for all forms of marine life that her name will never be forgotten. A surface view of a wreck is often particularly restricted as we are now so used to the freedom of the modern aqualung. But on wrecks such as the *Umbria*, surface observations are quite spectacular. In the shallow water around the starboard davits, the main gangway stretches along the side of the ship and provides a much-photographed, perspective-enhancing location as the uniform steelwork recedes into the sunlit background.

Slightly deeper in 15 metres (49 feet) but still visible from the surface on a good day is one of the massive propellers. The port screw is buried but the starboard one stands high above the seabed and, supported on its A frame, provides a rare "prop" for underwater photographers.

(Far left) The main companionway on the Umbria *lies in shallow, sunlit water and recedes into the distance. As she is on her side, the deck is on the left.*
(Left) One of the two huge propellers protrudes from the upturned keel. This bronze prize is prime salvage, but is well protected.

Umbria's modern visitors

Hass's explorations took him away from the *Umbria* soon afterwards, but by then he had brought it to the attention of the diving world and fired the imagination of non-divers with his tales of adventure. And this was at a time when the world's media were looking for anything to brighten up those drab post war years.

Despite the difficult and often uncertain journey to Port Sudan, the *Umbria* continues to attract divers who come from countries all over the world. Several groups have tried to organize diving centres but at the *Umbria*, they experience great problems not only coping with the authorities but also in attracting suitable local labour. Some of them managed to cater for visiting divers with remarkable ingenuity but the difficulties have forced most of them to give up.

One English company has consistently offered an almost uninterrupted facility, although recently this too has ceased to offer diving trips. It was very basic and was based on the lighthouse reef of Sanganeb where a small concrete platform, built to support the lighthouse, also served as a base for the divers. The continued survival of the company was due mostly to the efforts of an English couple, Jack and Babs Jackson, whose experiences organizing trips into the desert mountains of Sudan have given them invaluable local knowledge. The Jacksons have survived many years on the platform, and, despite working with the most primitive facilities, they have been able to sustain and support hundreds of divers who have been attracted over the years from all parts of the world to live right next to some of the most exciting diving in the underwater world.

The Jacksons greet divers in Port Sudan and then take them on the two-hour boat trip to Sanganeb — a route which passes the *Umbria*. The boat is always laden, not only with the newly arrived divers but also with exotic fruit and food from the Port Sudan markets. (The Sanganeb lighthouse boasts no luxuries other than mattresses and a couple of Calor gas cookers.) During the trip, the Jacksons relate the history of the *Umbria* to the new arrivals as they

motor past, and there is the promise that they will return to dive on her as soon as they are settled on their new "home".

Diving holiday companies, not surprisingly, establish themselves where

diving is good and also attracts enough visitors to be reasonably profitable. In Sudan, it was quite different. It was almost impossible to run a consistent holiday service. It was only the quality of the reef diving, plus the existence of

(Far left) *Visiting boats to the Sanganeb Lighthouse have to tie up to the end of the jetty and carry goods along to the main platform on the reef.*
(Top) *A makeshift habitat built by Cambridge University was the home for marine biologists who dived at regular intervals to record and measure the rate of coral growth in the area.*
(Left) *The towering lighthouse operates automatically and warns approaching ships of the treacherous reef.*

the *Umbria* that ensured that enough fee paying customers would brave the red tape and the very basic hospitality.

Hass returns

When Hans Hass decided to revisit the *Umbria*, exactly 30 years after he had first set eyes on her beautifully colonized structure, it was the Jacksons who played host to him. A great deal of change had occurred in those years: diving equipment and training techniques had been researched and developed so that almost anyone could, with proper training, dive in safety and comfort.

Kitted up with the latest air cylinders and demand valves, Jack Jackson and Hans Hass dived the site that brought back so many exciting memories for Hans, and that was now almost a second home for Jack. Armed with photographs taken by Hans during his first visit, they discovered that very little had changed on the wreck itself, apart from the collapse of the funnel, one mast and a lifeboat davit. However, the marine life had multiplied and spread dramatically to cover every area of the wreck.

(Above) *The stern section of the* Umbria *is a mass of curves and corals.*
(Above right) *The open structure of the wreck is a delight to swim around in the bright, clear waters.*

(Right) *Inside the* Umbria *there is no coral growth, just a layer of very fine silt, and divers must be careful not to stir this up.*

The wreck

When presented with such a wealth of fascinating marine life it is often easy to overlook the structure upon which such life depends. But the structure of the *Umbria* is still too impressive to be ignored, and has not become so overgrown that it is unrecognizable. Indeed the *Umbria* remains virtually intact and her colourful colonizers are an added decoration to an already graceful shape. Particularly impressive is the stern section where her sweeping curves and mainly intact railings slant up towards the sunlit surface. The area is open yet intact and allows divers unlimited and safe access from here to the main holds. The solid steel deck supports are still as strong as ever but the hatches have either rotted away or fell off when she sank. The holds lie at about 45° and are easily accessible to inquisitive visitors.

Inside each hold, the original cargoes are sometimes hard to identify, hidden by a coral coating. In some of the holds, small items have spilled out and lie in jumbled heaps. Elsewhere, large cans of food have been gradually opened by saltwater corrosion, their contents long since eaten by the fish. The holds containing ammunition are to be avoided

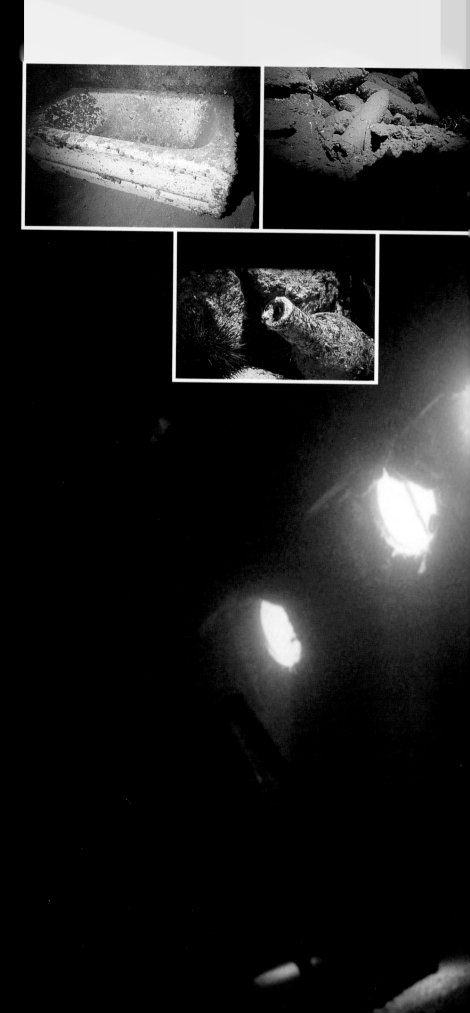

as some types of explosives become more volatile when steeped in salt water while other types are diffused in time by the marine penetration. There is no knowing which type is which, so total caution is the safest rule.

One of the great attractions of the *Umbria* is that she is so explorable inside. Being in shallow water the light levels are high, so the Umbria's internal areas are pleasantly lit once your eyes become adjusted. Most of the hatches are large enough to swim through and open enough not to worry about them suddenly closing with you inside. As with all wrecks, the internal structures are coated with a deposit of fine silt and care is needed when finning to keep disturbance to a minimum, especially if you wish to photograph the inside.

If the perspective-enhancing gangway is the external attraction on the *Umbria*, it is the porthole-lined internal gangways which are the most photogenic. The contrast between the bright beams of light streaming in through the port holes and the dark green internal decking provides irresistibly powerful compositions. The strongly directional lighting flickers on the decking and gives the internal areas a fireside-dappled, green glow.

Perhaps a few visiting divers have collected the odd small souvenir to remind them of their visits on the *Umbria*, but the larger exhibits still remain. The *Umbria* is a whole ship untouched by salvage or treasure hunters, with uniquely rich marine life and an ideal position.

(Centre) *The portholes allow light to stream inside onto the internal bulkheads adding colour, motion and mood.*
(Above, left) *This is one bath which has definitely overflowed forever.*
(Above, right) *The* Umbria's *cargo included munitions en route to Rangoon. These now lie covered in silt.*
(Above, centre) *Wine bottles have long since lost their corks and become a foundation for marine growth.*

Umbria's marine life

One of the major fascinations for divers on the *Umbria* today is the magnificent range of underwater sights; hard and soft corals have taken advantage of all suitable structures from bulkheads to ammunition boxes and from thin rigging to solid decking. The new habitat created by this gradual colonization has attracted a great variety of marine animals quick to take advantage of all it has to offer. Strange nooks and crannies on the old wreck have taken on new functions as ideal lairs for safety conscious creatures such as Moray eels. Crustacea of all kinds are also attracted by the new sources of food which generate rapidly. The *Umbria* has now found a new and much more interesting role with her natural cargo than ever she achieved in her working life on the surface.

The fast-growing soft corals were the first to take hold of the ship as their needs were ideally suited by these calm clear Red Sea waters. The *Umbria* provided a multitude of places to settle upon and the waters were rich with floating planktonic life — two essential ingredients for profuse marine growth. At the same time that the soft corals were discovering their new homes, bottom-dwelling crabs and lobsters discovered the *Umbria*'s array of wholely

unnatural but particularly suitable lairs. Whether made of iron, timber, hessian or rubber, the critical factor appeared to be position, safety and food supply.

The growth of the coral led to the cautious arrival of many varieties of reef fish. They found the changing face of the *Umbria* an easy source of food and, of course, shelter. Coral-eating Parrot fish, with their powerful beaks were spoilt for choice as they sauntered around the wreck, picking here and pecking there at the corals. The brightly coloured, oblong and rather stubby bodies of the Parrot fish have enough power to thrust themselves at the hard coral to break off food. Their reward from such thrusts is a mixture of algal food and coral. The coral passes through the Parrot fish's digestive system and is eventually deposited as fine sand. This group of fish, of which there are 13 species in the Red Sea, are the largest producers of sand. They feed during the day, flitting from one coral head to another, never resting but, at night, they secrete a veil-like mucus around themselves, settle down into the corals and rest.

Fish attract other fish: bottom-dwelling Lizardfish, for instance, are fun to watch. They lie motionless with their drooping mouths slightly open waiting for small fish to stray into their area. As

soon as one appears, the Lizardfish pounces with lightning speed, grabs the prey, gradually swallowing it whole.

There is no more striking example of effective camouflage than the Scorpion-fish, whose family are masters of two kinds of disguise. Not only can they change their colour to blend with the background but they can also change their texture to make seeing them extremely difficult. Like the Lizardfish, they lie on the bottom, motionless and invisible. They, too, rely on prey approaching them — whereupon they spring up to inject their victim with paralysing poison contained in their dorsal, pelvic and anal spines.

Within the same family are two of the underwater world's most famous fish, the Lionfish and Stonefish. The former are noted for their remarkable beauty and grace as they glide over the reefs like underwater galleons. The latter are grotesque but perfectly camouflaged carriers of the most deadly venom known underwater. They are difficult to see even when they are pointed out to you, for they take on the same warty mud-covered texture of their surroundings. Their stout dorsal fins contain the poison which is so painful when injected that it can, and frequently does, cause a fatal heart attack. Because they are perfectly disguised, we divers fortunately never know how

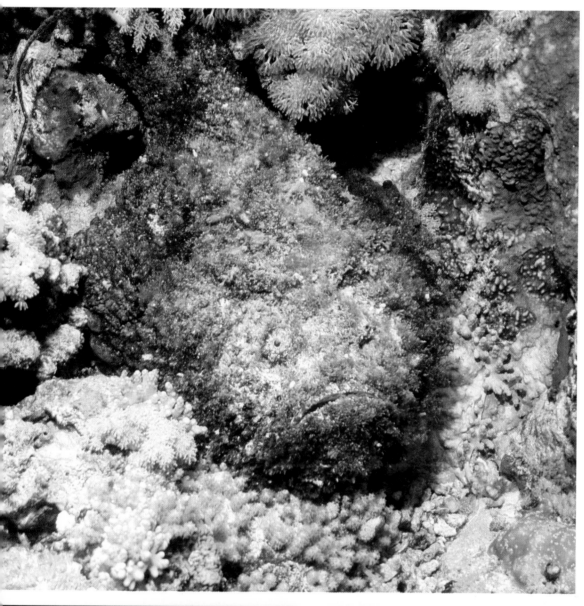

(Far left) *Pastel-coloured Parrot fish eat the corals, digest the nutrients and deposit the rest as sand.*
(Left) *This master of disguise is the Stonefish. It can change colour to blend perfectly with its background and the poisonous spines on its back can be lethal to those unfortunate enough to step on them.*
(Below, left) *The exotic Lionfish hovers majestically in mid-water. Despite its attractive appearance, the long top spines contain poison.*
(Below, right) *During the day, these Parrot fish dart around the corals, biting off chunks with their powerful beaks. At night they use holes in the same coral to sleep in.*

close a brush we may have had with these fish, and, though antidotes are available in some countries, the poison acts so fast that there is rarely time to bring a patient ashore, let alone to a local hospital.

On the lighter side, brilliantly coloured Squirrelfish seek the shelter of overhangs, of which there are many on the *Umbria*. When left alone, they hang motionless beneath their artifical umbrellas, but at the first hint of threat raise their dorsal fins in a fine aggressive display to repel invaders. Their large dark eyes and drooping mouths give them a sorrowful look which even the dorsal display cannot hide. If they are seriously challenged, they soon slip into the corals where the labyrinth of internal holes gives safety.

In the more open areas of the *Umbria*, such as the main holds, big Groupers are to be found. Prized for their size and taste, these fish were the main target for early spearfishers who snorkelled down as far as they could and for as long as possible to kill these docile and highly territorial creatures. The *Umbria* now is not so easily accessible to the casual fisherman and so has provided comparative safety for some really large Groupers in its dark holds.

Harmless to man, the Grouper family feeds mainly on small fish supplemented occasionally by crustacea. Their large mouths have a powerful suction force which effectively vacuums the prey into their mouths. But it is the smaller varieties of Groupers — the Anthias, whose presence most typifies all that is exciting about the Red Sea reefs. The Anthias constantly dart around in shallower water, hugging the coral reef for protection. An approaching diver will see them flitting to the safety of the corals but, within seconds, they are out again in more open water to feed on the plentiful zoo-plankton. Ironically, these little fish are frequently the food of their much larger relations.

The first fish the visiting diver will notice, are those that have learned to associate them with food. The advent of relatively cheap air travel and, even if difficult to organize, the diving package trips have ensured that the *Umbria* has become — for the fish — a renowned feeding station. The most commonly

(Centre) The majestic Emperor Angel fish glides around the wreck.

(Inset, above) Cardinal fish prefer the safety of overhanging table coral.

(Below, left) A food carrying diver becomes the centre of attention for Sergeant Major fish. They are voracious eaters and will peck at anything.

(Below, right) The graceful Queen Angel fish swims around on its own. They are usually very timid, but they have become so used to divers on the Umbria *that they will take food from their hands.*

used food is left-over bread. At the first appearance of a diver the area is instantly filled with countless small fish of all kinds. They seem to appear from nowhere.

Armed with a plastic bag full of bread, the diver is literally mobbed by silver and black Sergeant Major fish, Snappers of all colours from black and white to pastel yellows and pinks. Small Wrasse and Damselfish also join the riot

as a swirling ball of fishlife envelops the new arrivals. Anyone, it seems, remotely likely to bring food with them, is fair game for a peck from the fish. First-time divers often find their ears being nipped by hungry fish. Small they may be, but when you are underwater and you feel your ear being attacked, the instant reaction is to believe it is some big fish intent on inflicting much more damage on their next lunge. A rapid turn, of course, reassures that there is nothing more than the same swirling ball of small fish.

For a more sedate introduction to the *Umbria*, it is better to descend into slightly deeper water where the feeding fishlife becomes more individual and cautious. The larger and prettier Angelfish used to hold back until a diver had receded to a safe distance. But now, with the graciousness their names suggest — Queen, Emperor, Arabian and Royal — they have gradually become more used to human intruders and, after years of patient encouragement, will glide in towards bread held in the fingers and fearlessly suck it in their delicate mouths. The old hands take such activities for granted but, when a shy fish feeds like this for the first time, there is an excitement which is only perhaps equalled by the discovery of a new species.

To find larger fish, one has to look

(Above) *A large grouper hovers under an overhang. Despite their looks, they are very shy.*
(Top right) *Clown fish and anemonies live together in a symbiotic relationship.*
(Right) *Shoals of Barracuda swim relentlessly around the Umbria. They have a menacing appearance but have not been known to attack divers here.*
(Below, centre) *The smallest nooks and crannies are put to use by Blennies.*
(Far right) *Anthias abound in the wreck.*

more into the waters just away from the wreck where small shoals of Barracuda circle the area. The Barracuda shoals here are smaller than those off Sanganeb Reef where it is not uncommon to be totally surrounded by a wall of hundreds of barracuda, each measuring anything up to 1 metre (3 feet) in length. To see them in such numbers can give rise to panic as they have a menacing presence. But there is no record of any attacks on divers unless they have been seriously provoked. With a solid wall of these barracudas around you, you cannot help but feel only minor reassurance from these statistics.

The *Umbria* is an attraction of sorts for larger Sharks too, but these scavengers of the sea tend to find the ocean going, rubbish-depositing cargo vessels anchored off Port Sudan far more to their taste. These cargo boats dump the remains of their galleys into the sea, and this waste attracts sharks of all kinds in search of easy food. It is this plentiful supply within the environs of Port Sudan itself that helps keep the *Umbria* a safe place to dive.

The reefs around the Umbria are frequented by numerous varieties of shark. Their reputation makes any diver uneasy.

Jacques Cousteau and his team, on an expedition to observe sharks in the 1960s, set up underwater observatory cages 30 metres (98 feet) down from their underwater habitat on the Sanganeb reef. In those early days of underwater discovery, little was known about the habits of sharks. Tales of shipwrecked sailors being eaten alive as they waited to be rescued were accepted as fact. Cousteau and his team, no doubt very cautious at the prospect of finding out about sharks' habits the hard way, soon found that they were essentially shy creatures — quite capable of attacking man, of course, but only when he provoked the situation with blood-soaked fodder. And it is an interesting fact that nearly all of the most successful photographs of sharks have been taken after they have been attracted in this way.

(Top, right) The much-abused Puffer fish inflates himself to appear more fearsome. Once inflated, however, they can barely move.
(Centre, right) The rigid Box fish cannot swim very fast but is shy of photographers.
(Below, right) The delicate Butterfly fish usually swim in pairs around the wreck pausing here and there to peck at a piece of coral (far right) before moving on.

(Top, left) Small jellyfish pulsate their way through the water.
(Top, right) Coral trout are territorial and show strong aggression to approaching fish.
(Centre, left) Nudibranchs are seaslugs without shells. They have exotic markings and crawl slowly around the wreck.
(Below, left) The blue spotted lagoon ray is a frequent visitor. They bury themselves in the sand for improved camouflage.

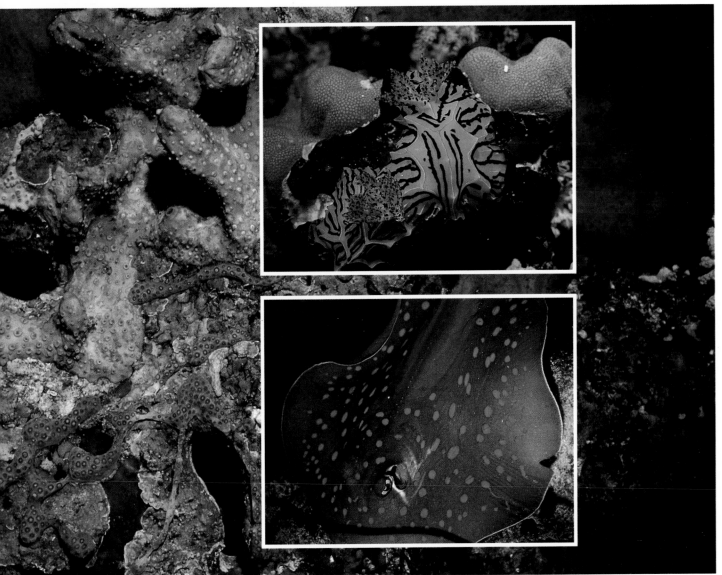

The profusion and diversity of corals on the Umbria are one of its main attractions. They abound in the bright clear waters and grow on every conceivable surface. Despite their profusion, the corals are extremely delicate and can easily be destroyed with a careless stroke of a diver's fin.

Visiting divers cannot fail to respond to the marine life that has colonized the Umbria. The rate of growth of the corals directly correlates with the increase in fish species and other plant and animal life.

THE ROYAL OAK

In 1939, a German U-Boat penetrated
Britain's main anchorage and sank one of
her capital ships. Over 800 men lost their
lives as the great battleship sank. H.M.S.
Royal Oak is a war grave now and may be
dived on only with permission from the
British Royal Navy.

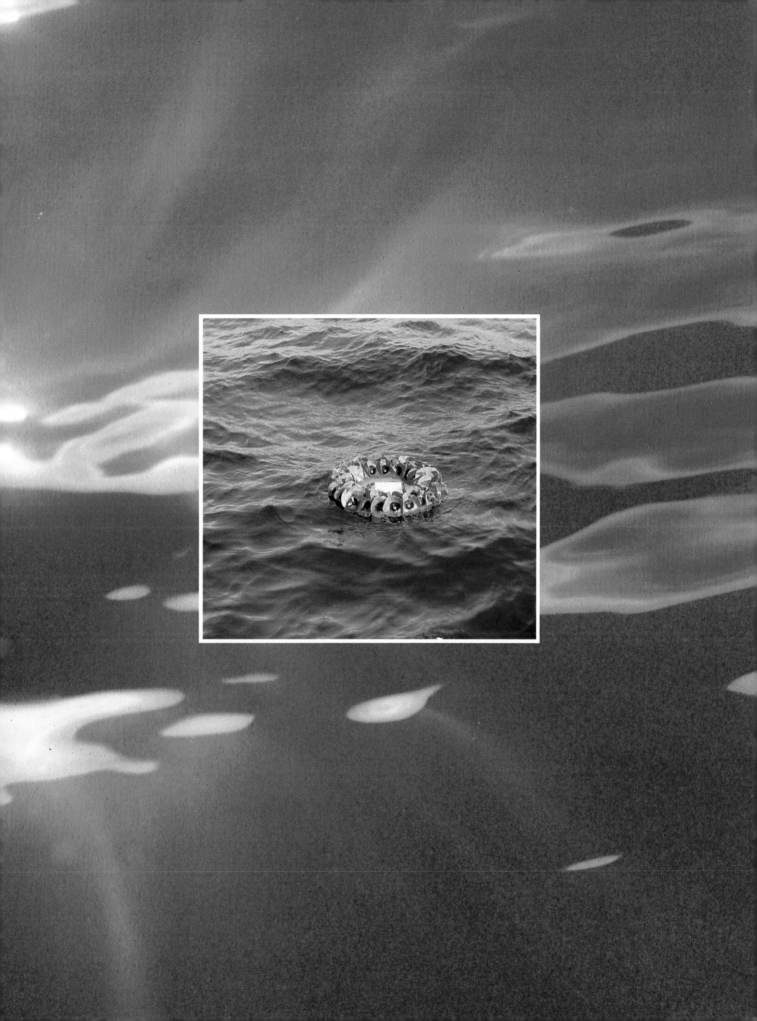

On the night of Friday, 13 October 1939, the British battleship *H.M.S. Royal Oak* was lying at anchor in the north east corner of Scapa Flow — a naturally protected area of water in the Orkney Islands just north of Scotland. What was to become World War 2 had just broken out and, for the second time this century, Britain was at war with Germany. Scapa Flow had once again been chosen as the main anchorage for the British Navy to provide the same facilities available during World War 1.

In one of the worst naval tragedies of World War 2, the light of dawn would reveal this huge 600 foot battleship lying upturned in 30 metres (98 feet) of icy cold water, her seemingly impenetrable hull, already fitted with extra protection side bulges, having been blown apart by the torpedoes from a German U-Boat in one of the most daring and successful raids in the history of maritime Germany. Over 800 British seamen were to lose their lives as the *Royal Oak* sank within minutes and

plummeted to the seabed just a few hundred yards from the safety of the cliffs at Gaitnip.

Miraculously, nearly 400 of her crew survived. Those who were not taken down with the ship were thrown into the icy oil-covered water in total darkness to make heroic attempts to reach the shore or to be plucked from almost certain death by the crew of the tiny tender *Daisy 2*. This boat, no more than 100 feet long and only 15 feet wide, managed to rescue 386 men. They

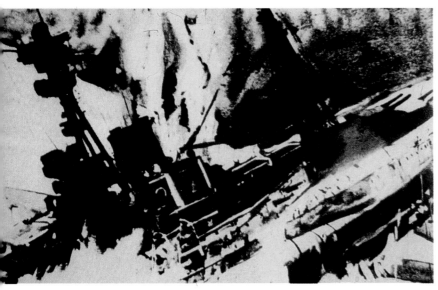

(Below left) *The 600-foot* Royal Oak *with her four pairs of 15-inch guns was built in World War 1 but, by 1939, was not as fast as the modern ships.*
(Below) *She displaced 29,000 tons and was just 100 feet wide.*
(Left) *Three massive explosions sent her to her grave.*

were crammed into every conceivable nook and cranny as the skipper navigated around the disaster area in the darkness of those early hours of Saturday morning.

The *Royal Oak* had been hit at a time when she was least prepared and with the majority of her crew turned in for what they believed would be another routine night. For the Germans it would be the first in a chain of victories that would give them a strong start to the war in which they wanted to reverse the defeat of World War 1.

As a tribute to the suffering of that night, a simple plaque was placed on the wall of St Magnus Cathedral, Kirkwall. The inhabitants of the capital were well aware that these lives were lost whilst providing protection for them. Out on the waters of Scapa Flow a green Admiralty wreck buoy marks the site of one of the most tragic and controversial losses in Britain's naval history.

The wreck of H.M.S. *Royal Oak* was immediately declared an official Navy war grave protected by law. It preserves the resting place of some of Britain's finest seamen who lost their lives in the worst possible way at a time of maximum impact for the German propaganda machine.

(Centre) *A green wreck buoy marks the war grave.* (Left) *Lucky survivors were picked up by the tiny tender* Daisy 2. *Had she not been there, nearly 400 more men would have died.* (Inset, centre) *The sign on the wreck buoy prohibits unauthorized diving.* (Inset, right) *A plaque in Kirkwall Cathedral has recently been enhanced by the addition of a bell from the Royal Oak.*

Scapa Flow

Located in the Orkney Islands, north of Scotland, Scapa Flow is a large area of naturally protected water whose facilities were considered ideal for the British Navy and her fleet.

Giving access to both the Atlantic and the North Sea, Scapa Flow is a good location from which to base strategic attacks whilst still providing shelter and security to anchored ships awaiting combat orders. Rarely over 50 metres (164 feet) deep, the Flow has an abundance of anchorages and only two main entrances. However, there are also five smaller channels but, prior to World War 2, these were thought to be impossible for a vessel to penetrate without being detected and sunk.

The collection of islands which comprise the Orkneys is best viewed from a light aircraft similar to those which provide the essential inter-island flight service for the inhabitants of the more remote outer islands. From the air you can take in the wide variation of scenery from the sheer 300 metre (980 foot) cliffs of Hoy, facing the uninterrupted power of the North Atlantic to the calm sheep pastures that flow down to the water's edge on the more sheltered east coast.

Approach from the south and you will fly from the northern shores of mainland Scotland towards the main entrance, Hoxa Sound. Hard to defend in times of war, this stretch of deep water would have been bridged with anti-submarine nets and constantly patrolled by armed ships. The tidal flow in this area is fast. One tide ebbs as the following tide starts to flow — given further turbulence by the waters of the Atlantic meeting the North Sea in the Pentland Firth. This stretch of water is notorious for its fierce currents caused by a gigantic volume of water trying to force its way through a narrow channel. This passage restricts the flow and causes the water to boil turbulently and swirl in powerful eddies as it waits to pass through from the Atlantic to the North Sea.

Continuing further north past the main entrance, you will see three much narrower channels which now have permanent stone barriers linking the islands which the channels separate.

(Top) The route of the German Commander's U-boat is now blocked permanently by solid stone barriers. In 1939, Kirk Sound was open, and the fierce tidal race together with old blockships were considered effective protection from enemy submarines.
(Below) The protected waters of Scapa Flow with Scapa Pier on the left. Royal Oak lies to the right, the oil seeping from her still clearly visible.

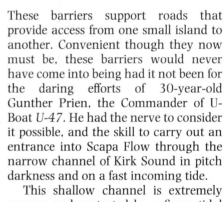

These barriers support roads that provide access from one small island to another. Convenient though they now must be, these barriers would never have come into being had it not been for the daring efforts of 30-year-old Gunther Prien, the Commander of U-Boat *U-47*. He had the nerve to consider it possible, and the skill to carry out an entrance into Scapa Flow through the narrow channel of Kirk Sound in pitch darkness and on a fast incoming tide.

This shallow channel is extremely narrow and protected by a fierce tidal flow. It was considered impossible to pass but old ships were positioned to restrict the width of the Sounds even further. Ironically enough, one of the blockships floundered on its way to Kirk Sound and sank before it could fulfill its final purpose. Despite its natural flaws, Scapa Flow is a sheltered anchorage that saw periods of intense activity during World War 1. Derelict buildings still remain as reminders of the active days when, at the end of World War 1, the German Imperial Fleet was interned in Scapa Flow following her surrender in 1918.

In a most surprising and bizarre

incident, the skeleton crews on board the German ships, rather than suffer the humiliation of surrender, opened up the seacocks and so, in one afternoon, sank their entire fleet. The scuttling happened so quickly and unexpectedly that only a few could be saved by beaching them. Most sank in deep water.

This incident has provided the Orkneys with a source of local employment ever since as salvage firms undertook to raise the wrecks and sell them for scrap metal. Most were raised in between the Wars but, for today's salvors, the remains of the Fleet have an added value in that the metal is free from nuclear contamination: they sank prior to man's nuclear activities. This added value helps to justify the heavy costs involved in raising the metal but few firms have made much money from their efforts. Nowadays, the wrecks are mostly left in peace for the diver to explore. They are unique underwater museums of World War 1.

With the onset of World War 2, the Orkneys and Scapa Flow once again became the focal point of British Naval strategy. The development of the aero-

plane meant that Scapa Flow was now more vulnerable to air attacks.

The Captain of *Royal Oak* was in charge of an ageing vessel whose orders were to act as anti-aircraft cover for Kirkwall, the capital of the Orkneys. Slow, compared to the more modern ships built between the wars, *Royal Oak* had just returned from exercises in the North Sea where she had received a battering from the harsh North Sea waves as she struggled to keep up with the Fleet. Her task of providing anti-aircraft cover was in response to fears that this war would be won or lost by the strength and effectiveness of either side's air attacks. To fulfill that task, the night of Friday, 13 October, she was lying half a mile south of Kirkwall. The night air was bitterly cold, the new moon was low in the sky and high tide was just before midnight. Everything was in Germany's favour.

H.M.S. Royal Oak

H.M.S. *Royal Oak* was built in the Naval dockyards at Devonport, Plymouth during World War 1. England, at war

(Far right) The first torpedo hit Royal Oak *in the bows. The second salvo was devastatingly effective.*
(Top, centre) Gunther Prien, Commander of U-47.
(Top, left) Metal from the German Fleet, scuttled in Scapa Flow at the end of World War 1, is valuable as it has never been contaminated by atomic radiation.
(Centre) Boom ships laid anti-submarine nets across the main entrance to Scapa Flow. They were opened to allow Navy ships into and out of the Flow.
(Right) Blockships are still in position today next to the Churchill Barriers which were built as a result of the Royal Oak *disaster.*

with Germany was urgently pushing forward with its naval shipbuilding policy in an era when battleships meant huge firepower and traditionally immense constructions whose very presence was enough to make any enemy think twice before engaging in combat.

Her keel was laid on 15 January 1914: she was launched on 17 November and completed six months later in May 1916. Nearly 600 feet in length and just over 100 feet wide, *Royal Oak* was equipped with a formidable array of firepower starting with 15-inch guns. They were the largest of their kind ever fitted to a British warship and there were eight in total in four turrets — two forward and two aft. Each barrel was capable of hurling their 900 kg (2,000 lb) shells to attack targets over 20 km (13 miles) away.

The scale of the machinery involved almost defies belief when compared to today's modern aluminium craft, fitted with computer controlled warheads capable of widespread destruction but fired from far smaller launchers. Supporting her main armament were 6-inch and 3-inch guns together with four submarine torpedo tubes although these were later removed as they took up too much space and needed too many men to operate them. Over 1,000 men were needed to keep *Royal Oak* at battle stations. She was a "Revenge" class battleship with four sister ships — H.M.S. *Ramillies, Resolution, Revenge* and *Royal Sovereign.* She served at Jutland in World War 1 and was capable of speeds in excess of 20 knots driven by her 40,000 horsepower oil-fuelled engines. It is this same oil that still seeps to the surface of Scapa Flow nearly 50 years later artificially calming the water and leaving an unmistakable patch, clearly visible from the air on a calm day.

On the night of Friday 13th, Prien approached Kirk Sound and, despite being half an hour later than planned, forced his way through Kirk Sound and into the calm waters of Scapa Flow. Once inside the Flow, Prien had to act quickly to capitalize on his chance of a surprise attack. His mind must have been racing as he surveyed the waters through the periscope of his U-Boat. His latest reports, based on aerial photographs, showed that several major British warships should have been at anchor in the Flow. Mercifully for the British Navy, all but the *Royal Oak* had set sail just a few days before to alternative anchorages, following fears that Scapa Flow was vulnerable to attack from the air. The Admirals were soon to discover that this misguided fear saved a tragedy from becoming a total and possibly terminal disaster.

With his crew at action stations and his torpedo tubes loaded, Prien fired a salvo towards the *Royal Oak* shortly before 1am. This first salvo scored a minor hit and helped to confuse the

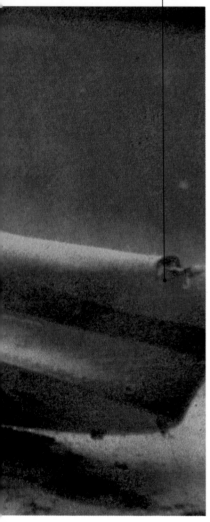

crew on board *Royal Oak* as they could only assume that the muffled explosion was an internal problem which did not seem to be causing too much alarm. Their misplaced nonchalance gave Commander Prien the vital time to reload and within 20 minutes he was ready to fire the salvo which would score three direct hits and send H.M.S. *Royal Oak* to the bottom of Scapa Flow in just over 10 minutes.

The huge battleship listed heavily to starboard as the crippling explosions ripped open her sides and allowed thousands of gallons of saltwater to flood into her. This unnatural shift of balance was given fatal momentum as the main guns swivelled in their turrets and forced the ship even more off balance until she finally keeled over and sank.

Pulled down by the massive guns, *Royal Oak* would have turned turtle had it not been that the same guns and the flying bridge halted the rolling turn and brought the wallowing ship to rest. Her upturned deck lay upside down at a 45° angle, her sleek keel uppermost and her superstructure crushed on the seabed – 30 metres (98 feet) below the surface of Scapa Flow.

Today *Royal Oak* lies as she settled nearly 50 years ago. Initially, nets were placed over her to stop bodies floating to the surface. More recently the bronze propellers were removed by navy divers. Apart from these two interventions, she remains intact, resting in her silent grave. Her massive hull reaches up to within 5 metres (16 feet) of the surface at low tide and appears to be a natural cliff-face, so large is her area. The keel strip which runs most of the length of the ship, gives the first clue to a diver that this structure is definitely not an underwater cliff, rather one of the most unusual wrecks in the world.

The years have not been kind to *Royal Oak*. Her keel and hull, being in shallower water have attracted a thick growth of marine weeds and kelp which bloom in the summer months when the waters are comparatively warmer. Even this growth cannot disguise her overall shape in shallow water. The upturned curves of her hull slope down into deeper water to the main rails where the hull meets the deck. It is at this point that the whole atmosphere of the wreck changes and she takes on a much more sombre feel.

(Centre) *An Airfix model shows how the wreck lies.*

A 15-in gun breaches
B Admiral's Barge
C Torpedo holes
D 6-in side armament
E Spotting top
F Side rails

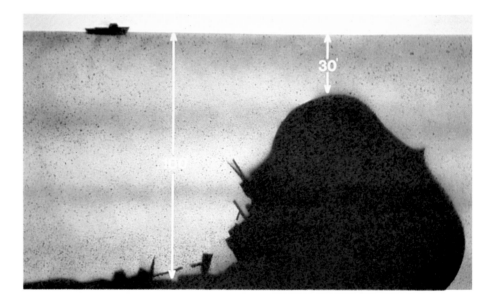

(Above) *The* Royal Oak's *upturned hull has covered most of her superstructure which lies crushed on the seabed.*

The upturned deck slopes away under the ship leaving a diver hovering in mid water with an 18 metre (59 foot) sheer uninterrupted drop to the seabed. Fortunately for divers, the gravitational pull of the earth is virtually eliminated underwater allowing you to glide down or rise up effortlessly.

Despite the confidence from near-weightlessness underwater, on the main rails of the *Royal Oak*, you have much more than physical emotions to control. Even the most experienced wreck diver will find it hard to equal the feeling of sheer excitement mingled with understandable fear as he leaves the rails to descend into the blackness.

The waters are dark and cold on even the brightest summer's day and the water clarity is poor. Visibility rarely exceeds 8 metres (26 feet). Plankton and other floating marine life cloud the water, hinder light penetration and give an eerie green tinge to the water.

As you slowly glide down, all you can hear is the sound of your own exhaled bubbles and the reassuring hiss of your demand valve as it supplies you with vital air. The dark outline of the wreck starts to appear out of the gloom and gradually you can begin to recognize detail. Everything is covered with a very fine silt which rises up in clouds if disturbed by even the gentlest fin stroke. Be careful when approaching for fear of reducing the visibility even further.

Out of the gloom your eyes search for detail. Gradually, as they become accustomed to the low light level, there emerges an enormous shape. Initially, you will not know what you are looking at or on what part of the ship you are, so it is best to start at a known point such as the stern or the bows and then follow the ship logically.

To dive on *Royal Oak* you have to be able to think upside down in order to recognize the various sections but, for a start, you can turn upside down for a while to view the ship as she would normally have been. This aids identification of a new area but soon you will start to think upside down and become familiar with large areas.

To swim from one end of the ship to the other would take an experienced diver at least 20 minutes. This is perhaps the best way of trying to appre-

(Top, left) The side rails now lie at a steep angle and point towards the seabed. Despite the cold, dark water, they have become the home for marine growth of all kinds.

Most common are plumose anemonies. At this point there is a 15-metre (50-foot) drop to the seabed.
(Above) The beam from a powerful underwater torch

helps to light a diver's way and to show the marine life in its true colours.
(Left) Loosened side rails dangle down towards deeper water festooned with plant life.

ciate the enormity of this once proud battleship now lying crumpled yet intact on the seabed of Scapa Flow.

Having found the area where the deck meets the hull with the main rails, you can start at the stern and work your way forward. The depth is about 18 metres (59 feet) so your dive can last 60 minutes before you need to consider any decompression stops. As the waters are cold, you may well become chilled before the 60 minutes are up or you may run low on air and need to end the dive. Whatever happens, you have plenty of time to begin to view the wreck and form your first impressions.

With your ability to hover, you are ideally placed to view the wreck without disturbing her or the fine silt with which she is covered. Starting at the stern you will swim over the large rear deck area which leads up to the first of the turrets containing the big guns. With the deck upside down at 45°, the reversed weight of the guns and their turrets is trying to rip them from the decking. It is only a matter of time before the already perilously thin decking rots and will not be able to support the weight, originally designed to act in the completely opposite direction.

The eight 15-inch guns were in four pairs — two aft and two forward. As you swim from the stern and pass the first turret, you will immediately see the second turret with two more massive breaches, each over 2.5 metres (8 feet) in diameter. At this point the main superstructure begins. It is an area which has suffered a great deal of impact damage. Though the full impact and effect of this damage was reduced by the support of the main guns as they dug into the sand, there is evidence, nonetheless, of heavy crushing and disformation.

It is hard to express or even pretend to be able to estimate the colossal forces that are exerted when a vessel of such immense size and weight becomes unstable and surprised by a sudden ingress of solidly heavy seawater. For massive bulkheads to be bent and crushed with apparent ease, the forces involved must be huge. Areas have been crushed and twisted leaving hanging debris that presents extreme danger

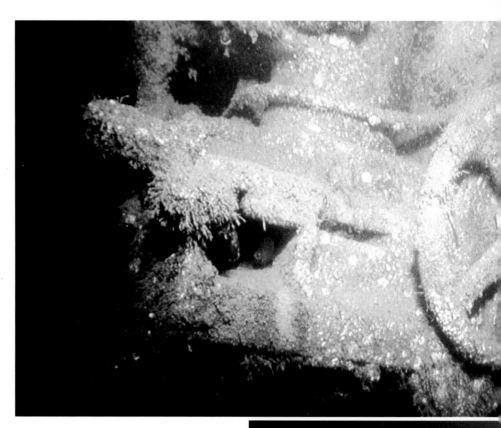

to the diver. Always keep well clear of any overhangs. The reverse gravity, combined with the rotting effect of saltwater, have produced potentially lethal hazards. Despite the cushioning effect of water which dampens motion, the mass of a structure remains largely unaffected and any falling metalwork could prove fatal to an over-curious diver.

It is for this very sound reason and with a view to remaining alive that a dive on the *Royal Oak* becomes more of a visit than a detailed exploration. Only open areas can be safely inspected, leaving the dangerous areas and overhangs to be viewed from a sensible distance. However, this limit on your access does not impair your ability to gain an impression of the enormity of this structure. As you swim to the superstructure you realise the colossal scale of the ship. The *Royal Oak* must be the largest most intact wreck in such shallow water in the whole of the northern hemisphere.

Finning forward from the second turret and the beginning of the superstructure, the area begins to resemble a large scrapyard as the funnel and fighting-top lie crushed and pinned to the seabed. In her floating state, the fighting-top would have reached up over 30 metres (98 feet) above the main deck.

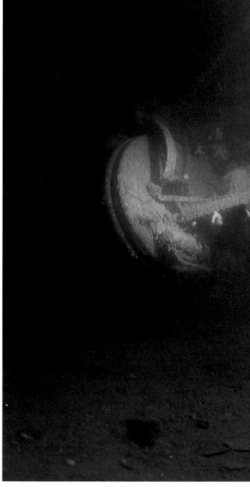

(Top left) *The main control wheel on the 15-in gun breach lies in 30 metres (100 feet).*
(Top right) *Outside the Imperial War Museum in London there are two identical 15-in guns to those on the* Royal Oak.
(Bottom left) *The breaches of the great guns on the wreck now lie in almost black water underneath the* wreck. *A diver's torch helps to show the detail.*
(Above) *Detail of the 15-in gun breaches outside the Imperial War Museum. The main control wheel is at the top and a shell stands to the left.*

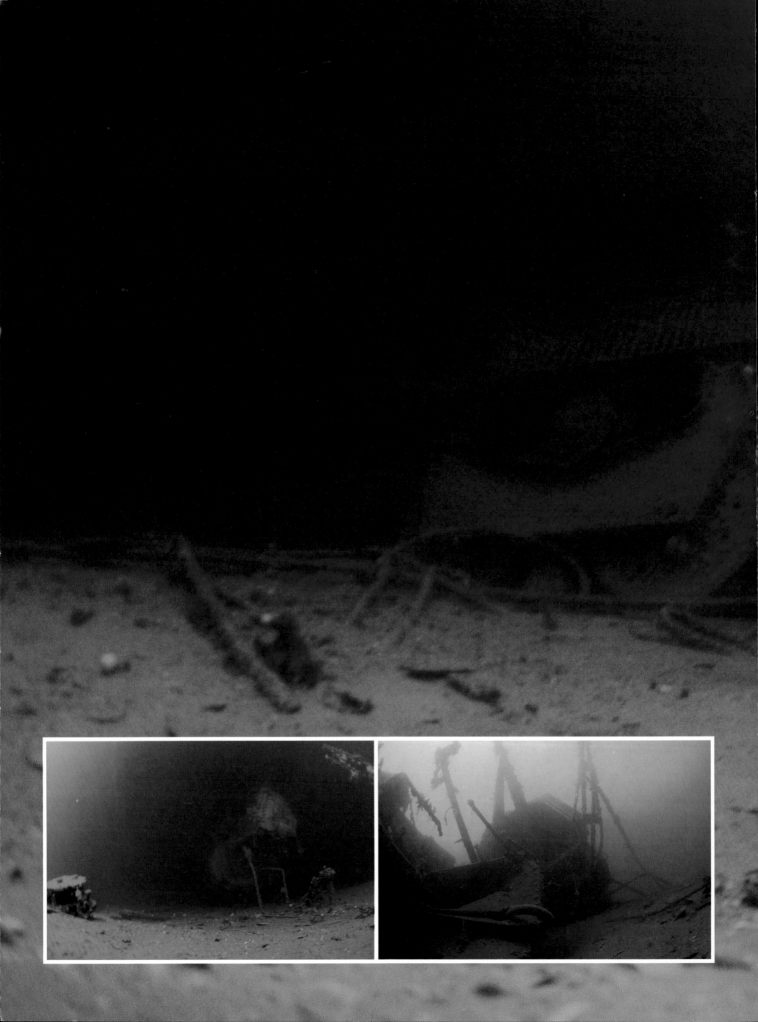

(Centre) *The section rear of the superstructure is a mangled heap of metal. There were no seaplanes on the Royal Oak at the time of her sinking but these are the remains of the launching mechanism. The seabed is littered with small debris.*

(Left inset) *The rear gun breaches are in much darker water than the forward ones. Here they lie right under the wreck in almost total darkness.*
(Right inset) *As the ship rolled over, the mast, flying bridge and spotting top buckled and came away from the ship. They now lie horizontally on the seabed.*

(Above) Water flooded in through these portholes and some survivors told of how they made a miraculous escape by getting out through them as the ship rolled over.
(Above, right) A 6-in side armament lies in 18 metres (59 feet). Most lie in line with the hull but this one seems poised for action.
(Below) The hull of the Royal Oak is lined with open portholes. They are over 50 cm (18 in) in diameter.
(Below, right and inset) The side armament plays host to marine growth which has taken nearly 50 years to form.

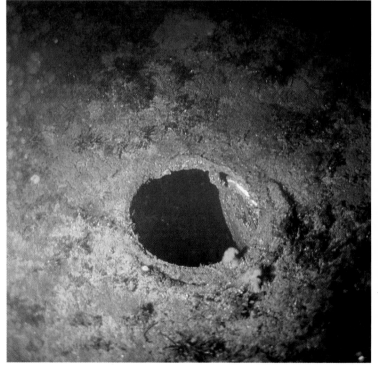

During the sinking, men in this area would have been helpless to escape as the structure quickly tilted over and drove into the sea as the ship rolled over. Only those who risked getting outside and jumping into the water stood any chance of survival. But they then had to contend with the ice cold, unforgiving northern waters. The choice was a hard one to make, and the time available to weigh up the options was fatally minimal.

In areas not crushed beyond recognition, you can discern the main gangways that provided covered access from one bulkhead door to another, with rows of portholes in between. Some portholes remain as open as they were that night whilst others are closed tight and even have their deadlights screwed down. The gaskets sealing the small area in between the deadlight and the glass of the porthole are still proving effective for there is air trapped in some of them — air from 1939 which sailors choked for and sadly found lacking as the chaos and panic of those 13 vital minutes passed by all too quickly.

Above these underwater gangways lie the side armament of 6-inch guns in single turrets. These guns are now above the gangway but when the *Royal Oak* was at anchor they would have been below and just above the extra protection bulges fitted to the sides of the ship to reduce the possible damage

from torpedoes. The bulges added a great deal of extra weight and affected the streamlining but the extra protection they afforded justified their inclusion. Unfortunately for the crew, if these

(Centre) *The ladder on the rear of the big gun cover now points upwards towards the deck.*
(Inset left) *A ladder in front of a 6-in gun gave access to the main deck.*
(Top) *The main gangway is now almost upside down, and the bulkhead door on the right remains closed.*
(Left) *A liferaft lies on the bottom. It might have saved more lives.*

side bulges had been twice the thickness, they may have withstood the attack.

Ladders lead from one gangway to another — up to some decks and down to others. They last resounded to the impact of heavy boots as panicking sailors desperately sought safety. Now these ladders attract silt and marine growth, their polished surfaces long since tarnished. Lights, with lightbulbs still intact, line the gangways but these would not have been lit on Friday 13 for fear of detection from the air. The safety of darkness suddenly became an added danger as the ship started to sink and sailors had to feel their way based on their memory of firedrills for just such an emergency.

Drop down towards the seabed now to view the scattering of small, unattached objects which must have fallen into the sea as the ship tilted. Of all these objects, none can be more poignant than the sight of a rigid liferaft lying upright on the seabed. Only some 4 metres (13 feet) long — she could still have saved the lives of many men had

she not been tossed into the sea or pulled down before they could embark.

At 30 metres (98 feet), a little further along the seabed, there is another small wreck. This is the Admiral's Barge, an ornate timber-hulled vessel tied alongside *Royal Oak* and used to transfer officers from the ship. She must have been pulled down with the Oak, and now lies upright and motionless on the seabed (see picture).

At this stage, the third of the four main turrets appears out of the green gloom. It has all but fallen away from the deck. The huge gun breaches are clearly visible on the seabed — the decking no longer able to hold their massive structures. Forward from here begins the large area of deck leading up to the bows. Here, the ratings would stand in neat formations at official ceremonies, proud in their crisp uniforms. Now this area, upside down, is a tangle of hanging ropes and a thick covering of marine growth. Vents that once supplied vital air to the decks below now are the homes of crabs and lobsters.

As you move along, the foredeck narrows until the bows appear, anchor chains stretching pathetically to the seabed. If you swim past the bows and look back, you can see the thin line of the bows which would have sliced through the water at speeds in excess of 20 knots. Drop down to the seabed again and you will see that the bows are in fact lifted off the seabed and light appears under the wreck. Only the foolish would swim under to explore. The sensible swim round and, if time permits, can begin to view the other side of the *Royal Oak*.

The other side is less revealing. As the *Royal Oak* lies at 45°, she is leaning on her starboard side. As a result, all there is to swim past on this side is a tall, near featureless structure reaching up from the seabed towards the surface. It resembles a vast, vertical cliff face, slightly softened by marine growth. You are faced with a 20-minute swim but with nothing to see en route.

Nothing that is, except for the first 30 metres (98 feet). It is in this area that the reason for the *Royal Oak's* rapid demise is revealed. It was in this forward area that the torpedoes struck.

The hull has been blown apart so extensively that you could swim into the hole and not be able to see either side until you stumbled on the inside of the ship. The metalwork is distorted beyond all recognition. Deck upon deck was flattened or reduced to mangled chaos. The area is in stark contrast to the other side where, even though there is extensive damage, the devasting explosions of the torpedoes did not reach. The twisted and mis-shapen metalwork that Prien's torpedoes achieved have not been disguised even by the camouflage of 50 years of marine growth.

Marine life

This north-east corner of Scapa Flow lacks the large tidal flow or water movement associated with the main entrance and small sounds. So the marine life that the wreck has attracted is plentiful but not profuse. Similarly, on the nearby World War 1 German Imperial Fleet, decades of underwater salvaging using hundreds of pounds of high explosives have discouraged fish. However, as salvaging work has receded so the fish have returned in both size and numbers.

(Right) The inside of the gunnery spotting top is a mass of wires and machinery. On the night of her sinking, Royal Oak *was looking for possible air attack, never imagining that a U-Boat could penetrate Scapa Flow. (Top, right) Marine growth now covers the once immaculate spotting top. This and saltwater corrosion are very slowly eroding this structure. (Bottom, right) The crumpled outriggers bear evidence of the forces involved when a ship of such size becomes unstable.*

Colourful wrasse inhabit the *Royal Oak's* kelp-covered keel, where ideal locations are to be found for their territories and nests. The abundance of nooks and crannies provides choice homes for all forms of crustacea such as edible crabs, velvet swimming crabs and small prawns.

In the deeper water, below 15 metres (49 feet), almost all areas are densely populated with attractive plumose anemones, some of which can reach up to 40 cm (16 inches) high with solid stems. Their base colours vary from orange to red and pure white, and their white polyps constantly stretch out in search of microscopic food floating past. Spider crabs scurry along the bottom as you swim past as if fearing you may suddenly swoop down and pick them up and abduct them.

If you could view the inside of the wreck in safety you would be sure to come across large conger eels who have grown fat in the safety of the structure. The labyrinth of passageways and tunnels provide ideal lairs for these long eels with the glazed unfeeling eyes, powerful jaws and muscular bodies, capable of propelling them far faster than any diver could swim.

These same lairs are shared with lobsters, whose night time feeding forays extend to the seabed. Armed with two large claws, one for cutting and the other for crushing their prey, these lobsters can reach up to 1 metre (3 feet) in length.

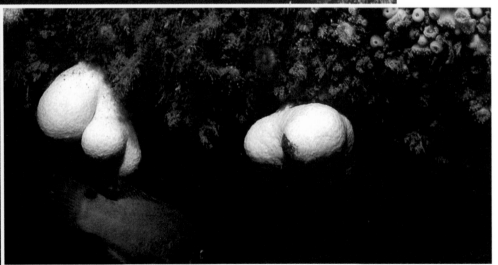

(Centre) The main torpedo hole is a large area surrounded by jagged metal. At one point a diver cannot see from one side of it to the other. Millions of gallons flooded in and the ship sank within minutes.
(Top, inset) Small anemonies now grow where once a sailor polished daily.
(Bottom, inset) Hauntingly named, Dead Men's Fingers grow on the wreck. Here their polyps are retracted.

Remembrance

Such are the living wonders of these waters. But a swim along the *Royal Oak* leaves an unforgettable memory of the dead, not the living. This huge battleship, lying contorted on the seabed, is a representative of a bygone era when the importance of a nation was indicated by the size and capability of her navy.

For the relatives of those men who lost their lives on H.M.S. *Royal Oak*, this wreck is a hallowed place. It is the grave of over 800 men who lost their lives in defence of Britain and as such is a sacred and protected site. The *Royal Oak* will remain on the seabed, protected by Navy law and visited once a year by Navy divers who, after a short service conducted on the local coastguard launch, dive down to the stern and ceremoniously unfold a battle ensign. On land, survivors meet annually in Portsmouth, their numbers dwindle as the years increase, but their short remembrance service keeps alive the love and respect for both the ship and her ill-fated crew.

(Top left) *A wreath is placed on the water after a service of remembrance.*
(Left) *A green wreck buoy marks the area.*
(Below, far left) *The Naval cemetery at Lyness contains the graves of the few bodies recovered.*
(Below, centre left) *An ensign is raised on the wreck each year by the Navy.*
(Below, centre right) *The wreath floats over the wreck.*
(Below) *A memorial plaque in St Magnus Cathedral, Kirkwall.*

H.M.S. *Royal Oak* is a designated war grave, and diving on her is strictly forbidden by law. Peter Rowlands was granted special permission to dive with the Royal Navy in order to document the wreck on film.

THE
CRISTOBOL COLON

The Island of Bermuda has for centuries
provided a stop off point for ships crossing
the Atlantic. Her shallow coral reefs have
also become the graveyard for many of
them. Over the years, a great variety of
coral has gradually colonized the wrecks,
decorating them, and eventually engulfing
them altogether. The three sections of the
wreck of the *Cristobol Colon* make up one
of the most beautiful wreck sites in the
world.

Beneath the surface of the waters that cover two-thirds of our planet's extent lie natural marvels that rival any land formation for beauty and spectacle. Modern mapping techniques enable us to reproduce accurate models of the undersea terrain as dramatic as any in the Grand Canyon or Yellowstone National Park. Recent discoveries include huge submarine trenches and sheer vertical walls on a scale unequalled on land.

Of course, those pioneers who took to the sea centuries ago understood and appreciated the basic detail of underwater terrain — without the aid of sophisticated modern techniques. They were well aware of hidden pinnacles that rise steeply from the depths to form hazardous obstacles. Their navigational and sailing skills were often keenly tested in the shallow water fringing the reefs of tropical islands.

And, yet despite Man's achievements in mapping the oceans to make them a safer place, ships still go aground. Early sailing ships, with their billowing sails and multi-mast designs, had the excuse of being completely at the mercy of the wind and waves. The wrong combination of wind and tide could overpower even the most knowledgeable skipper and leave his vessel to flounder on shallow reefs. The situation was doubly dangerous at night: the lack of navigation lights meant a crew could only listen for the breakers to judge how near they were to land.

Modern ships, with powerful engine rooms, radars and bridges full of the latest electronic satellite-fed navigational equipment, have no such excuses — yet they still go aground and sink. It seems that human error cannot be eliminated, however much is spent on instruments and controls.

Perhaps one of the world's most feared ocean areas is off the island of Bermuda in the Atlantic. A broad expanse of shallow water reefs has brought disaster to more than 350 ships over the years. It is not by chance that the Spanish, having lost several galleons, called her "The Isle of Devils". The island's natural ability to be both a maritime shelter and a graveyard must make it the undisputed capital of the wreck divers' world.

Bermuda

Completely alone in the middle of the North Atlantic, Bermuda, the world's most northerly coral outcrop, is over 950 kilometres (590 miles) from the nearest land. Volcanic action first thrust the island's land mass from the seabed, over 5 kilometres (3 miles) below to form an area no more than 33 kilometres (21 miles) long and 1.6 kilometres (1 mile) wide. For shipping, Bermuda is the main centre for the North Atlantic routes and this has brought trading prosperity to an island which has virtually no natural resources and is totally dependent on imports (the cost of which is supported by a financial tax-haven encouraging multi-national company investors).

Yet for all her attractions to outsiders, Bermuda has striven to build a stable, controlled society and temper a tourist trade which, if allowed to take hold on this small island, could destroy the very nature of her attraction. An equable climate and superb scenery are enhanced by summer temperatures that are truly tropical. Winters are mild, warmed by winds blowing over the Gulf Stream which, at this stage in its journey across the Atlantic, is over 400 kilometres (250 miles) wide.

This mild and consistent climate has produced exotic flora and fauna on land with lush growths in frost-free soil. The lack of heavy industry leaves a sparklingly clean atmosphere with bright

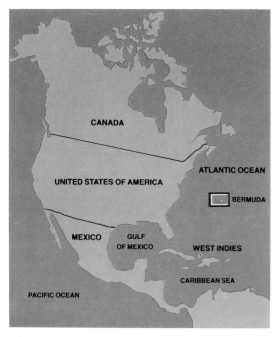

(Left) Bosses Cove provides a sheltered anchorage for small boats.

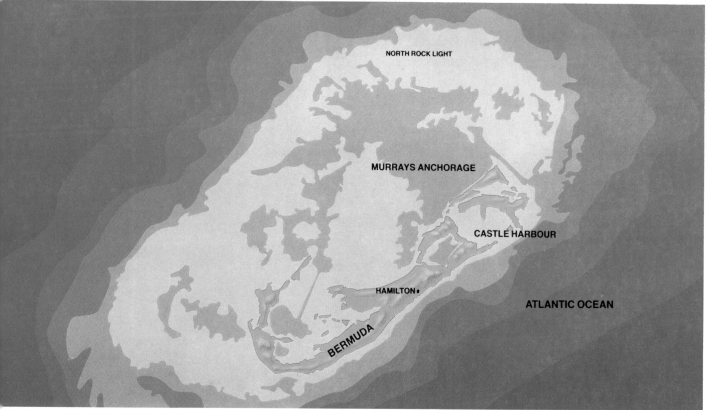

CANADA

ATLANTIC OCEAN

UNITED STATES OF AMERICA

BERMUDA

MEXICO

GULF OF MEXICO

WEST INDIES

PACIFIC OCEAN

CARIBBEAN SEA

NORTH ROCK LIGHT

MURRAYS ANCHORAGE

CASTLE HARBOUR

HAMILTON

ATLANTIC OCEAN

BERMUDA

(Above) *The pounding waves have formed arches rising out of the pure white sand.*
The lush Bermudan climate supports (Above, centre) Frangipanni, (Plumeria Rubra), (Above, right) Bottle Brush tree, (Calistemon Sp.), (Below, right) Yellow Lily (Lilium Sp.) and (Far right) Royal Poinciana, (Delonix Regia).

colours and naturally sandy beaches. A single airport limits the number of plane arrivals and Bermuda's laws do not allow visitors to come without accomodation booked in advance. Such controls keep Bermuda pleasantly uncrowded and encourage a society which derives the best from both British and American cultures. Bermuda has built up a reputation as being exclusive and therefore expensive — but for good reasons. To complement her land-based attractions, the Bermudan marine life is special enough to be considered unique. As well as supplying warm winds during the winter, the Gulf Stream provides a consistent supply of comparatively warm water. Even in the coldest winter, the water temperature does not drop below 15°C (59°F) between January and March while the summer sun warms the shallow waters to 29°C (84° F) between July and September. This consistency provides a comfortable marine climate in which the underwater life thrives. Creatures have no need to migrate to warmer waters during the winter but can remain in their habitats the whole year round.

For divers, the consistent temperature means comfortable diving for 12 months of the year. The clarity of the northern waters rarely falls below 20 metres (66 feet), and good calm conditions can increase this to at least 50 metres (164 feet). Despite these ideal conditions, the waters are not infested with boat loads of divers. Bermuda is surrounded by a shallow water fringing reef that covers nearly 500 square kilometres (193 square miles). In this sheltered area, the marine life is undisturbed and allowed to flourish in "greenhouse conditions".

Corals require clean, shallow, sheltered water to multiply and Bermuda has this in abundance. This naturally expanding location is the home of fast growing and rock solid corals which create natural structures of immense size and complexity. It is these structures that have caused so many ships to come to grief in the crystal clear waters surrounding Bermuda.

Bermuda – The wrecks

With such a history and supply of shipwrecks, Bermuda has a local diving population that spends most of its underwater time in search of and exploring the hundreds of wrecks around the coastline. The attraction is such that some divers have actually migrated to Bermuda for the diving alone. Almost all sites must be approached by boat – preferably of a shallow draft design to reduce the risk of damage on the coral heads. At low tide, proceed cautiously, with a look-out seated as high as possible to warn the skipper of approaching obstacles.

Boat journeys to wrecksites vary from 10 to 90 minutes depending on the site of your choice. The waters to the north where most of the known wrecks are situated are usually calm and clear. But judging distances offshore in the absence of any suitable landmarks can make exact location a time-consuming and sometimes fruitless exercise. There are times when the only way to find a wreck is to jump into the water with a mask and snorkel and be towed along by the boat!

In the Bermudan divers' catalogue there are about a dozen wrecks whose reputation distinguish them from the rest. They receive regular visits from the

(Right) *The wave action has opened up the wreck of the* Montana *for easy exploration.*
(Far right) *The bow section of the* Montana *is open and safe enough to enter.*
(Inset) *A diver examines glass ampoules on the* Constellation.

local dive clubs and dive tour operators.

The *Sea Venture*, which sank in 1609, can claim to be the very first shipwreck on the island. It was the survivors of this tragedy who went ashore to colonize the uninhabited island. As for the most recent wreck, it would be unwise to offer a name: new ones are added regularly.

The wreck with the most glamorous reputation is the *Constellation*. Most of her fame comes from her association with the film *The Deep*, from the novel by Peter Benchley, himself a keen scuba diver. The *Constellation* now lies six miles northwest of Bermuda but in 1943 was carrying medical provisions and general supplies to Venezuela. The cargo included several hundred bags of

(Left) *The huge paddle wheels on the* Montana *are breaking up but are still recognizable.*
(Below) *Two cannons from the* L'Hermenie *lie on the sandy seabed.*

(Above) *Soft corals silhouetted against the sunlit surface.*
(Top, far right) *An iron propeller which will rotate no longer, gripped by the seabed and covered in small marine growth.*

(Right) *The ribs of the* Caraquette *lie upright in the clear Bermudan waters.*
(Above, left) *The bow of the* Iristo *which sank in 1937. Her large winch wheels are encrusted with marine life.*

cement. These bags have long since split open and have concreted together to form a massive underwater pile – and to serve as a useful underwater landmark to locate the wreck.

The variety of the rest of the *Constellation's* cargo makes it a divers' treasure-trove where interesting small items are still easily found. The most extraordinary part of the cargo was a collection of small ampoules containing a light brown liquid being shipped to laboratories for processing into painkilling morphine. It was these ampoules that gave Peter Benchley the idea for his book, *The Deep*, which was to be a follow up to his hugely successful first novel *Jaws*. In *The Deep*, the wreck containing the ampoules is discovered underneath another wreck found by two tourist divers (played in the film by Jacqueline Bisset and Nick Nolte). Peter Benchley did not, in fact, depart far from the

truth, for this is almost what has happened to the *Constellation*. Just 50 metres (164 feet) away, 80 years before, the *Montana*, a paddle-wheel-driven ship struck the same coral head and sank. It is still visible today: especially the 8 metre (26 feet) diameter paddle-wheel which now lies on its side in no more than 20 metres (66 feet) of water.

In a similar sequence of events, the H.M. Brig of War *Carnation* sank in 1810 on a reef near the *Constellation* and was followed 28 years later by *L'Hermenie*, a first class French Navy frigate whose 60 double-banked cannons were strewn over the seabed in just 8 metres (26 feet) of water. At least 25 are still clearly visible, together with piles of cannon balls and cannon supports. The rest have been gradually covered and disguised by the fast growing hard corals.

(Centre) *A diver framed in the wreckage of the* Madiana *which went down in 1903.*
(Far left) *Portholes are a prize for the souvenir-hunting diver but they do not come off without a struggle.*
(Left) *The elegant lines of the anchor of the* Caraquette *provide a perfect "prop" for underwater photography.*
(Right) *Marine life is quick to colonize and very soon disguises its host.*

In another incident, the *North Carolina* sank in 1880 but this time it was not the coral heads that were to cause the damage but the ship's own anchor which pierced her hull and sank her 8 kilometres (5 miles) offshore in 8 metres (26 feet) of water. Being southwest of the island the visibility is not as clear as the northern reefs but the *North Carolina* is an attractive site with an intact bowsprit.

The list goes on, well documented in local archives, and is being expanded each year as more wrecks are discovered. But, if one person could be singled out as the most successful wreck locator it would be a local man named Teddy Tucker. His maritime experiences include – to name but a few – wreck location, treasure hunting and shark catching for research. His reputation has spread worldwide and it was on him that Peter Benchley based the character Romer Treece, the boat skipper in *The Deep*, played so successfully in the film by Robert Shaw.

From such a rich harvest of shipwrecks, the one that is both the largest and most beautiful of all on the surrounding coral reefs is the *Cristobol Colon*.

The Cristobol Colon

Built in 1923, the *Cristobol Colon* was an impressive vessel, 480 feet long and displacing 10,833 tons. A three-decked passenger liner, she was built to cater for luxury-seeking clients and, in October 1936, set sail from Cardiff, Wales, heading for Vera Cruz in Mexico via Bermuda. She was under the indirect command of the Spanish Government, who had seized her during the summer to assist them during the Spanish Civil War.

The *Cristobol Colon* had taken on a cargo of coal in Cardiff but it was widely rumoured that she might be calling at Cuba to take on arms and munitions for the war effort. There were no fare-paying passengers on board so the crew of 160, which included six stewardesses, had a simple task during the voyage. It was the simplicity of this voyage which was to cause it to be her last.

At around midnight on 25 October 1936, a full moon was shining on the clear waters around Bermuda but the radio operator had his mind and ears tuned to a broadcast from Spain. Had he been listening more attentively to the much more relevant navigational signals, he would have been informed that the North Rock Light was out of order. As a result, the uninformed captain misjudged the channel lights leading towards Hamilton, the main port and capital, and the *Cristobol Colon* ran aground eight miles northeast of Bermuda. At the time, she was steaming ahead at her full speed of 15 knots and so ended up high and dry, with very little hope of refloating on the next high tide.

For two days after the grounding Captain Crescencia Navarro Delgado refused all offers of salvage. A New York firm was on standby with a quote of $1,800 a day plus $50,000 if they were successful. Even the local Admiralty joined in the negotiations but the captain was adamant. Local tugs tried

(Right) *The bows of the* Cristobol Colon *can be seen from the surface.*
(Far right) *The propeller on the* Cristobol Colon *stands above the wreckage.*

to pull her off at successive high tides but it soon became obvious that the *Cristobol Colon* was destined to remain on the reef.

Standing so high and dry, she looked afloat from a distance and was a hazardous decoy for other shipping. Just under one year later, the Captain of the *Iristo* assumed that he was in safe waters following the *Cristobol Colon* but found himself and his Norwegian freighter aground on a nearby reef. To try to reduce this possible confusion, the masts and funnel were immediately removed from the *Cristobol Colon.*

For another five years, she sat on top of the reef, rusting and attracting a rich coral growth on her submerged hull. She seemed destined to crumble as the elements gradually took their toll but, in 1942, the American Air Force decided to use her as target practice for their pilots. They literally blew her off the edge of the reef and into deeper water. Her presence could no longer

confuse approaching shipping and her structure began to take on a new role in the underwater world supplying a perfect sanctuary for corals and fish.

Diving the Cristobol Colon

Any journey over the coral reefs to the north of Bermuda is an extremely hazardous business. The area is so vast that it is impossible to stick to or remember a safe route. All you can do is to take things one at a time and keep a look out for local coral heads, whilst trying to steer a compass course in the direction of the wreck. Once on the outer edge of the fringing reef, marker buoys are often left to indicate the wrecksite as exact location so far off-shore can be time consuming and sometimes totally unproductive.

Nearly 500 feet long, the *Cristobol Colon* was blown up and scattered over a very large area. Some estimates claim

between you and the sky. Light flurries of wind mark the surface with ever-changing patterns and give an enhanced three-dimensional feel to your dive.

So many wreck divers spend the whole of their time gazing down that they completely miss one of the most rewarding visual aspects of a wreck dive. The effect of sunlight on the dramatic structure of a wreck provides unlimited enjoyment for the eye and,

that her wreckage covers over 9,000 square metres (97,000 square feet) but there are at least three main sections — the bow, mid-section and the stern. Of these, the bow is in the shallowest water and a diver can enter at 5 metres (16 feet) and emerge at 15 metres (49 feet). Most of the finer detail has been eroded away over the years but deck railings still exist in this section. Here, passengers would have looked out to sea as they walked on deck after dining in the sumptuous ballroom. Large swaying seafans now replace orna-mental flags as decoration with their roots firmly attached to the wreckage.

Most evident in this bow section are two very large propellers. This appar-ently odd position for items normally associated with the stern is explained by the fact that these two are spare propel-lors, one of which lies bolt upright. Each blade is 2 metres ($6\frac{1}{2}$ feet) high and these would have been bolted to the deck for safekeeping until needed. Being in such shallow water, the bows are gradually being covered by rapidly growing corals but it will take many years before these growths are sufficient enough to disguise this section of the wreck. Of all the sections, the bows are the most interesting and photogenic: you can swim in and out of large open areas. As a result you can access parts from below and look up to see the silvery surface that marks the frontier

more especially, the underwater camera.

Most divers on the *Cristobol Colon* tend to spend a whole dive on each of the three main sections, and so have plenty of time to absorb the detail and scenery. In such shallow water, you can anchor over the wrecksite with two or three tanks of air and spend most of the day on the site. After all, it can take over 90 minutes to reach the wreck from the mainland so to do one rapid dive and return home would be a little extravagant.

With a fresh tank on your back and after a brief rest in the warm Bermudan sunshine, a short swim from the bow area brings you over the mid-section. You can see it clearly from the surface as it starts in 6 metres (20 feet) of water and drops down to 15 metres (49 feet).

(Above) Delicate Sea Fans
(Gorgonia ventalina)
take many years to reach
this size.
(Left) The solid metal
sections of the Cristobol
Colon *will withstand the*
sea's erosion for decades to
come.
(Top, left) The huge
engines on the Cristobol
Colon.

CRISTOBOL COLON

On a good, clear day after settled weather, you should be able to see right down to the seabed. Two large boilers lie with their tubes now corroded open providing ideal lairs for moray eels and small crabs. There were six altogether that provided the steam for the four 1,775 h.p. turbine engines that were running flat out when she went aground. The area is littered with the pipework associated with steam power much of which was made from high quality brass and copper.

Large numbers of valves and gauges emerge from the coral encrustation, easily identifiable since the glass fronts are too smooth to support the same marine growth. Still in evidence are two giant flywheels, both at least 2.5 metres (8 feet) in diameter, that once transmitted the power from the engines to the propellers. They are attached to the long propeller shafts which slope down into slightly deeper water. Although she was not damaged internally when she went aground, the subsequent damage inflicted by the American Air Force has reduced this part of the Cristobol Colon to a mangled and mainly flattened mass but, the cautious explorer can make out objects such as baths and toilets together with quality floor tiles.

The *Cristobol Colon* was designed and built as a first class passenger liner with plush carpets, mahogany-lined cabins and ornate light fittings. There was a chapel on board, complete with patterned floor tiles. In the mid-section area, lines of port holes make picturesque subjects for the photographer. Closer inspection reveals that they are just holes — the original brass fittings have been removed as souvenirs. Steeped in mild acid to remove the marine growth, they are then sandblasted before being polished back to the original gloss.

Ships that were designed and built as ornate vessels for the well-to-do are a wreck divers' dream. They always offer the chance of retrieving such small and fascinating pieces as finely inscribed

The powerful winches on the Cristobol Colon *play host to hard corals and divers.*

nameplates hidden under a pile of debris (the timber doors upon which they would originally have been attached having long since rotted away). On ships that carried wealthy passengers, a host of personal effects may remain to be discovered. But, unfortunately for divers on the *Cristobol Colon,* her last voyage was without well-heeled fare-paying passengers. Had that not been the case, her reputation would have been even further enhanced as a treasure-trove.

Lying slightly deeper in 15 metres (49 feet) is the stern section with some of its railings intact but, once again, target practice has reduced this once large section to a widespread area of flattened plates and buckled structures. Being deeper, a diver's time is limited in this area and there are still some

complete portholes, albeit in less accessible areas.

One drawback to this wreck from a tidy diver's point of view is the ship's main cargo: coal, that is now scattered all over the site. You may surface looking more like a coal miner than a diver if you are ferreting around under sections to try to find interesting and possibly valuable artefacts. Despite the warm water, most divers choose to wear a thin wet suit for physical protection rather than warmth. The wreckage can be very jagged and, with your view restricted by a mask, it is easy to snag or bump into it unintentionally, with the possibility of a nasty cut.

Being a civilian ship, the *Cristobol Colon* does not have any dangerous cargo, nor was she armed, despite being commandeered to help the Spanish in

(Far left) *The twisted wreckage of the* Cristobol Colon *frames a diver. The waters in summer are warm enough to dispense with a full wetsuit.*
(Left) *Large sections of the wreck are open and can be entered safely.*
(Below) *Huge nuts and bolts have been completely covered and will soon be unrecognizable.*

the Civil War. But, some of the airborne rockets and shells launched at her by the USAAF may survive undetonated and could be lying under the wreckage you are about to lift up. Salt water corrosion and seepage into the powerful detonation charges can make such ammunition more volatile. Caution is the best course: as a rule, never handle any munitions that look intact. Despite this slight risk, the *Cristobol Colon* has a good supply of brass shell cases which, when retrieved and polished, make excellent ornaments. In addition, when the shells are cleaned, intricate engraved markings reappear. Most relate to the year of manufacture but, on some, there will be details of flight patterns and of the type of explosives contained. It is the revelation of such detail long after the dive is over that makes wreck hunting so exciting and unpredictable.

The marine life

When you first enter the waters of a coral reef, your eyes will be greeted by a constantly moving colourful world of marine animals and plants. The corals that have set up home on the *Cristobol Colon's* structure include the evocatively named Brain, Tree and Staghorn varieties. All thrive in the shallows where light and clarity are excellent. Brain coral gets its name from its uncanny resemblance to the human brain once removed from the skull. But there the similarity ends. The underwater Brain is extremely hard and, although there are heads which closely resemble the size of a human brain, they mostly grow to over three metres (10 feet) in diameter. At such sizes they become perfect shelter for Gobies — small fish about the length of a matchstick with large eyes out of all proportion to their bodies.

The more flexible corals known as Sea Rods and Sea Fans are attached to a variety of foundations. Some mistake rope for a safe foundation and sway precariously in the current, their deep purple colour and intricate pattern of growth making them most attractive. As their name suggests, the Sea Fans are graceful, looking like intricately-

(Left) Elegantly shaped
hard corals thrive in the
warm shallow waters.
(Above) Detail from a
picture of Brain Coral
shows why it is so called.

patterned fans. The Sea Rods, more tree-like, could perhaps better be likened to giant cacti — without the spikes. Their colours vary between purple, brown, blue, black or yellow depending on their location on the reef.

Despite the wreck's position on Bermuda, the most northerly coral island, the marine life is typical of the region. But the *Cristobol Colon* has attracted some unusual inhabitants, such as the Yellow Coneys. These fish are a smaller version of the commonly found Coney (which resemble small Groupers). The Yellow Coney is quite rare and is a vivid golden colour. Aquarists who try to keep these fish at home are in for a disappointment. After about a month, the bright gold fades to a disappointing brown. As a saving grace, the flesh is succulent and tasty!

Most amusing are Trumpetfish. Very long and thin, they rely for survival upon a resemblance to thin strands of the Sea Rod corals. They hang vertically in their camouflage but are capable of fast acceleration out of the coral towards their unsuspecting prey. Being on the edge of the Bermuda Outer Reef, the *Cristobol Colon* often plays host to the open water species such as Barracuda with occasional visits from Tuna and Bonito. These fast swimming fish are large and valued for their texture.

It is not inconceivable that you could come across some small sharks, as you are over 9 kilometres (5½ miles) from the mainland and just 2 kilometres (1 mile) from the Atlantic Ocean floor. In particular you may see Nurse sharks

which spend most of their time on sandy bottoms. Their eyes are very small and fortunately their mouths and teeth are too. Despite being related to the more feared species of sharks, the Nurse is docile and easily scared off.

Perhaps the most exciting sight in summer months would be a large Manta Ray. These can reach up to 6 metres (20 feet) across but they too are harmless, feeding on plankton and staying close to the surface where they sometimes warm themselves on sunny days when the water is calm. For most of the time they keep on the move: you are more likely to see one swimming past the wreck on its way to find more plankton. They have been known to circle around and apparently pose for the cameras, and then depart for open water, simply and effortlessly transported by a flap of their huge wing span.

As with so many underwater sites where ships have come to grief and formed a new marine environment, you never can predict what you will see next. You are merely being allowed a brief visit into a constantly changing world. However, the sights and experiences revealed to you, on even the most mundane dive, will not cease to captivate you and drive you to the marine identification books to try and establish the name of your latest find. The beauty of shipwrecks is that they combine the best of diving with a view of human history. Add to this the unforgettable sight of the marvels of the marine life that make wrecks their kingdom and the picture is complete.

Bermudan marine life is both colourful and very varied.
(Far left, top) Angelfish;
(Far left, centre) Porgy fish;
(Far left, bottom) Grouper.
(Below) Large clams are sensitive to light and movement.
(Below, far left and left) General scenes in shallow water illustrate the attractions of Bermuda's reefs.

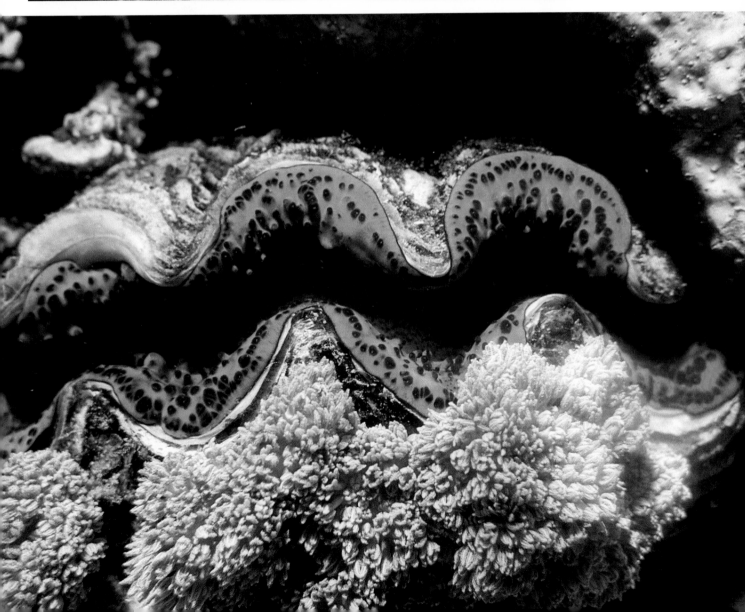

TRUK LAGOON

The events of World War 2 have left the
diving world with a host of shipwrecks to
discover and explore. The most extensive
collection lies in Truk Lagoon where
American planes took their revenge for
Pearl Harbour and sank most of Japan's
cargo ships. The Philippine Government
has protected the wrecks by law
preserving them as an underwater
museum.

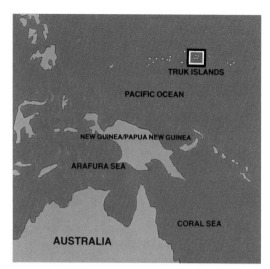

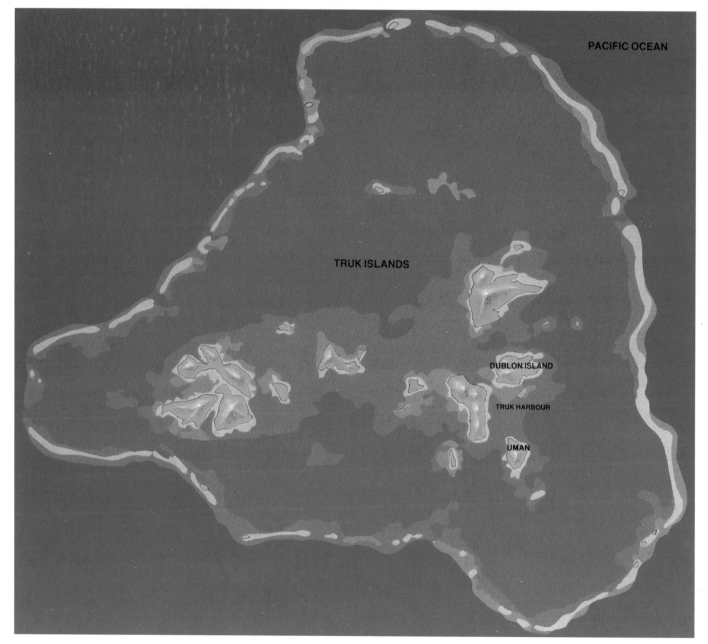

Once the debris and destruction of man's warring nature has been removed from the battle-scarred land, a natural regeneration takes place. Although the result is environmentally pleasanter, the removal can destroy much of historical interest and deny us the chance of observing Nature's own regenerative powers.

In the same way, salvage of wrecks of naval battles, whether by governments for political reasons or by individuals for financial gain, takes place. Such removal denies divers the enjoyment of visiting the wrecks or their deep water locations. Occasionally, a governing body acts to save underwater wartime evidence *in situ*. When this happens wrecks can be preserved both for divers to view and for nature to change gradually.

Fortunately, many wrecks remain and become legendary dives in the subaqua world. Despite extensive salvage operations, the German Fleet, scuttled in Scapa Flow after World War 1, is one of the most accessible collection of warships in the world. There is, however, one location which can boast over 60 wrecks which have remained untouched for over 40 years. This is at Truk Lagoon in the northern Pacific. Here, successive governments have banned salvage and individual bounty hunting. The result is a unique underwater museum and laboratory. To divers, Truk is undeniably the seventh wonder of the world.

Truk is a natural lagoon about 64 kilometres (40 miles) across at its widest point and has a fringing reef over 161 kilometres (100 miles) long. This vast area contains 11 main islands and over 100 much smaller ones. For wreck divers, among its attractions is the evidence of a successful American attack on the Japanese Imperial Fleet in February 1944.

(Above) The beautiful tropical beaches of Truk Lagoon are sometimes scarred with the evidence of conflict.
(Top, middle) All wreckage is protected by law.

(Main) *Two Helldiver SB2c's fly over Guam during the Saipan Invasion in search of enemy shipping.*
(Inset) *Dublon Town, Truk Islands, was Japan's naval base in the Carolines. US carrier-based planes took this aerial shot just before the attack of 16 February 1944.*

As the Japanese Navy's main Pacific anchorage, Truk was under a constant threat of air attacks and its presence represented a hindrance to America's domination of the Pacific. On 16 February 1944, American forces began "Operation Hailstorm", an operation which at first took the Japanese forces by surprise. It was originally thought that most of the Japanese Fleet was at anchor there but, unknown to the Americans, just a few days before the attack, most of the capital ships had upped anchor and left the area.

In the attack, American Hellcat fighter planes swarmed over Truk's waters and inflicted a decisive blow to Japan's naval strength. They were followed by Avenger torpedo bombers, Helldiver dive bombers and finally the Douglas Dauntless bombers. The Japanese lost over 40 ships and 270 aircraft together with vital fuel depots. Further attacks the same year and in 1945 put paid to Truk's strategic importance. Once the war was over, the area returned to its former calm. The evidence of the American attack lay

hidden below the lagoon water. It would still have been forgotten had there not been a plague of Crown of Thorns starfish in the early 1960s. To prevent these coral-eating starfish from destroying the reefs, the local inhabitants learned to dive. It was during this period of diving activity to stem the spread of the starfish that they discovered the wrecks and saw how nature had colonized them successfully.

World-wide, divers soon learned the attractions of Truk — wrecks, perfectly preserved, in warm clear water. Each successive dive revealed more and more wrecks. Over 100 wrecks have now been charted in and around the lagoon. Such is the number of wrecks that space is not available to describe them all in detail but there are two in particular which deserve to be singled out.

(Centre) The seaplane base on Dublon Island being attacked on 16 February 1944. Fragmentation clusters and incendiary bombs are being dropped.

(Left, top) A Japanese warship on fire after being attacked by fighter planes from the Carrier USS Intrepid.

(Left, below) Just off Dublon Island a Japanese ammunition ship explodes after a dive-bombing attack from a US plane.

(Below) A Japanese destroyer tried to escape from Truk, but was successfully caught by US planes.

(Bottom) The rich coral growths are the main diet of the Crown of Thorns starfish.

Fujikawa Maru

Lying upright in 34 metres (112 feet), the *Fujikawa Maru* at 435 feet long is one of Truk's best wreck dives. She was sunk by a single torpedo striking her starboard side just aft of the superstructure. Despite the fact that she sank in 34 metres (112 feet) of water, the tips of her two masts break the surface: they provide ideal mooring points for visiting dive boats. Over the years hundreds of divers have kitted up in the tropical heat, anticipating spectacular dives and, over the years, the *Fujikawa Maru* has never disappointed her visitors.

Diving off a large wreck in such clear water is ideal for most divers. The *Fujikawa Maru* is a wreck which can be enjoyed at all levels and by divers of all capabilities. The surface-dependant snorkeller can see the shallow water coral and can detect the shapes which lie in deeper water. Novice divers sensibly limiting themselves to 15 metres (49 feet) are able to inspect the main bridge, while the experienced wreck diver can spend each dive in a different area and still want to return for more.

As you hit the warm water and adjust your buoyancy prior to descending, you look down into the deep blue depth. There below you is a breath-taking sight. A blaze of soft corals grow on every available space on the two masts. Their colours vary from deep crimson red through to crisp yellows and light blues. Their polyps are all out-stretched to capture the minute food particles which float past. Their stems reveal an intricate sub system of arteries resembling veins. They never fail to make an underwater photographer take just one more picture.

Descending down either of the two masts, you can see the main superstructure with the top of the bridge lying in no more than 13 metres (40 feet) of water. Since any sunlit area is inhabited by marine life, from a marine biologist's viewpoint, these artificial reefs are a productive area for study. Since the dates of the wrecks are known, the age of the growths of corals and molluscs can be accurately gauged. This makes the wreck a perfect base from which to establish growth rates and study the preferred habitats of these comparatively recent marine growths.

(Far left) *The scale of the Truk wrecks both in quantity and size provides divers with a unique site. The mast of the* Fujikawa Maru *towers over two visiting divers. They are only allowed to look and take photographs of these protected wrecks.*
(Left) *A decaying lorry is the focus of attention after years' underwater.*
(Below) *A diver hovers over the huge hold of the* Fujikawa Maru *with deck cargo still in position.*

(Below) The marine life has colonized every space on the wrecks. Both hard and soft corals compete with clams and colourful Butterfly fish come in search of food.
(Right) Intricate soft corals have delicate pastel colours and intricate patterns.
(Below, right) Hard corals cover the metalwork and soft corals add the final decorations.

As well as corals, fish have settled into the *Fujikawa Maru* as if it was always part of their underwater world. Large shoals of Glass Sweeper fish swirl around the wreck while Groupers guard their individual territories from unwanted predators. Moray eels take advantage of man-made lairs to house their long bodies, while beautiful Lion fish hide in the dark overhangs, waiting for night to signal their time to hunt and feed. Close inspection reveals an abundance of much smaller marine life but, for divers, it is the view of the larger areas of the wreck itself and its fascinating cargo that appeals the most.

The hub of any ship is the bridge. From this vantage point, the captain surveyed the scene and gave his orders.

This was the communication and control centre of the entire ship. On the *Fujikawa Maru*, marine silt now covers most parts of the bridge, but it cannot hide the details. Ship's telegraph, compasses, voice tubes and the main wheel, now interspersed with corals and the inevitable shoals of small fish, conjure up life as it once was on the bridge. Marine creatures make no distinction between the various pieces of navigational equipment. Their only criteria is that they should provide a stable platform for growth.

The *Fujikawa Maru* was intended to supply munitions and spares to support the war effort: in the holds, divers can see the massive amount of equipment needed to sustain a fighting force.

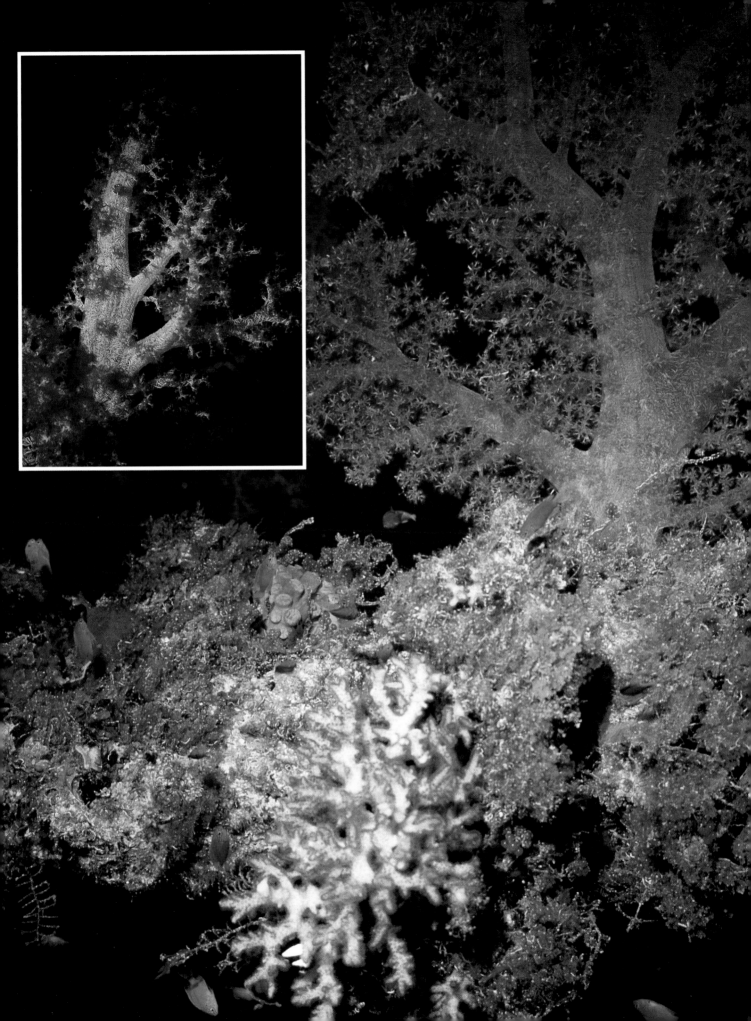

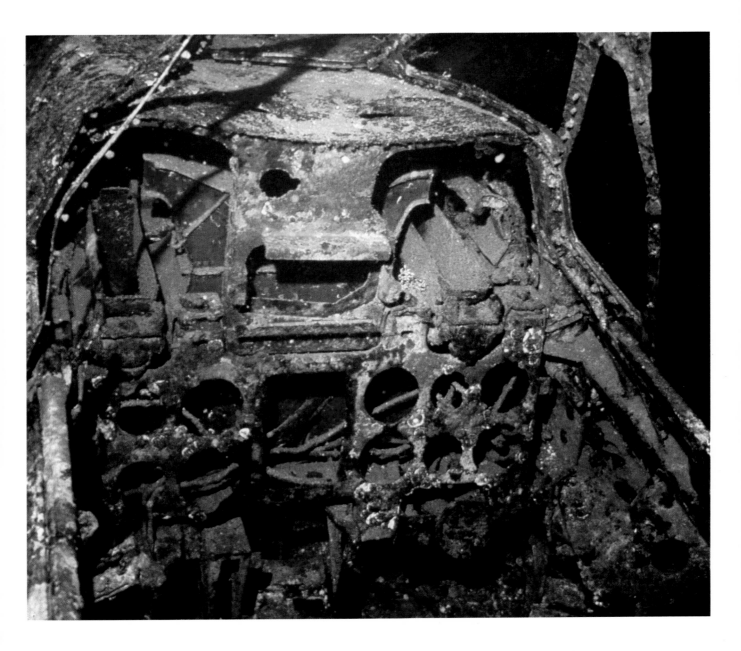

Of all the holds, perhaps the most popular is No. 2 where fighter aircraft lie on top of each other. In here the bright clear water allows us to see the cockpit of a Mitsubishi A6M Risen, commonly known as the Zero fighter plane. The instrument panel, complete with its radio dials and gauges, fills the space in front of the pilot's seat. The all important joystick is still there, giving the impression that the plane is ready to defend against all comers. Spare propellers lie scattered on the floor together with the various spare parts needed to maintain the planes.

Even though the ambient light levels are quite good, a torch is essential to see the colour and detail in the darker areas. The beam of a modern dive torch will penetrate great distances through clear water, but take care not to stir up the fine sediment which covers most areas. Once disturbed, it will take a long time to settle and it reduces the visibility instantly.

The light of your torch will reveal the true colours of the corals. Without the torch you would not see these colours, since water absorbs light and therefore colour. Reds disappear in shallow water and then oranges and yellows, until at 30 metres (98 feet) all you will have left

(Left) A fighter plane remains almost intact. Its windows have been shattered in the attack. (Above) The remains of a Zero fighter cockpit.

is blues and blacks. What looks like a dull grey coral at 15 metres (49 feet) could be transformed into a vivid red plant as your torch beam picks it out. Your torchlight will guide you while you examine the inside of the large wreck. The holds, large enough to swim in and out of, are safe to enter, but you should always be on the look out for hanging debris which when dislodged, is dangerous.

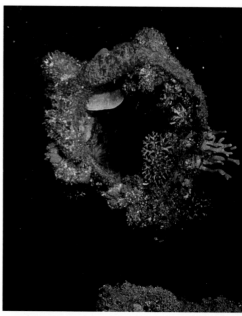

Examination of other holds reveals more about the *Fujikawa Maru's* varied cargo. Rows of 4-inch armour piercing shells together with row upon row of machine gun bullets litter the forward hold. Despite a thick layer of sediment over the whole area their neat stacking is still visible. Smaller less war-like stores include dozens of *sake* bottles and piles of pottery destined for the canteens on land and aboard warships. The glazed surfaces on the plates restricts marine growth so a quick wipe shows up the patterns as if they had been made yesterday. Some of this crockery would have been used in the ship's galley, still intact with its coal burning stove and array of cooking utensils.

Diving in and out of the wreck will almost certainly keep you at depths below 20 metres (66 feet) so you will have to keep one eye on your watch to make sure that you do not exceed your safe time. If you do, you will then have to decompress before surfacing so that gases absorbed at pressure are allowed to dissipate from your bloodstream without forming dangerous bubbles which would result in "the bends". The *Fujikawa Maru* is too large to be taken in on a single dive so most dive tours will cater for a second afternoon dive. A lunchtime break is an ideal opportunity to discuss your finds and learn from the experiences of other divers so that when you next dive, you will have a more productive time. The break is also ideal for an inevitable snooze in the midday heat after a light lunch!

To the north of the area lies Dublon Island and to the south is Uman. The waters around these two islands contain many of the wrecks but these are mostly lying in up to 60 metres (197 feet) of water. The safe maximum depth for air diving is 50 metres (164 feet) or less but, in the warm clear

(Top, left) The light of the flashgun restores the natural colours of the corals in these pictures. (Top, top left) The vivid colours of the marine growth have replaced the original paintwork.

(Centre) Marine growth cannot cope with smooth pottery surfaces so it is immediately recognizable. (Above) Small fish dart over the wrecks in search of food and shelter.

waters of Truk, many dives are made below this without incident. The wrecks are a magnetic attraction and justify the extra preparation needed for such deep dives. Being in comparatively shallow water, the *Fujikawa Maru* is probably the most dived Truk wreck both in terms of the number of divers and the time spent diving on her.

On a second dive you can go into areas missed on the first dive or not

(Above) A small gun fitted to a cargo vessel would have been helpless in the attack.
(Right) A diver takes aim on the underwater world. The only shooting done now is with underwater cameras.
(Far right) Large sponges filter the clear waters providing contrast to the mast looming in the background.

attempted during the morning's dive. With a little more experience of the layout you can swim to areas with much more confidence.

Whether you swim from the main superstructure to the bows or the stern you will arrive at a 6-inch gun. There is one at either end of the ship. These were fitted in 1940 when the Japanese Government commissioned her to be converted from a general cargo ship into an aircraft ferry armed with two 6-inch guns and an array of machine and anti-aircraft guns. The main guns date back to the Russo-Japanese war of 1899. They were certainly not the newest of guns then, but they would still have been capable of inflicting severe damage on any vessel which strayed within range.

Most divers want to have some sort of souvenir to remind them of their dives, and in this case, of a most memorable dive. Since it is forbidden to take anything off the wreck, underwater cameras are the ideal way of capturing the wreck without moving it. The host of corals make colourful foregrounds and the inclusion of a buddy diver will help to give an idea of the scale. Electronic flashguns help to restore the faded colours but, once again, take care not to stir up the sediment. This will be picked up by the flash and reduce the clarity and quality of the image.

It is almost impossible to know where to start when photographing such a photogenic wreck. The angles are limitless and the subjects abound. With only 36 frames in your camera you will soon run out of film. Particularly impressive are the two masts that reach up from the deeper water towards the sparkling surface.

A view up to the surface will show the sparkling sunlight dappling on the water and a deep blue circle known as Snell's window. This is caused by light being reflected from the surface. Shoals of fish are silhouetted against the bright surface as they swim in and out of their underwater habitat.

In Truk there are enough wrecks to last a wreck-diver's lifetime. The variety of wrecks is wide, their condition is preserved and there are new discoveries to be made on each.

Aikoku Maru

To the east of Dublon Island there is a concentration of wrecks which lie in much deeper water and so can only be dived by experienced visitors. The most amazing of these is the *Aikoku Maru* which sank in 73 metres (240 feet). She was 150 metres (492 feet) long and never had the chance to serve in civilian life. As soon as she was completed, she was commissioned to support the Japanese war effort and never fulfilled her original purpose as a freight-carrying passenger liner. Her forward holds were filled with munitions for her and other members of the Japanese fleet. In addition, she carried mines and other high explosives.

When an American Avenger torpedo bomber scored a direct hit on these stores, the resulting explosion disintegrated the whole of the forward section of this large vessel. The force of the explosion was such that one of the attacking planes was hit by the shock wave and it too disintegrated. The ship's fall to the seabed was instant as the debris of the explosion rained down over the site. Huge sections of metal were hurled 800 metres (2,600 feet) through the air and when the smoke cleared, the waters were thick with floating debris and fuel oil. The *Aikoku Maru* had literally been blown apart.

For those with sufficient deep diving experienced, the *Aikoku Maru* does not represent many difficulties as most of the interesting areas start at 40 metres (131 feet) but such a wreck needs time and close examination. Once inside her, you will discover a wealth of detail and tragic evidence of the human losses. You will soon be swimming down decks where the added depth will restrict dive times and so increase the time needed to decompress before surfacing.

This means that extra air is needed which is provided by using twin sets. The resulting increase in volume enables a diver to dive for longer and yet still have sufficient air to supply him while decompressing. Such a large supply of air in the hands of an inexperienced diver could result in a massive bend.

Suitably kitted up, the descent into the deep water is a time for adjusting buoyancy as the neoprene wetsuit com-

presses at depth and so reduces your buoyancy. Buoyancy compensators allow you to bypass small amounts from your main air supply into a life-jacket to give reassuring lift as you slowly fall down into the blue area where, as yet, you cannot see anything at all.

During such descents some divers experience a feeling of unease and disorientation. There are few indications of direction and the only obvious sign is from your bubbles which must be going upwards. As you fall deeper and deeper, the air being supplied by your demand valve changes not in taste, but in smoothness. The movements in the

valve are cushioned at these greater depths resulting in the provision of a rich smooth supply of air. This change is also amplified by the narcs. Like being tipsy, it is pleasant, but could lead to your becoming over-confident and therefore a danger to yourself and those with you.

The narcs has varying effects on divers and occurs at different depths but as a general rule a diver at 30 metres (98 feet) will probably start to feel some effect. Below this he will definitely be affected by the nitrogen increased air supply. The combination of the narcs and the *Aikoku Maru* itself test even the most experienced diver.

Just as the narcs start, the wreck appears out of the blue. The light levels have been getting gradually lower as the sunlight is absorbed. Your eyes become accustomed to picking out detail below and finally, the wreck appears. At first sight, the wreck is confusing for there seems to be something missing. She is smaller than you thought and this is puzzling. It is also disorientating, since you are trying to establish your location. It is then that you realise the cause of the confusion. The area forward of the main superstructure just doesn't exist. It was, of course, blown away in the attack. All that is left is an area of mangled metal,

twisted out of all recognition.

Fortunately, the rear section is intact. Inspection reveals a passenger liner with attractive lines and a wealth of detail to explore. With one eye on your dive timer, you know there will never be enough time to see it all on one dive, so you must decide on an area and concentrate on it.

Swimming around the outside of the *Aikoku Maru* from the damaged bridge towards the stern, you will experience the eerie silence of the deep. This time the contrast seems even more extreme when you imagine the noise of the explosion which sank the ship. Now the only sign of that tremendous noise is in

(Left) The US attack on 16 February 1944 took the Japanese by surprise, and led to the end of Truk's strategic importance. (Right) Grumman Avengers flying in formation proved too much for the unprepared fleet.

the shattered wreckage. Your eardrums will register a slight pain as the pressure increases during descent and you have to "clear" your ears periodically to stop the pressure inside your sinuses building up to dangerous levels.

Anti-aircraft guns, which were almost certainly still firing as the ship sank, lie pointing to the sky. Rows of ammunition lie neatly stacked on one side and piles of exhausted shell cases are scattered on the other. The sun deck, originally intended as a relaxing area for the fare paying passengers, is now covered with thick marine growth. This is the most accessible area and is the starting point for an exhilarating dive of discovery.

At 50 metres (164 feet) the light is low and a dive torch is essential if you are to venture inside. Light can be seen through the ship which helps to keep down the rising claustrophobia which these locations inevitably encourage. Inside the ship, the electric cables, released from the bulkheads as their fixings rotted, dangle down and are a constant threat to the careless diver. As you navigate your way deeper into the wreck, the light disappears and you can only be guided by the light of your torch. You must know where you are heading. More importantly, you must be fully aware of your route for the return journey. That may sound simple on land, but underwater the rising bubbles from your demand valve crash against the ceiling and dislodge silt and debris which floats down and reduces the visibility straight away. Swimming forward is fine as you approach undisturbed water but as soon as you turn round you are faced with a completely different situation.

As if the ceiling debris were not dangerous enough, there is a layer of fine silt on the floor which can be over 30 cm (12 in) deep in places. Careless finning will raise this debris into a cloud which will take days to settle down.

The light of your torch concentrates your vision as you carefully navigate your way down passageways and through holds. The munitions in the rear holds which didn't explode, still pose a threat. Over the years saltwater can make them volatile so touching is forbidden, sensibly.

In the gloom, flick your torch from side to side to cover as large an area as possible to give you a chance to orientate yourself. On the *Aikoku Maru* your beam is just as likely to fall on human remains, marking the underwater grave of numerous Japanese sailors, as it is to fall on cargo. The skeletons and human remains throughout the ship are now made even more eerie by their covering of fine silt, as if smothered rather than drowned.

Personal effects can be recognized in the bunkbed dormitories. Metal picture frames, plates and glasses are easily discerned as they attract far less marine growth than items such as metal framed bunkbeds. The internal waters are still, protected from any currents, and the atmosphere is undeniably heavy. By now, we are deep inside the ship and it is time to leave. Our visit must be well timed to make sure that enough air is left to decompress but the hardest journey is yet to come. The return journey through the silt disturbed passageways is not pleasant.

Your experience now is tested to the limit. Even the most competent can question the correct route, and any change from the proper course is potentially fatal. Ropes and guidelines, which must be taut, are there to point the way, but any slack rope is a serious hazard that can entangle and trap.

Nearly always there is the sickening feeling that the return journey seems to be taking far longer than you expected. The thought that you may have made a directional error looms larger by the second. With these feelings mounting up, the sight of the external deep blue water again is almost like a breath of fresh air. For you know that you are safe by comparison, even though you are still 50 metres (164 feet) below the surface of Truk Lagoon.

The remainder of the dive is workmanlike and functional. Your dive timer tells you how long you have been down and you will have precalculated your decompression time so you know when and how long you will need to surface. As you slowly rise to shallower water you will be aware of the dark shape of the *Aikoku Maru* disappearing into the blue depths. Decompressing gives you valuable time for reflection on a dive which has been a series of contrasts – depth, destruction and the discovery of one more of Truk's wrecks that will continue to lie here protected in its unique atmosphere.

GLOSSARY

Airlift
A suction device that uses compressed air from the surface to dredge up soft material from the seabed for examination at the surface.

Aqualung
A device to enable divers to breathe underwater. Invented in the 1940s by Cousteau and Gagnan, it consists of a metal cylinder that stores compressed air and a valve or regulator with mouthpiece that delivers the air to the diver at the right pressure.

Bends
This is the name given to a condition that occurs if excessive nitrogen forms bubbles in the bloodsteam of a diver. Circulation is restricted and very severe cases can result in death or paralysis. Once the bubbles have formed the only way to remove them is by repressurizing the diver in a recompression chamber.

Buddy
A jargon term used to indicate a diving partner. It is always recommended that divers dive in pairs.

Decompression
After diving at depth for a long time it is necessary to control the rate of the ascent so that excess nitrogen can be released gradually from the bloodstream to prevent the formation of minute circulation-stopping bubbles. This is done by stopping at specific depths for a certain time before reaching the surface. The length of time is laid down in tables issued by all major diving authorities. Failure to adhere to these time limits could result in the BENDS.

Drysuit
This is an insulated, waterproof suit used for cold water diving. It has a waterproof zip and seals on the neck, wrists and ankles to prevent water entering the space around the body.

Marker buoy
A float with a line attached that the diver secures to an underwater "find" to make it simple to locate later.

Nitrogen Narcosis
A temporary euphoric effect caused by the pressure of nitrogen in the bloodsteam. It usually starts at a depth of around 30 metres (100ft). It is also known as "narcs" or "raptures of the deep".

Recompression chamber
This is a sealed compartment, usually cylindrical, into which divers are placed for recompression if they show any symptoms of the BENDS. It allows them to be pressurized as if they were underwater. The pressure is controlled from outside the chamber.

Slates
Rigid plastic sheets with waterproof markers attached, on which divers can write messages to each other underwater.

Tanks
Also known as cylinders or bottles, they contain compressed air and are attached to the diver's back by a harness.

Thermocline
This is the dividing point between layers of water of differing temperatures. There can be as many as three in divable depths.

Valve
Also known as a regulator, it is fitted to the compressed air cylinder and delivers air via the mouthpiece to the diver.

Weightbelt
A belt containing varying amounts of lead. It is used to adjust a diver's buoyancy underwater.

Wetsuit
Usually made from neoprene, it is a suit that traps a thin layer of water around the diver's body. The layer of water is heated by the body and insulated by the neoprene. It is widely used in all areas of diving, though in really warm waters it would probably only be worn as a form of protection.

INDEX

Page numbers in *italic* refer to the illustrations

ACKNOWLEDGEMENTS

T = top, B = bottom, C = centre, R = right, L = left

PHOTOGRAPHERS
Paul Arbiter 24BL, 25, 29T, 30C, 35.
Geoff Barker 63, 70–79.
BBC Hulton Picture Library 8R.
Steve Birchall 45TR, 120C, 121BR.
Mensun Bound 13, 18B, 19TL, 19TR, 19C, 19B, 21T, 21B, 22, 23, 24R, 26, 27, 28TR, 28BR, 28CL, 28BL, 29BL, 29BR, 30T, 31TR, 31C, 31B, 32CL, 34, 37T, 37BL, 37BR.
Canada House, London 64, 66–67.
Horace Dobbs 167, 174–177, 182T, 182B, 186–187, 188.
Alex Double 87B, 91, 94–95B, 100–101, 101BL, 102T, 103TL, 108CL.
Tamara Double 88–89.
Laurence Gould 141, 142–161.
Imperial War Museum 112–113.
Jack Jackson 82–83T, 86–87T, 86B, 92, 93B, 95T, 96TL, 99T, 99BR, 100CT, 100BR, 103BL, 104–105, 106TR, 106C, 107TL.
Bill Lewis/Bruce Bailey 168TR, 169T, 179, 180TL, 180TR, 180BR, 181T.
The Mansell Collection 7L, 9L.
Michael Holford Library 16BL, 17T, 17B.
Leo Mastogastino 36.
Keith Morris Title Page 1, Title Page 2, 18T,
56L, 58BL, 58–59, 59TR, 60–61, 81, 83B, 84–85, 93T, 96TR, 96CL, 98, 102B, 103BR, 106–107, 106BL, 107TR, 107CR, 107BR, 108 except CL, 109, 137B, 162–163, 164–165, 177TL.
National Archive Washington DC 170–171, 172–173(B/W), 184–185.
Oxford University World Ship Trust 14–15, 20TR, 31TL, 32T, 33.
Peter Rowlands End papers; 12–13, 38–39, 42B, 43, 44, 45B, 46TL, 46BL, 47, 48BL, 49, 50–51, 52T, 52B, 53, 54–55, 57T, 57BR, 62–63, 80–81, 90, 94TL, 96–97, 99BL, 110–111, 113TL, 114, 119, 120TL, 120TR, 120BL, 120CB, 120BR, 122–136, 137T, 138–141, 166–167, 173BR.
Peter Sieniewicz 69T, 69B.
Herwath Voigtman: Planet Earth Pictures: 178, 180–181B, 183, 189.
Adam Woolfitt: Susan Griggs Agency 6BL.
World's Edge Picture Library 7R, 8L, 8R.
ILLUSTRATIONS
Mensun Bound 20, 23, 26, 30–31, 34.
Caroline Caldwell 16. **John Charles** 15, 40–41, 65, 68, 82, 116, 143, 168.
Simon Dobbs 37. **Hugh Morrison** 36.
Francis Rankin 32. **Mike Wright** 33.